Leeds Studies in English

New Series XLII

© *Leeds Studies in English* 2012
School of English
University of Leeds
Leeds, England

ISSN 0075-8566
ISBN 978-1-84549-551-0

Copyright
All rights reserved. No part of this publication may be reproduced in any material form (including photocopying or storing it in any medium by electronic means, and whether or not transiently or incidentally to some other use of this publication) without the written permission of the copyright owner, except in accordance with the provisions of the Copyright, Designs and Patents Act 1988, or under terms of a licence issued by the Copyright Licensing Agency Ltd, 33-34, Alfred Place, London WC1E 7DP, UK. Applications for the copyright owner's permission to reproduce part of this publication should be addressed to the Publishers.

Printed in the UK

Publishing Office
Abramis Academic
ASK House
Northgate Avenue
Bury St. Edmunds
Suffolk
IP32 6BB

Tel: +44 (0)1284 700321
Fax: +44 (0)1284 717889
Email: info@abramis.co.uk
Web: www.abramis.co.uk

Leeds Studies in English

New Series XLII

2011

Edited by

Alaric Hall

Editorial assistants
Helen Price and Victoria Cooper

Leeds Studies in English

<www.leeds.ac.uk/lse>
School of English
University of Leeds
2011

Leeds Studies in English

<www.leeds.ac.uk/lse>

Leeds Studies in English is an international, refereed journal based in the School of English, University of Leeds. *Leeds Studies in English* publishes articles on Old and Middle English literature, Old Icelandic language and literature, and the historical study of the English language. After a two-year embargo, past copies are made available, free access; they can be accessed via <http://www.leeds.ac.uk/lse>.

Editorial Board: Catherine Batt, *Chair*
Marta Cobb
Victoria Cooper, *Editorial Assistant*
Alaric Hall, *Editor*
Paul Hammond
Cathy Hume, *Reviews Editor*
Ananya Jahanara Kabir
Oliver Pickering
Helen Price, *Editorial Assistant*

Notes for Contributors

Contributors are requested to follow the *MHRA Style Guide: A Handbook for Authors, Editors, and Writers of Theses*, 2nd edn (London: Modern Humanities Research Association, 2008), available at <http://www.mhra.org.uk/Publications/Books/StyleGuide/download.shtml>. Where possible, contributors are encouraged to include the digital object identifiers or, where a complete free access text is available, stable URLs of materials cited (see *Style Guide* §11.2.10.1).

The language of publication is English and translations should normally be supplied for quotations in languages other than English. Each contributor will receive a free copy of the journal, and a PDF of their article for distribution. Please email all contributions to <lse@leeds.ac.uk>.

Reviews

Copies of books for review should be sent to the Editor, *Leeds Studies in English*, School of English, University of Leeds, Leeds LS2 9JT, United Kingdom.

Contents

Purity and *Pueritia*: The Anti-Theme of Childhood Innocence in Late Medieval English Courtesy Books	1
Joanna Bellis *Cambridge University*	
Reading Between the Lines: The Liturgy and Ælfric's *Lives of Saints* and Homilies	17
Stewart Brookes *King's College London*	
Looming Danger and Dangerous Looms: Violence and Weaving in Exeter Book *Riddle 56*	29
Megan Cavell *University of Cambridge*	
The Nun's Priest's Identity and the Purpose of his Tale	43
Carol F. Heffernan *Rutgers University*	
The Yew Rune, Yogh and *Yew*	53
Bernard Mees *RMIT University*	
Sententia in Narrative Form: Ælfric's Narrative Method in the Hagiographical Homily on St Martin	75
Hiroshi Ogawa *Showa Women's University*	
Infinitival Complements with the Verb *(ge)don* in Old English: Latin Influence Revisited	93
Olga Timofeeva *University of Zurich*	
Errata to Domenico Pezzini, 'An Edition of Three Late Middle English Versions of a Fourteenth-Century *Regula Heremitarum*'	109

Reviews:

Rachel Koopmans, *Wonderful to Relate: Miracle Stories and Miracle Collecting in High Medieval England*. Philadelphia: University of Pennsylvania Press, 2011	111
[Heather Blurton]	
Massimo Verdicchio, *The Poetics of Dante's 'Paradiso'*. Toronto: University of Toronto Press, 2010	113
[Ruth Chester]	

Katharine Breen, *Imagining an English Reading Public, 1150–1400*.   115
Cambridge: Cambridge University Press, 2010
    [Joyce Coleman]

Peter Brown, *Authors in Context: Geoffrey Chaucer*. Oxford: Oxford   117
University Press, 2011
    [Cathy Hume]

Dinah Hazell, *Poverty in Late Middle English Literature: The 'Meene'*   119
and the 'Riche'. Dublin: Four Courts Press, 2009
    [Mike Rodman Jones]

Dana M. Oswald, *Monsters, Gender and Sexuality*. Cambridge: 120
Brewer, 2010
    [Liz Herbert McAvoy]

Kiriko Sato, *The Development from Case-Forms to Prepositional*   122
Constructions in Old English Prose. Bern: Lang, 2009
    [Olga Timofeeva]

Purity and *Pueritia*: The Anti-Theme of Childhood Innocence in Late Medieval English Courtesy Books

Joanna Bellis

The starting-point for this article is the linguistic resemblance between *puer* and *pur*, the tempting etymological simulacra that represent a crux in the patristic debate about childhood. Medieval theologians were divided over whether the native quality of childhood was purity, or whether the child was corrupted by original sin from conception. This article investigates the ramifications of the conflicted theology of childhood innocence for the English courtesy literature of the later Middle Ages, whose practical purpose was the education of noble children. It contends that medieval children's literature, although often dismissed as textually unsophisticated, is far less simplistic in its understanding of childhood than the theological models to which it responded. The contradictory theological models of childhood were a reductive, problematic but ineluctable context for those writers whose task it was to educate real children in the habits of courtesy.

    The article will propose two things: firstly, that while the religious literature reduced children to a symbolic object of adult imitation, the social literature sought to school children in imitation of adult behaviour, and thus at its heart was a crucial conflict with mainstream Christian writing on childhood. The courtesy authors found their own, pedagogically orientated, depiction of childhood diametrically opposed to spiritual paradigm of the respected and authoritative patristic and scholastic texts, and thus they were forced to sublimate the ironic circularity in which they were bound. Contradiction defines their response to other philosophies of childhood, but it is a contradiction that, although central, is necessarily unspoken. The theme of childhood innocence in their sources becomes an anti-theme in these texts, simultaneously central and intensely problematic. Secondly, the article will argue that it was not only from spiritual, but in secular culture, that the pressure from idealised models of childhood was felt. The courtesy manuals were written for noble and gentry children, to instruct them in how to conduct themselves in a manner suitable to their pedigree. But secular courtly literature is full of examples of children whose nobility is innate and self-authenticating. The courtesy books' negotiation of these two literatures, sacred and secular, whose culturally dominant philosophies of childhood fundamentally undermined their own, is a subtle one. But, for all its caution and thoughtfulness, it constitutes a rebuttal and a re-examination by one of the lowliest of medieval genres, vernacular instruction for children, of the claims of major theologians, as well as the dominant models for conceptualising childhood that were circulating in secular literature.

Purity and 'Pueritia'

The discussion will begin by examining the contradictory theological paradigms available for conceptualising childhood in the Middle Ages: one emphasising the innate sinfulness of the child from conception; the other, the purity of the pre-pubescent, pre-sinful age. Its first section will discuss the tension in the patristic literature, and the second will show how it was inherited by vernacular religious writers of the late Middle Ages. The third will turn to the courtesy books, contrasting the literature written *about* with that written *for* children. Setting these texts in their religious context, the ideological differences between them crystallise into a binary between theologised idealisation and sentimental exemplarity, on the one hand, and pragmatic reality on the other. The courtesy manuals' explicit advice for children entails a mediation of these models that constitutes a third way: an innocence that is acknowledged, but unsentimental and unspiritualised. Their shift in focus from the child as object to the child as subject means that their interpretation of childhood, although it is inflected by theological discourse, rejects and corrects its paradigms. The discussion will end by examining the social context of courtly literature, and the even more acute pressures its models of innate childhood innocence placed on instructional literature for children. The meme of the innocent child that is prominent in both secular and sacred cultural matrices demanded a cultural reappraisal by the courtesy books, which acknowledged its force, but quietly undermined its validity.

It is half a century since Philippe Ariès's controversial book *L'Enfant et la Vie Familiale sous l'Ancien Régime* argued for 'the complete absence of the modern notion of childhood' in the medieval period, yet his ideas were largely responsible for the energy that has since been poured into investigating childhood in history.[1] His book is the given anterior to P. J. P. Goldberg and Felicity Riddy's recent essay collection *Youth in the Middle Ages*, whose introduction, entitled 'After Ariès', counters his allegation that 'the modern idea of the family ... produced the idea of the child', and that before the early modern period medieval parents saw their children essentially as miniature adults.[2] Ariès held that the high rate of infant mortality, coupled with the necessity that children perform the same manual tasks as adults, did not allow for the concept of an extended period of 'childhood' as a stage between infancy and maturity — evinced by the fact that children appear as small adults in many artistic representations. And although Ariès is now refuted, his work continues to be a point of departure, and responses to and rebuttals of it have formed some of the best modern studies of medieval children. Shulamith Shahar's *Childhood in the Middle Ages* states that its central thesis is a refutation of the allegation that 'a concept of childhood' did not exist in the medieval period; likewise, reviewing a comprehensive set of evidence, Nicholas Orme's recent book claims 'it cannot be over-emphasised that there is nothing to be said for Ariès's view of childhood in the middle ages'.[3] This article will not recapitulate arguments comprehensively made elsewhere: it makes the assumption that the Middle Ages did have a concept of childhood, and will not martial more evidence in support of this. But it will

---

[1] 'L'absence complète du sentiment moderne de l'enfance' (my translation), Philippe Ariès, *L'Enfant et la Vie Familiale sous l'Ancien Régime* (Paris: Plon, 1960), p. 102.

[2] P. J. P. Goldberg, Felicity Riddy, and Mike Tyler, 'Introduction: After Ariès', in *Youth in the Middle Ages*, ed. by P. J. P. Goldberg and Felicity Riddy (York: York Medieval Press, 2004), pp. 1–10 (p. 2).

[3] Shulamith Shahar, *Childhood in the Middle Ages* (London: Routledge, 1992), pp. 1–6; Nicholas Orme, *Medieval Children* (New Haven: Yale University Press, 2003), p. 9. See also Barbara A. Hanawalt, *Growing Up in Medieval London: The Experience of Childhood in History* (Oxford: Oxford University Press, 1995); R. C. Finucane, *The Rescue of the Innocents: Endangered Children in Medieval Miracles* (Basingstoke: Macmillan, 1997); Pierre Riché and Danièle Alexandre-Bidon, *L'Enfance au Moyen Age* (Paris: Aubier, 1994); and Sally Crawford, *Childhood in Anglo-Saxon England* (Stroud: Sutton Publishing, 1999).

interrogate the complexities of that concept, informed as it was by conflicting theological and social pressures. It responds to Goldberg and Riddy's comment that 'the inherent tendency of the evidence to reflect ideology rather than social practice' leaves a blinkered picture of medieval children.[4] In analysing some of the lesser-known conduct literature, it suggests that this distinction between social practice and ideology is crucial to understanding medieval paradigms of childhood, and it is precisely because the courtesy books occupy a hinterland between the two that they are in hermeneutic conflict with the very culture whose mores they seek to instil.

The theological background

Before turning to the courtesy literature that is the main focus of this article, this section will contextualise the paradigms of childhood innocence that the Middle Ages inherited, and will demonstrate that already in patristic literature the idea of childhood innocence was complex and contradictory. The particular crux of this debate was whether the proper quality of childhood was native purity; or whether the infant, sharing the sin of the first parent, was from birth innately as sinful as the adult. Augustine, responding to the Pelagians, held that the lustful act of conception passed original sin to the baby in the very moment of its coming into existence. He maintained that 'the feebleness of the infant limbs is innocent, not the infant's mind'.[5] He goes on to give the example of a baby who, although incapable of speech, was more than capable of feeling envy, as he contemplated his brother sharing his mother's milk. In this formulation, the child's heart is just as corrupt as the adult's, and lacks only the ability to give outward expression to its sinful nature. And when *pueritia*, the age of speech, succeeds *infantilium* in Augustine's schema of childhood, the sinful soul gains only a better means of exercising its corrupted humanity.

Augustine was pondering Job 14. 4–5, where he read that 'none is pure from sin before you, not even an infant of one day upon the earth',[6] and it would be unfair to reduce his sometimes agonised theology of children to one of complete and wholly developed depravity. In a letter to Jerome, he agonises over the fate of unbaptised infant souls:

> where, in the case of infant children, is sin committed by these souls, so that they require the remission of sin in the sacrament of Christ, because of sinning in Adam from whom the sinful flesh has been derived? or if they do not sin, how is it compatible with the justice of the Creator ... that unless they be rescued by the Church, perdition overtakes them, although it is not in their power to secure that they be rescued by the grace of baptism? ...

---

[4] Goldberg, Riddy, and Tyler, 'Introduction: After Ariès', p. 7.
[5] 'Imbecillitas membrorum infantilium innocens est, non animus infantium'. *St Augustine's Confessions with an English translation by William Watts. 1631*, Loeb Classical Library, 2 vols (London: Heinemann, 1960–61), I, 20; Augustine, *The Confessions*, trans. by Henry Chadwick (Oxford: Oxford University Press, 1991), p. 9.
[6] 'Quoniam nemo mundus a peccato coram te, nec infans, cuius est unius diei vita super terram?' Augustine, *Confessions*, ed. by Watts (I, 18–20), trans. by Chadwick (p. 9).

it is not lawful for us to deny that nothing else than perdition is the doom of souls, even of little children, that have departed from the body without the sacrament.[7]

Yet, despite his heartache over the fate of the unbaptized, Augustine could not escape the conclusion that children were born as inheritors of the sin of Adam, and not as blank slates. Martha Ellen Stortz suggests that 'between innocence and depravity Augustine posed a third possibility: non-innocence.'[8] He maintained that children were born with the seed of original sin in their hearts, that would bud and blossom in due proportion to their competence. However, the earlier church fathers Hermas (whose writings were included in the apocrypha) and Clement of Alexandria, both writing in the late second century, had offered a very different theology of childhood in their concept of *nēpiotés*, which is defined by Peter Brown as 'the artless simplicity, candor and lack of affectation of the child':

> the child before puberty was 'blameless'. He enjoyed without disruption the precious gift of 'singleness of heart', of 'absence of malice'. Sexual urges and sexual imaginings had not yet come to divide his 'face' from his 'heart'. The world of adult cunning, of adult self-interest, and of adult hypocrisy — of which the rise of sexual feeling at puberty was a first, premonitory symptom — had not yet closed in upon him.[9]

Népiotés is not a positive quality, but the absence of a negative: it is the opposite of Stortz's 'non-innocence', it is the absence of sin. And it is noticeable how often the word 'absence' is used in these patristic descriptions of childhood. Clement defined *népiotés* as 'the absence of pretence or complication, the absence of duplicity, of cunning or hypocrisy; frankness, sincerity'.[10] Hermas's second mandate similarly defined the innocence of children as the absence of sin: 'have simplicity and be innocent and you shall be as the children who do not know the wickedness that destroys the life of men'.[11] In both, the emphasis is on moral vacuity, not positive purity; neutrality not active virtue. These theologians saw childhood essentially as a pre-sinful age. They took their cue from the words of Christ:

> Amen I say to you, unless you be converted, and become as little children, you shall not enter into the kingdom of heaven.[12]

Jesus had told the disciples that without an imitation of childlikeness, they were occluded from the kingdom of heaven: there could not be a stronger endorsement of childhood as a blessed state. He did not say that it was because the child was *sinless* that he had this special

---

[7] Augustine, *Letters of Saint Augustine*, trans. by J. G. Cunningham, 2 vols (Edinburgh: Clark, 1875), ii, 304 (letter 166). 'Ubi in paruulis peccent, ut indigeant in sacramento Christi remissione peccati peccantes in Adam, ex quo caro est propagata peccati, aut, si non peccant, qua iustitia creatoris ita peccato obligantur alieno [...] ut eas, nisi per ecclesiam subuentum fuerit, damnatio consequatur, cum in earum potestate non sit, ut eis possit gratia baptismi subueniri. [...] neque negare fas nobis est eas, quae sine Christi sacramento de corporibus exierint, etiam parvulorum non nisi in damnationem trahi.' *S. Avreli Avgvstini Hipponiensis Episcopi Epistulae*, ed. Alois Goldbacher, Corpus Scriptorum Ecclesiasticorum Latinorum, 34, 44, 57–58, 5 vols (Vienna: Tempsky, 1895–1923), III 560–61. For a summary of Augustine on this issue, see Martha Ellen Stortz, ' "Where or When Was Your Servant Innocent?": Augustine on Childhood', in *The Child in Christian Thought*, ed. by Marcia J. Bunge (Grand Rapids, Michigan: Eerdmans, 2001), pp. 78–102 (pp. 78–79).

[8] Stortz, 'Where or When Was Your Servant Innocent?', p. 82.

[9] Peter Brown, *The Body and Society: Men, Women and Sexual Renunciation in Early Christianity* (New York: Columbia University Press, 2008), pp. 127, 70–71 respectively.

[10] 'Absence de prétension ou de complication, absence de détour, du ruse ou d'hypocrisie, franchise, sincérité' (my translation). Clement of Alexandria, *Le Pédagogue*, ed. by Marguerite Harl and Henri-Irénée Marrou, 3 vols (Paris: Éditions du Cerf, 1960), I, 25.

[11] Hermas, 'The Shepherd of Hermas', in *The Apostolic Fathers*, ed. by Kirsopp Lake, 2 vols (London: Heinemass, 1913), II, 71.

[12] 'Amen dico vobis nisi conversi fueritis et efficiamini sicut parvuli non intrabitis in regnum caelorum.' Matthew 18. 3. All biblical quotations from *The Douai-Rheims Vulgate* <http://www.drbo.org/> [accessed 25 August 2011].

grace; indeed his words have been interpreted by many Christians as suggesting that it is the incapacity of children to do anything but receive the grace of God freely that makes them the perfect model of repentance, by definition a post-sinful state. However, most medieval readings of this text took it as a straightforward advocation of the simple, pure, childlike nature.

These contradictory patristic philosophies filtered into the church teaching of the Middle Ages to competing degrees. Isidore of Seville's influential *Etymologiae* (early seventh century) derived the etymology of *puer* from *pur*, constructing a linguistic identity between the concepts of childhood and innocence, a self-authenticating etymological proof alleging the innate purity of children.[13] He defined *pueritia* as the 'pure [*purus*] age, during which a child is not yet suited for procreating.'[14] For Isidore, the child's bodily immaturity mirrored an internal purity in which the temptations of lust were as unimaginable as the procreative act was impossible. He imagined childhood as a state in which both the body and the character were not fully formed, and in which the power of sinful human nature had not yet budded.

Scholastic theologians tempered the Augustinian scheme of childhood with Isidorean purity. In the thirteenth century, Thomas Aquinas stated that 'infants are heirs of Adam's sin, otherwise they wouldn't die. So it was necessary to baptize infants so that those on whom Adam brought damnation at birth might achieve salvation through rebirth through Christ.'[15] For the sacrament of baptism to be efficacious, Aquinas allowed that original sin must be present in the infant; but Aquinas, whose thought was influenced not only by Augustine, but by Aristotle, offered a more developmental understanding of the fallenness of humanity.[16] He followed Augustine in dividing childhood into the three stages of *infantia*, *pueritia* and *adolescentia*: yet where Augustine's categories delineated the limited competence of the child to *enact* its sinfulness, Aquinas's limited the *sinfulness* of the child. What characterised *infantia* was the inability to reason, and Aquinas held that there was no need for children to receive the sacraments of penance or unction.[17] The child before the age of seven was incapable of mortal sin, and confession and communion did not commence until puberty. The Augustinian schema became, ironically, a measure of declining innocence, and the process of maturity one of increasing sinfulness.

Cristina L. H. Traina, commenting on the paradox of these two patristic theologies of childhood, remarks that 'to adopt an extreme version of either of these convictions would be to choose one of two heretical positions: deterministic nihilism, the belief that the human will is essentially and irretrievably evil and sinful; or Pelagianism, the belief that people are

---

[13] Isidore of Seville, *The Etymologies of Isidore of Seville*, ed. by Stephen A. Barney (Cambridge: Cambridge University Press, 2006), p. 241 (xi. ii. 10).

[14] 'Pura et necdum ad generandum apta.' *Etymologiarvm sive Originvm*, ed. by W. M. Lindsay (Oxford: Clarendon, 1911), xi. ii. 2; *Etymologies*, ed. by Barney, p. 241.

[15] Thomas Aquinas, *Summa Theologiæ: A Concise Translation*, ed. and trans. by Timothy McDermott (London: Eyre and Spottiswoode, 1989), p. 565 (lvii, 68: 9). 'Pueri autem ex peccato Adae peccatum originale contrahunt: quod patet ex hoc quod sunt mortalitati subjecti [...] Unde necessarium fuit pueros baptizare, ut, sicut per Adam damnationem incurrerunt nascendo, ita per Christum salutem consequantur renascendo.' *Summa Theologiae: Latin Text and English Translation*, ed. and trans. by James J. Cunningham, 60 vols (London: Blackfriars, 1964–81), LVII, 108.

[16] For a description of Aristotelian philosophies of childhood on medieval theologians, see Orme, *Medieval Children*, pp. 13–15.

[17] For more on Aquinas's theology of childhood, see Cristina L. H. Traina, 'A Person in the Making: Thomas Aquinas on Children and Childhood', in *The Child in Christian Thought*, ed. by Marcia J. Bunge (Grand Rapids, Michigan: Eerdmans, 2001), pp. 103–33.

essentially good.'[18] Medieval ecclesiastical teaching on children did hold the two in tension, without pushing either to its natural conclusion. The holy innocents were venerated as infant martyrs, although they were unbaptised — 'Childermas' was celebrated on the 28th December, when a boy-bishop would take part in leading the liturgy, surrounded by a retinue of other boys in clerical clothing. Nicholas Orme records how at this festival in Salisbury, the boy was formally installed and led services and administered blessings; in St Paul's, he preached a sermon; and in other cities boys toured the parish, being feasted by and blessing the people.[19] Children were frequently used as living symbols of purity in church ceremonies. Shulamith Shahar cites the statutes of the Norwich Furriers' Guild, which stipulate that 'the candle in the religious procession shall be borne by an innocent child'.[20] The acolyte encapsulates the reductive symbolism of childhood purity: taken out of a natural context and placed in a ritual one, he becomes purely a symbol for something which has very little to do with real childhood, but everything to do with the spiritualised idealisation of it. The most extreme example of childhood innocence is of course the *puer senex* of hagiography. The child saints are frequently found shunning the frivolous activities of their peers: they lie in their cradles in attitudes of devotion, arms folded and eyes raised heavenward, serious and sad as old men. The infant Nicholas 'in his tendre age' is said to have 'eschewed the vanitees of yonge children',[21] and Gregory wrote that Benedict 'had even from the time of his boyhood the heart of an old man.'[22] In the saints' lives we have children without a childhood, possessing a distinct kind of *népiotés*: gravity beyond their years. In these various literary depictions of childhood innocence, the common thread is negativity: eschewing vanity, avoiding guile, being unable to lie. Rather than finding positive virtue in childhood, the *népiotés* concept and its actualisation in church ritual reads childhood retrospectively, as the unspoiled form of adulthood, as the absence of sin.

Childhood in vernacular spiritual literature

This archetype was widely influential outside Latinate culture, the subject of popular proverbs, such as 'childerne and fooles can not ly', and often discussed in vernacular religious literature.[23] This section discusses how the patristic paradox was developed by popular vernacular literature, focusing on a carol of the early fifteenth century, by John Audelay:

> And God wold graunt me my prayer,
> A child agene I wold I were!

[18] Traina, 'A Person in the Making', p. 106.
[19] Orme, *Medieval Children*, pp. 188–89.
[20] Shahar, *Childhood in the Middle Ages*, p. 19.
[21] Jacobus de Voraigne, *Gilte Legende*, ed. by Richard Hamer and Vida Russell, Early English Texts Society, o.s., 327–28 (Oxford: Oxford University Press, 2006), I, 12.
[22] 'Ab ipso pueritiae suae tempore cor gerens senile.' Gregory, *Dialogues. Tome 2, Livres I–III*, ed. by Adalbert de Vogüé and trans. by Paul Antin, Sources chrétiennes, 260 (Paris: Cerf, 1979), p. 126 (Prologue, 1); trans. by J. A. Burrow, *Ages of Man: A Study in Medieval Writing and Thought* (Oxford: Clarendon, 1988), p. 98.
[23] John Heywood, *A Dialogue of Proverbs*, ed. by Rudolph E. Habenicht (Berkeley: Univiersity of California Press, 1963), p. 125. See also the Pearl-maiden's defence against the accusation that 'I my peny haf wrang tan': *The Poems of the Pearl Manuscript: Pearl, Cleanness, Patience, Sir Gawain and the Green Knight*, ed. by Malcolm Andrew and Ronald Waldron (London: Arnold, 1978), pp. 82 and 85 (ll. 614 and 671–72); and, on the Augustinian side of the issue, the infant protagonist's assertion in *Mundus et Infans* that he was 'gotten in game and in great sin': *Three Late Medieval Morality Plays: Mankind, Everyman, Mundus et Infans*, ed. by G. A. Lester (London: Black, 1981), p. 112.

Joanna Bellis

Fore pride in herte, he hatis alle one;
Worchip ne reverens kepis he non;
Ne he is wroth with no mon —
In chareté is alle his chere!
    And God wold graunt me my prayer,
    A child agene I wold I were!

He wot never wat is envy;
He wol uche mon fard wele him by;
He covetis noght unlaufully —
Fore cheré stons is his tresoure.
    And God wold graunt me my prayer,
    A child agene I wold I were!

In hert he hatis lechori —
To here therof he is sory! —
He sleth the syn of gloteré,
Nother etis ne drynkis bot fore mystere.
    And God wold graunt me my prayer,
    A child agene I wold I were!

Slouth he putis away, algate,
And wol be besé erlé and late —
Al wyckidnes thus he doth hate,
The seven dedlé synus al in fere.
    And God wold graunt me my prayer,
    A child agene I wold I were!

A gracious lyfe, forsothe, he has —
To God ne mon doth no trespas —
And I in syn fal, alas,
Everé day in the yere!
    And God wold graunt me my prayer,
    A child agene I wold I were!

My joy, my myrth is fro me clene —
I turne to care, turment, and tene —
Ded I wold that I had bene
When I was borne, and layd on bere —
    And God wold graunt me my prayer,
    A child agene I wold I were!

Fore better hit were to be unboren,
Then fore my synus to be forelorne,
Nere grace of God that is beforne,
Almysdede, and holé prayere!
    And God wold graunt me my prayer,
    A child agene I wold I were!

Now other cumford se I non
Bot schryve me clene with contricion,
And make here trew satisfaccion,
And do my penans wyle Y am here —

> And God wold graunt me my prayer,
> A child agene I wold I were! [24]

Little is known of Audelay apart from that which can be gleaned from his fifty-five poems, preserved uniquely in Bodleian Library MS Douce 302. For the most part they are monitory and penitential, lamenting the poet's blindness and deafness, which he understood as a judgment on his sins. The carol espouses a view of children which exemplifies their spiritualised, metaphoric function, framing childhood naïvety within the paradigm of the deadly sins. However, the axes of its contrasts are not really sin and innocence, but knowledge and ignorance: it is not because the child is virtuous that he 'wot never wat is envy', but because his experience has not opened him to the possibility of it. The carol's depiction of innocence is one of profound simplicity. It suggests that children are incapable of committing mortal sin because their experience of the world is insufficient to school them in it. Audelay looks back with wistfulness to a time of life at which the remorse that he feels 'eueré day in þe yere' was not yet possible. His lament, 'a child agene I wold I were', retrospectively imagines a world of simplicity that was impermeable to his darkened adult experience and the temptations of a future age. The manuscript of heading of the carol, *Cantalena de puericia*, locates it specifically in the context of the patristic debate about childhood, and it is the anti-Augustinian counter-strain that is dwelt upon by Audelay. The child of his carol 'wot never wat is envy' and 'hatis lechori' because greed and lust are too sophisticated for him; he 'doth no trespas' because he has not yet learned how. He belongs to a world apart, beyond the reach of sin and its penalty. He is occluded from the realm of adult temptation — and his blessed ignorance becomes a model for Christian adult imitation.

Both the theological models of childhood — somatic sinfulness and innate sinlessness — were current in the vernacular religious culture of the later Middle Ages, neither foreclosing the other. Both also misrepresented childhood by reducing it to its symbolic theological function. It is as idealistic and sentimental (as anyone who knows any children knows!) to say that they are free from the vices of humanity, as it is perverse to ascribe to them the wickednesses of the adult world. However, there is a third and more sophisticated reading of childhood that emerges in the vernacular meditations on the theological symbolism, which locates it between these binaries. In his attempt to characterise *népiotés* as a real child, Audelay hints at a more naturalistic picture, which emerges distinct from his idealisation of negative purity. Alongside the statement that the child has the 'seven dedlé synus al in fere', is the image, 'cheré stons is his tresoure'. The interpretation of the child's simplicity as precocious resistance of sin happens in parallel with the poet's tacit acknowledgment of the casuistry of such a manoeuvre: while he suggests that the child holds the deadly sins 'in fere', 'putis away' sloth and 'hatis lechori', this theologised depiction is undermined by the natural childishness at the heart of the industry which is credited with such spirituality. The child is 'besé erlé and late' — but with 'cheré stons', satisfying his juvenile pleasures, because unaware of any others. Audelay's child may be offered as a spiritual example, but he is also a real child, genuinely and sincerely absorbed in his world of play, and approaching it with no special grace. His cherry stones are not an ascetic

---

[24] John the Blind Audelay, *Poems and Carols* (Oxford, Bodleian Library MS Douce 302), ed. by Susanna Fein (Kalamazoo, Medieval Institute, 2009), <http://www.lib.rochester.edu/camelot/teams/fsjac14f.htm>, carol 14 [accessed: 28 July 2011]. See also *The Poems of John Audelay*, ed. by Ella Keats Whiting, Early English Texts Society, o. s., 184 (London: Oxford University Press, 1931), pp. 197–198 (no 41). See also Michael Bennett, 'John Audelay: Some New Evidence on His Life and Works', *The Chaucer Review*, 16 (1981–82), 344–55; and Susanna Fein, 'Good Ends in the Audelay Manuscript', *The Yearbook of English Studies*, 33 (2003), 97–119.

renunciation of riches symbolising spiritual victory over covetousness; they are real riches in a child's world. Attempting to depict genuine childishness, but in a theologically conditioned light, is problematic: Audelay is forced simultaneously to applaud the child for his virtue, and acknowledge that that virtue is unconscious.

Audelay touches upon, but circumnavigates, the problem that is unavoidable and acute for those authors whose writings were directly concerned with the bringing–up of real children. This section has shown how the conflicting theological models problematised the depiction of children in vernacular spiritual literature; the remainder of this article will analyse how the secular courtesy books, responding to the opposing available paradigms of childhood, interrogated this dilemma. They engaged the question of childhood innocence from an utterly different heuristic perspective: practical not spiritual, literal not symbolic. The conflict in the theological literature created a central but sublimated crux in the social literature. Accommodating the spiritual models of childhood was unavoidable, but the courtesy books' mediation shows a fundamental departure from them.

The courtesy books: at odds with the spiritual *and* the secular meme

The literature that was written *for* children and was concerned with the practicalities of their upbringing, rather than recommending to adults the imitation of childlike virtue or spiritualising childhood as an object for Christian imitation, offers an understanding of childhood that is neither somatic corruption nor sentimentalised unspoiledness. The courtesy books and other instructional literature for children negotiate and ultimately reject both doctrinal positions on childhood. It confronts the slovenliness of children that is ignored by the idealising literature, instructing them to behave courteously in a household, not to spit, belch or blow their noses, tear their meat or chew it with open mouths, brandish the bones between their teeth, have dirty nails, scratch their heads, pick their teeth, talk over their superiors, gossip about their peers, or be rude to their servants. Injunctions such as these are commonplace:

> Ley not þyne Elbowe nor thy fyst
> Vpon the tabylle þat thow etist,
> Bulk not as a Bene were in þi throte,
> As a karle þat comys oute of a cote.[25]

> Belche thou neare to no mans face
> with a corrupt fumosytee,
> But turne from such occasion, friend,
> hate such ventositye.[26]

> Blow not thy nose, nor looke thereon;
> to most men it is loath.[27]

These admonitions acknowledge the gluttony, unmanneliness and selfishness of children that are no less reprehensible for juvenile. They confront the reality that children are not pure by nature, and need to be educated in clean and courteous habits. Theirs is an ideology focused *upon* social practice, rather than a romanticisation of it: they dwell upon what the exemplary depiction glosses over.

---

[25] 'The Lytyll Childrenes Lytil Boke', in *The Babees Book*, ed. by F. J. Furnivall, Early English Text Society, o. s., 32 (London: Trübner, 1868), p. 18 (ll. 45–48).
[26] Hugh Rhodes, 'The Book of Nurture', in *The Babees Book*, ed. by F. J. Furnivall, p. 77 (ll. 229–32).
[27] Ibid., p. 80 (ll. 335–36).

The style of the courtesy books is simple: they are usually written in rhyming quatrains, sometimes alphabet acrostics, such as 'The a.b.c. of Aristotel'. Caxton stipulates that children 'muste entretyde be | With esy thyng, and not with subtilte',[28] and these poems' style is one of straightforward and mnemonic maxims. Nonetheless, their negotiation of the theme of innocence is a complex one. They cannot but acknowledge the dominant meme of childhood simplicity, yet their changed inflection inverts the theological paradigm: the principal addressee becomes the child, and polished adult behaviour the principal object of emulation. Courteous conduct and perfect manners are the desired object, contrasted with lack of self-control and ignorance of social grace; whereas in the adult literature, childlike lack of affectation is presented as virtuous simplicity and moral probity, in contrast with the secret, sinful soul of the adult reader, concealed behind a front of decorum. The one praises as lack of deception what the other castigates as lack of self-control. Emulation is a key aspect in which the change of addressee makes all the difference. It is not that there is no place for the theme of innocence in the courtesy books, but their scrutiny and correction of actual childish conduct leads them to react against and reframe the available models of it.

This is not to say that the courtesy books are explicit about their rejection of the paradigms of spiritual literature: overtly to contradict Aquinas and Isidore would be too bold a manoeuvre. But they do subtly reverse the direction of the theological discourse. The author of 'The Lytyll Childrenes Lytil Boke', for example, considers the same assertion as Audelay, that the child 'is wroth with no mon', appealing to the well-known archetype in his attempt to encourage children to be 'tretable':

> To children it longithe nat to be [vengeable];
> Sone meeved and sone forgyvyng;
> And as it is remembrid bi writyng,
> Wrathe of children is sone ouergone,
> With an apple the parties be made atone.[29]

The theme of innocence is there in the background: 'remembrid bi writyng' suggesting that it is in clerical discourse that the author is familiar with the topos that 'to children it longithe nat to be vengeable'. The theological aspect is not dismissed: it is held up as an ideal, while simultaneously undermined by the fact that the admonition needs to written at all. There is a certain irony in that the idealisation of children, designed for adults to imitate spiritually, is made into a goal for children to aim at practically. The influence of the ideal child is tangible, even though the author's minute engagement with the undesirable behaviour of the real child subtly undermines any credence that might attach to it. The prevailing characteristics of the real child are temper and contrariety, not sentimentalised amiability. But there is also tenderness in the realism of the characterisation: the statement 'with an apple the parties be made atone', reminiscent of Audelay's 'cheré stons', indicates an appreciation and positive understanding of childishness as a separate category from *népiotés*, innocence as something different from sinlessness, and a genuine simplicity of experience distinct from a religious imitation of it. A similar depiction of play is discernible in the poem 'Ratis Raving':

> Sa lang havis child wyl alwaye
> With flouris for to Jap and playe;
> With stikis, and with spalys small,
> To bige vp chalmer, spens & hall.

---

[28] William Caxton, *The Book of Curtesye*, ed. by F. J. Furnivall, Early English Texts Society, e. s., 3 (London: Trübner, 1868), p. 53 (ll. 524–25).

[29] Anon., 'The Lytyll Childrenes Lytil Boke', in *The Babees Book*, ed. by Furnivall, p. 30 (ll. 80–84).

The 'flouris', 'stikis' and 'spalys small' signify solely within the child's world of play, rather than being read as symbols in an overlaid interpretation of it. The poet does not praise native childishness as though it were Christian imitative purity. And his verdict on childhood is the more cautious:

> This eild is lycht and Innocent,
> Suppos It want gud Jugment:
> For-thi I bles it nocht as best,
> Na ȝit I wary it nocht as verst.[30]

Innocence and 'gud Jugment' are two distinct qualities in this literature. The author, as he ponders the patristic terminology, does not equate sinlessness with virtue: *pueritia* is not 'best', although neither is it, in the Augustinian formulation, equal with the 'verst'. In this poem, 'innocent' means something very different from 'sinless'. The author uses the same language as the religious literature, but defines it fundamentally differently. Where religious writers conformed their understanding of the *res* to the *verbum*, the courtesy manuals reappropriate and redefine the theologised concept to fit the reality. The place in the courtesy books where the theme of childhood innocence is most acutely subverted is in the pedagogical poems, 'How the Wise Man tauȝt His Son' or 'How the Good Wijf Tauȝt Hir Douȝtir'. Parental address is a common enough topos to assume that it is indeed a topos, as much as a reality: 'Ratis Raving' is written to 'my gud sone';[31] Caxton's 'lytil Iohn' is the object of his advice in *The Book of Curtesye*;[32] Chaucer's 'lyte Lowys' is addressed in 'A Treatise on the Astrolabe';[33] Geoffrey de la Tour-Landry's 'wel bylouyd doughters' are the intended readers of his collection of cautionary tales, *The Book of the Knight of the Tower*.[34] The form occupies an ambiguous space between the cliché of an established formula and the genuine tenderness of parental address.[35] For example, every stanza of 'The Good Wif Thaught Hir Doughtir' ends with the refrain, 'my leue childe' or 'my der childe'.[36] The frequency of this appellation makes it formulaic, but its function in the mnemonic structure of the poem does not nullify its authenticity by repetition. Rather its regular punctuation of the otherwise rigid advice to 'make þou non iangelyng', 'laughe þou noght to lowde', and 'go þou noght to toune',[37] with a continually and comfortably repeated note of affection, mixes the tenor of sternness with affection.

In this genre, although innocence is acknowledged, it is not cherished: rather, there is emphatic recommendation to the child to learn the ways of adulthood. The principle that

---

[30] *Ratis Raving and Other Moral and Religious Pieces, in Prose and Verse*, ed. by J. Rawson Lumby, Early English Texts Society, o. s., 43 (London: Trübner, 1870), pp. 57–58 (ll. 1128–31 and 1142–45).

[31] *Ratis Raving*, ed. by Lumby, p. 26 (l. 15).

[32] Caxton, *The Book of Curtesye*, ed. by Furnivall, p. 45 (l. 435).

[33] Prologue to 'A Treatise on the Astrolabe', in Geoffrey Chaucer, *The Riverside Chaucer*, ed. by Larry D. Benson, 3rd edn (Oxford: Oxford University Press, 1987), p. 662 (l. 1).

[34] Geoffrey De La Tour-Landry, *The Book of the Knight of the Tower*, ed. by M. Y. Offord and trans. by William Caxton, Early English Texts Society, s. s., 2 (Oxford: Oxford University Press, 1971), p. 12 (l. 35).

[35] The canonical exemplar of parental advice was of course the end of the book of Proverbs, 'the words of king Lamuel. The vision wherewith his mother instructed him' ('verba Lamuhel regis visio qua erudivit eum mater sua'; Proverbs 31. 1–5), which is similarly frank about the realities of adult temptation. It is no coincidence that elsewhere the book of Proverbs exhibits a similarly pedagogic view of childishness to that expressed by these poets: 'folly is bound up in the heart of a child, and the rod of correction shall drive it away' ('stultitia conligata est in corde pueri et virga disciplinae fugabit eam'; 22. 15; see also 20. 11).

[36] *The Good Wife Taught Her Daughter, The Good Wyfe Wold a Pylgremage, The Thewis of Gud Women*, ed. by Tauno F. Mustanoja, Suomalaisen Tiedeakatemian toimituksia, series B, 61 (Helsinki: Suomalaisen Kirjallisuuden Seura, 1948), pp. 159–72.

[37] *The Good Wife Taught Her Daughter*, ed. by Mustanoja, pp. 159–61 (ll. 15, 41, and 50).

guides the advice is 'Loke what woman þou wolt be, and theron set thy thowʒt.'[38] Whereas the carol-narrator complains, 'a child aʒene I wold I were', these poems are designed to teach children how to lose their innocence — but to lose it to maturity, and not to sin. In 'The Good Wyfe Wold a Pylgremage', the young girl's sexual innocence is, in one sense, lost, because the wife-narrator seeks to acquaint her with the truth before she learns the hard way:

> Doʒttor, seyd þe good wyfe, hyde thy legys whyte,
> And schew not forth thy stret hossyn, to make men have delytt;
> Thow hit plese hem for a tym, hit schall be thy despytt,
> And men wyll sey of þi body þou carst but lytt.

Lack of experience is figured not as a precious thing to be guarded or emulated, but a dangerous thing, such that the wife concludes,

> Better wer a childe vnborn þan vntaught,
>   My leue childe.[39]

Audelay's idealisation of a world in which sin has not yet entered is not, in this context, a good thing. When Audelay wished himself 'unboren', it was in order to re-enter a pre-sinful state. But the ignorance he wistfully regretted appears here as a dangerous lack of knowledge: without wisdom, the child is better off 'vnborn'. The wife needs to introduce her daughter to the adult world, even if it involves destroying her innocence, because for better or worse she moves in it. Ignorance, in this literature, is *not* bliss.

Similarly, the father's advice to his son is to recognise and forget the frivolity of his childish pastimes and see the world the way the adult does:

> Sonne, sette not bi þis worldis weele,
> For it fariþ but as a cheri faire.[40]

This image is almost the exact reversal of Audelay's, which made the cherry hoard a symbol of the purity and simplicity of the child's uncovetous mind, and held out such a state as the ideal for the aspiring Christian. But to the father, 'cheri faire' represents only transience and immaturity. This phrase, referring to a festival at the time of the cherry harvest, was also a common metaphor for the transience of wordly joys (see the MED definition). The father doesn't sentimentalise the 'cheri faire': his advice to his son is to leave his cherries behind as he adopts a maturer and more pessimistic understanding of the world. This is a long way from the 'cheré stons' as 'tresoure': the child is encouraged to abandon his ephemeral treasure for the sake of treasure in heaven. Rather than celebrating the ingenuousness of play, the poet exhorts the child to forget his foolishness, and to come to a more disillusioned understanding of the ephemerality of the 'worldis weele'. In an exact reversal of Audelay's metaphor, the secular manuals advise that children should learn as soon as possible imitate the adult world.

But they do so not by contradicting but by co-opting the imagery of the spiritual paradigm. Instead of rejecting *nēpiotēs* out of hand, these authors negotiate and accommodate the theme of negative purity. Caxton begins his Book of Curtesye by analysing the morality of infancy:

> [l]ytyl Iohn/ syth your tendre enfancye
> Stondeth as yet vnder, in difference
> To vice or vertu to meuyn or applye ...
> But as waxe resseyveth prynte or figure,
> So children ben disposide of nature.[41]

---

[38] *The Good Wife Taught Her Daughter*, ed. by Mustanoja, p. 175 (l. 61).
[39] *The Good Wife Taught Her Daughter*, ed. by Mustanoja, pp. 173–74 (ll. 25–28); p. 172 (ll. 208–9).
[40] 'How the Wise Man tauʒt His Son', in *The Babees Book*, ed. by Furnivall, p. 52 (l. 143).
[41] Caxton, *The Book of Curtesye*, ed. by Furnivall, p. 3 (ll. 1–7).

This is very different from the treatment of the same theme in theological literature. Negative innocence, stemming from inexperience, not resistance, of temptation, is still present: the child is like soft wax, able to receive the impression of either 'vice or vertu'. But Caxton does not use this image to signify the untouched state of sinlessness. Instead, he inverts the theme, using inexperience as the pretext to present adult conduct to children as the object of imitation, rather than childish naïvety as object of imitation to the adult world. Instead of celebrating innocence, these poems provide a practical manual of how to lose it. They explore, deeply and unsentimentally, the native quality of their addressee, not applauding as a spiritual feat the natural condition of being young. They do not despise innocence, but they resist the conflation of ignorance and innocence in their differentiation between sapient virtue and nescient naïvety, between the adult's informed and active purity and the child's unconscious purity. They are closer to a different gospel exhortation, one that encompasses shrewdness in its definition of innocence: 'be ye therefore wise as serpents and simple as doves.'[42]

It is the prevailing ethic of practical morality that differentiates the didacticism of the courtesy books from that of the religious literature. Courtesy and piety may be sister-virtues, but the emphasis of the former is on earthly assimilation and socialisation, and not renunciation of corruptive worldly society. However, the courtesy books still use the language of virtue to categorise the social as the moral. One author calls it 'honestye' to 'eate thy meate somewhat close': the semantic blending of propriety, decorum, purity, chastity and moral uprightness in this word suggesting a semantic matrix in which moral virtue and social mannerliness collided.[43] The advocation of courtesy has a fundamental embrace of, not withdrawal from, the world, configuring spirituality within a framework of obeisance and advancement. In this paradigm, heavenly reward is held out to social aspirants, not social ascetics: success lies in learned behaviour and not innate quality. Novices must abandon their rude childish manners and embrace refined adulthood to attain perfection, rather than the other way round. 'The Babees Book' concludes with the wish

> That thurhe your nurture and youre gouernaunce
> In lastynge blysse yee mowe your self auaunce![44]

It is not that the courtesy literature is unspiritual in its depiction of childhood, but that the promise of 'lastynge blysse' coincides with the idea of self-advancement and social harmony. Holiness is presented as something achieved *through* appropriate socialisation, and not the rejection of societal ethics. Part of the mediation of the influential spiritual ideas in this literature is its borrowing and redefinition of the same vocabulary and imagery.

However, in their move from the spiritual to the social, the courtesy books found in social paradigms an equally problematic tendency to overlay the adult world onto the juvenile. By nature, noble children are as unrefined as the base-born, their habits just as vulgar — demonstrated by admonitions against spitting and belching. The final irony, which makes the idea of childhood innocence so problematic for the courtesy manuals, is that secular culture offered a model of childhood that was every bit as problematic as the spiritual one. The courtesy manuals were designed to educate noble children in noble behaviour that *should*, according to courtly literature, have been innate and inalienable; to educate them, in other words, to be what they already were. In the romances, examples abound of lost children whose striking beauty and moral superiority mark them as noble, whether by kinmarks blazoned on

---

[42] 'Ergo prudentes sicut serpentes et simplices sicut columbae'; Matthew 10. 16.
[43] Hugh Rhodes, 'The Boke of Nurture', in *The Babees Book*, ed. by Furnivall, p. 79 (ll. 299–300).
[44] 'The Babees Book', in *The Babees Book*, ed. by Furnivall, p. 9 (l. 216–17).

their body, or by their peculiar dignity and prowess.[45] Nobility, in the romances, is a self-authenticating ontological reality. And just as the religious metaphor of the child exerted a pressure on the reality of social pedagogy, the fictional world of the court exerted a peculiar pressure on its original. Educating the noble child to act as who he innately is (or should be), in the light of the literature of self-evincing legitimacy, is the paradoxical premise of the courtesy writing. Noble by nature, children have to be taught how not to behave '[as a ka]rle þat comys oute of a cote.'[46] The formula 'lerne or be lewde' appears as the title of one poem and is quoted in several others. This paradox is as problematic for the courtesy book authors as the religious concept of *népiotés*. Both secular and sacred literature had a model in which children were pure or noble by nature, and in which their innocence or dignity manifested itself spontaneously and untaught, as the authenticating evidence of their pedigree. Yet those who had the care of real noble children had the difficult job of impressing upon them these expectations while confronting their palpable unreality. Courtesy literature is neither an exclusively sacred nor secular genre: it blends religious and social language, it promises both treasure in heaven with rewards in earth, its instructions are a mixture of moral imperative and social decorum. Yet in both secular and sacred literature the theme of childhood perfection collided with the discrepancy with reality. The paradoxical job of the courtesy literature was to teach noble children how to be *innately* noble; or to teach beings of inherent simplicity how to act without duplicity: to instil the kind of innocence that the very act and necessity of instruction proved not to exist. In this sense, the courtesy manuals, although thoroughly immersed in their culture, were also profoundly counter-cultural, as they negotiated cultural memes that were inherently contradictory.

Moreover, the success of the paradoxical enterprise of teaching noble children to be noble had social ramifications in which pedagogy was certainly implicated: Hugh Rhodes comments, 'by the Chylde yee shall perceiue the disposytion of the Gouernour.'[47] Manners were no casual matter in the networking of the elite: and yet, in instilling them in their charges, teachers had to accommodate the the secular, as well as the sacred models, that held them to be intrinsic. The 'Babees Book' poet writes:

> O yonge Babees, whome bloode Royalle
> With grace, Feture, and hyhe habylite
> Hathe enourmyd, on yow ys that I calle
> To knowe this Book; for it were grete pyte,
> Syn that in yow is sette sovereyne beaute,
> But yf vertue and nurture were withe alle;
> To yow therfore I speke in specyalle,
>
> And nouhte to hem of elde that bene experte
> In governaunce, nurture, and honeste.[48]

The poet contrasts the beauty and ability with which royalty has 'enourmyd' them with the virtue and nurture which have to be acquired: it is a cautiously qualified assertion of what is and isn't innate in the noble child. 'Grace, Feture, and hyhe habylite', and not to mention 'sovereyne beaute', are innate, the poet allows, although this statement is couched with careful caveats: the assertion 'in yow is sette sovereyne beaute' does not allege beyond all doubt that beauty

---

[45] See for example *Havelok the Dane*, ed. by G. V. Smithers (Oxford: Clarendon, 1987), p. 21 (l. 605).
[46] 'The Lytyll Childrenes Lytil Boke', in *The Babees Book*, ed. by Furnivall, p. 18 (l. 48).
[47] Preface to 'The Boke of Nurture', in *The Babees Book*, ed. by Furnivall, p. 63.
[48] 'The Babees Book', in *The Babees Book*, ed. by Furnivall, p. 1 (ll. 15–23).

is a product of nature and not nurture; and even more ambiguous is the term 'enourmyd', meaning 'ornamented'. Having been *decorated* with the qualities of royalty, then, they are importuned 'in specyalle' to *learn* the code of conduct, framed in moral terms: 'vertue and nurture', 'nurture, and honeste.'

And this is the nub of the problem: if the noble child had to acquire its courteous conduct by imitation and instruction, surely the aspiring bourgeoisie could assimilate imitative nobility also — another of the rippling circles of emulation — which undermines the very claim to innate status. This was the question for Caxton, who wrote his prologues ostensibly for an aristocratic readership, yet relied upon and courted the patronage of burghers and merchants. Tracy Adams remarks that the courtesy books were 'appropriated and re-deployed by non-noble readers for their own self-fashioning'.[49] Throughout the fifteenth century intermarriage between the gentry and lower nobility was increasing, and by the 1430s, £40 per year was enough to qualify for the knighthood: nobility was affordable. Statements such as '[thys] book is not requysyte to every comyn man to have, but to noble gentylmen that by their vertu entende to come and entre into the noble ordre of chyvalry', and 'this present booke is not for a rude uplondyssh man to laboure therin ne rede it, but onely for a clerke and a noble gentylman'[50] are frequent in Caxton's prologues and epilogues, and while there is truth in Richard Firth Green's assessment of them as 'advertising talk, designed in part to entice non-noble clients with the promise of initiation into aristocratic mysteries', they also indicate a theoretical crisis over heredity, a need to articulate exclusivity under threat.[51] Caxton, himself an upwardly mobile merchant, advised his son to

> Take hede to the norture/ that men vse
> Newe founde/ or auncyent whether it be,
> So shal no mon your curtiosye refuse.
> [...] haunte
> The guyse of them / that do most manerly.[52]

Copying the breeding of the 'most manerly' attains the likeness, if not the birthright, of 'curtiosye'; and the oblique animadversion that the hallmark conduct of the elite may be either 'newe founde, or auncyent' hints that it is indeed a 'guyse', not a property. The aspect of social advancement exposes the paradox that the courtesy books have been hedging around from the beginning: that so-called innate behaviour needs to be learned. Caxton's advice indicates that creating an external impression is the real goal of courteous conduct,

> that men may of you saye
> A goodly chylde.[53]

The courtesy literature preserves the theoretical veneer of innate nobility, but in practice it recognises that social identity is conferred rather than natural; just as it did lip-service to the theological analogue of childhood innocence, while acknowledging its fallacy. Caxton's ambition for his son is that people will say well of him: the difference between the social classes is principally one of language not of ontology, as Chaucer's Manciple's recognises:

> Ther nys no difference, trewely,
> Bitwixe a wyf that is of heigh degree,

---

[49] Tracy Adams, 'Noble, wyse and grete lordes, gentilmen and marchauntes: Caxton's prologues as conduct books for merchants', *Parergon*, 22 (2005), 53–76 (p. 53).

[50] Epilogue to 'The Order of Chualrye' and Prologue to 'Eneydos', from William Caxton, *Caxton's Own Prose*, ed. by N. F. Blake (London: Deutsch, 1973), p. 126 (ll. 6–9); p. 80 (ll. 68–70).

[51] Richard Firth Green, *Poets and Princepleasers: Literature and the Court in the Late Middle Ages* (Toronto: University of Toronto Press, 1980), p. 159.

[52] Caxton, *The Book of Curtesye*, ed. by Furnivall, p. 45 (ll. 436–38 and 449–50).

[53] Ibid., p. 9 (ll. 69–70).

> If of hir body dishonest she bee,
> And a povre wenche, oother than this —
> If it so be they werke bothe amys —
> But that the gentile, in estaat above,
> She shal be cleped his lady, as in love;
> And for that oother is a povre womman,
> She shal be cleped his wenche, or his lemman.[54]

The difference between a *lady* and a *lemman*, a *wyf* and a *wenche*, is one of register: linguistic stratification is the henchman of social differentiation, and as much as the Manciple protests himself a 'boystous' man for whom word and deed possess an integrity free from such euphemistic relabelling, there *is* a 'difference'. The problem of having to *seem* what you *are* is that people are defined by language, and the familiar categories of word and thought that classify and contain social experience. The authors of the courtesy books are forced to accommodate both the myth that noble identity is integral and the reality that it is socially conferred: to labour under a mirage of semantic and social identity held to be referential and essential, while in practice universally understood to be relational and conditioned.

Archetypal presentations of childhood innocence, therefore, were confronted by literature that addressed itself directly to children. Its conception of childhood is complicated not only by the pedagogic imperative to correct the kind of behaviour that proves innocence not to be intrinsic, but by the social pressure to pretend that such correction is unnecessary. Both the secular and the spiritual models were at odds with the courtesy authors' understanding of the reality of childhood, yet both were too prevalent to be easily rejected. As a result, the paradox at the heart of courtesy literature is left largely unspoken. In the final analysis, it is appropriate that the problem is essentially one of textual decorum, saying something that can't be said and acknowledging something that can't be acknowledged, in the schooling of children in behaviours that they must simultaneously somehow pretend were completely natural.

Conclusion

This article has argued both that religious and secular literature had models of childhood innocence that were incommensurable with the reality of childhood experience, and that the response of medieval children's literature was subtle and pragmatic. With the reversal of the addressee, theme became anti–theme. The allegorised and idealised image of childhood was the pretext for the pedagogic exhortations of 'kembe your hede' and 'purge your nose'.[55] Ironically, these ostensibly lowly texts expose some of the absurdities and inconsistencies of the august adult literature. The very fact of their composition involved a rebuttal of the sentimentalisation of childhood innocence, but instead of articulating this rebuttal explicitly, the courtesy authors adopt it as part of their complex ethic of emulation. The perfect children of hagiography and romance are co-opted as objects of emulation for real children, in a circular cultural matrix which had originally made them objects of adult imitation themselves. With appropriate irony, it is by carefully hedged deference to these dominant theological and social models that the allegedly unsophisticated texts expose something that we knew all along — that the symbol is always a simplification of the original.

---

[54] Chaucer, 'The Manciple's Tale', in *The Riverside Chaucer*, ed. by Larry D. Benson, pp. 284–85 (ll. 212–20).
[55] Caxton, *The Book of Curtesye*, ed. by Furnivall, p. 7 (ll. 36–39).

Reading Between the Lines: The Liturgy and Ælfric's *Lives of Saints* and Homilies

Stewart Brookes

Source investigation has played a significant part in the study of Old English literature for many years, with scholars seeking to identify the biblical verses, patristic commentaries, and treatises upon which the Old English texts are based.[1] As Charles Wright recently commented, 'The recovery of [Latin] sources has been one of the great undertakings — and one of the great successes — of Old English literary scholarship since the late nineteenth century.'[2] Despite this emphasis upon Latin sources, little attention has been paid to the presence of occasional quotations in Latin in Ælfric's Old English saints' lives and homilies beyond the observation that the inclusion of Latin is a characteristic feature of Ælfric's later writings, a sign of a more educated target audience.[3] Certain questions occur to me about these Latin citations, however, that have not adequately been resolved by the explanations which have thus far been offered. First, why does Ælfric single out particular Latin lines for inclusion in his saints' lives and homilies? And secondly, why does he include Latin at all in texts which are otherwise written exclusively in the vernacular?[4]

Looking behind the use of Latin quotations

In order to investigate Ælfric's inclusion of Latin quotations in his *Lives of Saints* collection and homilies I will begin by examining his 'Life of Cecilia'. This saint's life offers a useful

---

[1] An example of what has been achieved in the field of source studies is the *Fontes Anglo-Saxonici* project which set out to identify all 'written sources which were incorporated, quoted, translated or adapted anywhere in English or Latin texts which were written in Anglo-Saxon England (i.e. England to 1066), or by Anglo-Saxons in other countries': <http://fontes.english.ox.ac.uk/whatisfontes.html> [accessed 20 February 2012].

[2] Charles D. Wright, 'Old English Homilies and Latin Sources', in *The Old English Homily: Precedent, Practice, and Appropriation*, ed. by Aaron J. Kleist (Turnhout: Brepols, 2007), pp. 15–66 (pp. 15–16).

[3] M. R. Godden, 'The Development of Ælfric's Second Series of *Catholic Homilies*', *English Studies*, 54 (1973), 209–16 (p. 216).

[4] For Ælfric's saints' lives, see *Ælfric's Lives of Saints*, ed. by Walter W. Skeat, Early English Text Society, o. s., 76, 82, 94, 114 (London: Oxford University Press, 1881–1900; repr. as two volumes 1966). Hereafter cited as *LS* with item number. For his homilies, see *Ælfric's Catholic Homilies: The First Series: Text*, ed. by Peter Clemoes, Early English Text Society, s. s., 17 (London: Oxford University Press, 1997); *Ælfric's Catholic Homilies: The Second Series: Text*, ed. by Malcolm Godden, Early English Text Society, s. s., 5 (London: Oxford University Press, 1979); and *Homilies of Ælfric: A Supplementary Collection*, ed. by John C. Pope, Early English Text Society, s. s., 259, 260 (London: Oxford University Press, 1967–68). Hereafter cited as *CH 1*, *CH 2*, and *SH*, respectively. For a study of Ælfric's textual output, see *A Companion to Ælfric*, ed. by Hugh Magennis and Mary Swan, Brill's Companions to the Christian Tradition, 18 (Leiden: Brill, 2009).

test-case because it is a vernacular translation which features Latin quotation in a way that is typical of many of the other pieces in the *Lives of Saints*. The 'Life of Cecilia' opens with Ælfric setting out the dilemma faced by Cecilia, a devout Christian from childhood, when she is told that she must marry the worthy, but heathen, Valerian. Cecilia has no way out and the wedding celebrations begin. In the description of the festivities we see the first of two Latin lines that Ælfric includes in his Old English text:

> Þa betwux þam sangum and þam singalum dreamum, sang Cecilia symle þus Gode, '*Fiat cor meum et corpus meum inmaculatum ut non confundar*' ('Beo min heorte and min lichama þurh God ungewemmed þæt ic ne beo gescynd'). And sang symle swa. (lines 16–19)[5]
>
> Then in the midst of the songs and the constant melodies, Cecilia sang continually to God in this way, '*Let my heart and my body be unstained so that I might not be put to shame*' ('Let my heart and my body be undefiled through God so that I might not be put to shame.') And she always sang in this way.

Shortly afterwards Cecilia and Valerian find themselves in bed together:

> Cecilia sona, þæt snotere mæden, gespræc hire brydguman and þus to Gode tihte, 'Eala þu min leofa man, ic þe mid lufe secge, ic hæbbe Godes encgel þe gehylt me on life, and gif þu wylt me gewemman, he went sona to ðe and mid graman þe slihð þæt þu sona ne leofast. (lines 20–24)
>
> [I]mmediately Cecilia, the wise virgin, spoke to her bridegroom and thus allured him to God, 'Oh, my beloved husband, I say to you with love, I have an angel of God who guards me while (I am) alive, and if you wish to defile me, he will turn to you at once and strike you in anger so that instantly you will not live.

Valerian does not expect this speech from his bride on their wedding night; nor do Cecilia's words have the effect she wants, to 'allure' him to God. Rather, Valerian is afraid, demands to see evidence of this angel for himself and, suspecting that Cecilia has a secret lover, threatens to kill them both. Eventually, Cecilia persuades Valerian that he will not merit an angelic visitation until he has been baptised and has embraced Christianity. This accomplished, an angel appears to Valerian, bearing 'anum gyldenum gewrite' ('a golden piece of writing', line 40). We then see the second of the Latin lines:

> On þam gewrite wæron þas word gelogode, '*Unus Deus, una fides, unum baptisma*' ('An ælmihtig God is and an geleafa and an fulluht'). (lines 42–44)
>
> In the piece of writing were arranged these words, '*There is One God, one faith, one baptism*' ('There is one almighty God and one faith and one baptism').

Ælfric goes on to describe the persecutions, and eventual martyrdom, suffered by Cecilia, Valerian, and others. Aside from these two lines in Latin, however, his narration is entirely in Old English. A source study approach would point to Psalms 118. 80 and Ephesians 4. 5, respectively, as the texts lying behind these quotations, adding the information that Ælfric's Latin is of a non-Vulgate form.[6] This still leaves unanswered the question as to why Ælfric

---

[5] Quotations from Ælfric's 'Life of Cecilia' are from *Ælfric's Lives of the Virgin Spouses*, ed. and trans. by Robert K. Upchurch (University of Exeter Press: Exeter, 2007), pp. 72–85.

[6] For Psalm 118. 80, the Vulgate has 'fiat cor meum inmaculatum in iustificationibus tuis ut non confundar' ('Let my heart be undefiled in thy justifications, that I may not be confounded'), lacking 'et corpus' which is in Ælfric's Latin, and adding 'in iustificationibus tuis' which Ælfric does not have. In the case of Ephesians 4. 5, the Vulgate has 'unus Dominus, una fides, unum baptisma' ('One Lord, one faith, one baptism'), using 'Dominus' whereas Ælfric has 'deus'. Several, though not all, of these differences can be found in the variants printed in the edition of the Vulgate used in this paper, *Biblia Sacra Iuxta Vulgatum Versionem*, ed. by Robertus Weber (Stuttgart: Deutsche

should choose to quote these two lines in Latin, and only these two lines, since the Latin does not appear to add anything to the understanding of the story.

Latin quotation in other of Ælfric's writings

A strong clue as to Ælfric's motivation for including Latin in his vernacular translations is provided by a pair of comments in his adaptation of the Book of Judges. Summarising the biblical account in chapter four of the Book of Judges, Ælfric narrates the Israelite victory over Yabin and his army, and the demise of Sisera at the hands of Yael. He then pauses for a moment to draw his audience's attention to the fact that this event is alluded to in the Book of Psalms:

> We secgað nu eac þæt we singað be þisum on urum sealmsange, swa swa hit sang Dauid þurh þone halgan gast, God heriende þus: '*Ecce inimici tui sonauerunt et qui oderunt [te e]xtollerunt capud. Fac illis sicut Madian et Sisare sicut Iabin in torrente Cison.*' Ðæt ys on urum gereorde, he cwæð to his Drihtene: 'Efne nu Drihten þine fynd hlydað and þa þe þe hatiað ahebbað heora heafda. Do him swa swa Madian and swa swa Sisaran and swa swa Iabin æt þam burnan Cyson.'[7]
>
> Also, we say now that we sing about this in our singing of the Psalms, just as David sang it inspired by the Holy Spirit, praising God in this way: *Your enemies have made a noise: and they that hate you have lifted up the head. Do to them as you did to Midian and to Sisera: as to Yabin at the brook of Kishon*. That is in our language, he said to his Lord: 'Even now, Lord, your enemies clamour and those who hate you raise up their heads. Do to them just as to Midian and just as to Sisera and just as to Yabin at the stream of Kishon.'

Up until this Latin verse, with its authorial explanation, the adaptation of the Book of Judges has been entirely in Old English. Ælfric explains that he quotes the Latin in order to underline the link between the Israelite victory in the Book of Judges and the reference to this in Psalm 82. 3, 10.[8] A few passages later, Ælfric once more quotes in Latin from this psalm (Psalms 82. 12), and again he draws attention to the fact that this is a Latin verse that is sung regularly as part of the recitation of the Psalms:

> Be þisum we singað eac on þam foresædan sealme ongean Godes wiðerwinna þe willað æfre þwyres, swa swa se halga gast us sæde þurch Dauid: '*Pone principes eorum sicut Oreb, Zeb et Zebee et Psalmana.*' Ðæt is on Engliscre spræce, 'Sete ðu ure Drihten heora ealdormen swa swa Horeb and Zeb and swa swa Zebee and Salmana.'[9]
>
> We also sing about this in the aforementioned Psalm against the adversaries of God, who always wish perversely, just as the Holy Spirit told us through David: *Make their princes like Oreb, and Zeb, and Zebee, and Salmana*. That is in English, 'Make you, our Lord, their leaders just like Oreb and Zeeb and just like Zebah and Zalmunna'.

In contrast to his inclusion of Latin in the 'Life of Cecilia', there is no mystery here as to Ælfric's intention. He informs his audience that these Latin verses ought to be familiar from the liturgy: 'We secgað nu eac þæt we singað be þisum on urum sealmsange' ('Also, we say

---

Bibelgesellschaft, 1994). Translations from the Vulgate are from *The Holy Bible: Douay Version. Translated from the Latin Vulgate* (London: Catholic Truth Society, 1956).

[7] *The Old English Heptateuch and Ælfric's Libellus de Veteri Testamento et Novo*, vol. *1*, ed. by Richard Marsden, Early English Text Society, o. s., 330 (London: Oxford University Press, 2008), pp. 192–93, lines 91–98. Emphasis is mine.

[8] Psalm numbers in this paper refer to the Vulgate's numbering. This psalm is Psalm 83 in the Hebrew original and many modern English translations.

[9] *Heptateuch*, ed. by Marsden, p. 194, lines 150–55. Emphasis is mine.

now that we sing about this in our singing of the Psalms') and 'Be þisum we singað eac on þam foresædan sealme' ('We also sing about this in the aforementioned psalm'). The need for this explanation is because the Book of Judges did not occupy a central place in the daily worship of the Anglo-Saxons and so the defeat of Sisera and Yabin would not have been well known. Similarly, the reference in Psalm 82 to Oreb, Zeeb, Zebah and Zalmunna would not have been understood without the background story. That Ælfric includes these two, arguably obscure, references in his highly-selective adaptation of the Book of Judges is significant. The adaptation condenses whole chapters into a few succinct lines of summary and typically omits exotic names.[10] It seems evident that Ælfric's reason for including these two episodes in his adaptation of the Book of Judges is because he wants to explain the verses from the Psalter for the monastic contingent in his audience. Governed by The Rule of St Benedict these monks followed a regime which stipulated that all 150 psalms should be recited each week, beginning afresh at the Night Office on Sunday.[11] The monks had to commit the entire psalter to memory and sing it every day, but understanding the context of what they were singing was another matter, even for those who were fluent in Latin. Recognising that the psalmist's allusions to characters from the Book of Judges were likely to be lost on his audience, Ælfric cites these verses in Latin in order to aid the process of recognition and he explains their meaning in order to add greater significance to the recital of the liturgy.

For Ælfric, obedience stems from understanding, and he aims to combat ignorance with frequent explanations. He stresses the importance of understanding key liturgical texts in his homily for Ash Wednesday:

> Ælc cristen man sceal cunnan his pater-noster, and his credan. Mid þam pater-nostre he sceal hin gebiddan, and mid þam credan he sceal his geleafan getrymman. Se lareow sceal secgan þam læwedum mannum þæt andgyt to þam pater-noster and to ðam credan, þæt hi witon hwæs hi biddað æt gode, and hu hi sceolon on god gelyfan.[12]

> Every Christian man must know his Pater Noster, and his Creed. With the Pater Noster he shall pray, and with the Creed he shall confirm his faith. The master shall teach the unlearned men the meaning of the Pater Noster, and of the Creed that they may know what they ask of God, and how they are to believe in God.

Addressing this very requirement, Ælfric's 'De Dominica Oratione' supplies a phrase-by-phrase analysis of the Latin in which the Pater Noster was recited.[13] Catering for both the unschooled and more learned, the homily provides a clear example of Ælfric's commitment to explaining primary Latin texts such as the Pater Noster and the Psalms in the vernacular.

With Ælfric's commitment to explaining primary texts in mind, I suggest that he includes the Latin lines in his 'Life of Cecilia' in order to provide the background to Latin verses with which his audience ought to have been familiar. The context in which an Anglo-Saxon congregation, particularly one which included the laity, would have been most likely to encounter Latin scripture was in the recitation of the liturgy. In his adaptation of the Book of Judges, Ælfric points explicitly to the liturgical source behind the Latin he quotes: 'sealmsange' ('the singing of psalms'). As we have seen, he does not indicate the source of the Latin quotations in the 'Life of Cecilia' and so consideration of their place within the liturgy

---

[10] The omission of 'superfluous' names is Ælfric's practice throughout his writings; see, for instance, his comments in 'De Sancta Maria', *CH* 2, 31. 6–10. Even in his translation of the Book of Genesis, where he generally follows the biblical text closely, Ælfric omits lengthy genealogies.

[11] *The Rule of St Benedict*, ed. and trans. by O. H. Blair (Fort Augustus: Abbey Press, 1948), ch. 17.

[12] *LS* 12, lines 261–67.

[13] *CH* 1, 19. In *CH* 1, 20, 'De Fide Catholica', Ælfric turns his attention to the Creed.

is required. Conveniently, the liturgical sources known to Ælfric are listed in a letter that he wrote to Wulfstan, outlining the service books required for effective prayer as part of his effort to educate those with ecclesiastical responsibility:

> Mæssepreost sceal habban mæsseboc and pistelboc, and sangboc and rædingboc and saltere and handboc, and penitentialem and gerim.[14]
>
> A mass–priest must have a massbook and a Book of the Epistles, and an antiphoner and a lectionary and a Book of Psalms and a manual and a penitential and a computus.

After examining the items in this and the corresponding lists in Ælfric's Old English 'Letter to Wulfsige' and his Latin 'Letter to Wulfstan', I believe that the service book known as the antiphoner ('sangboc') is the liturgical text which explains Ælfric's use of Latin in his 'Life of Cecilia'.[15] Antiphoners contained the text, and often musical notation, for the sung parts of the Divine Office (the daily cycle of liturgical prayer), gradually coming to include hymns, responsories, versicles, and psalms, in addition to the antiphons which give the book its name.[16] In his guide to the liturgical observances of the monks, the 'Letter to the Monks of Eynsham', Ælfric makes frequent reference to the antiphoner. For example: 'Nam his tribus noctibus canimus sicut antiphonarium nos docet' ('In these three nights we sing as the antiphoner instructs us') and 'tribus psalmis totidemque lectionibus cum responsoriis agitur nocturna laus, ut in antiphonario titulatur' ('The Office of Nocturns is said with three psalms and the same number of readings and responsories, as in the antiphoner').[17] It is clear that Ælfric assumes that the monks will have ready access to a copy of the antiphoner for the precise details about the various psalms and chants that he mentions.

The antiphoner was of fundamental importance to the functioning of monastic life: the antiphoner's chants were designed to complement the readings from the life of the particular saint being commemorated, and the completion of the lection was signalled by a sung antiphon and response. Examination of the kind of antiphoner to which Ælfric refers is complicated by the fact that no complete antiphoner has survived from the Anglo-Saxon period. Nevertheless, it is still possible to get some idea of the contents of Anglo-Saxon antiphoners by turning to examples from earlier periods which are likely to have formed the basis from which Anglo-Saxon service books would have been constructed. One such exemplar is the Compiègne Antiphoner (*Liber Responsalis*), a mid ninth–century compilation of antiphons and responses which was erroneously attributed to Gregory the Great.[18]

---

[14] *Die Hirtenbriefe Ælfrics in Altenglischer und Lateinischer Fassung*, ed. by B. Fehr, Bibliothek der angelsächsischen Prosa, 9 (Hamburg: Grand, 1914), Ælfric's 'First Old English Letter for Wulfstan', p. 126, 15.

[15] *Die Hirtenbriefe Ælfrics*, ed. by Fehr, 'Letter to Wulfsige', p. 13, l. 52, and 'Letter to Wulfstan', p. 51, l. 137. For the identification of the 'sangboc' with the antiphoner, see Helmut Gneuss, 'Liturgical Books in Anglo-Saxon England and their Old English Terminology', in *Learning and Literature in Anglo-Saxon England*, ed. by Michael Lapidge and Helmut Gneuss (Cambridge: Cambridge University Press, 1985), pp. 91–141 (pp. 103–4). Close discussion of the function of service books, and a detailed account of the extant witnesses to these service books from the Old English period, is provided by the essays in *The Liturgical Books of Anglo-Saxon England*, ed. by Richard W. Pfaff, Old English Newsletter: Subsidia, 23 (Kalamazoo: Medieval Institute Publications, Western Michigan University, 1995). See also, Richard Pfaff, *The Liturgy in Medieval England: A History* (Cambridge: Cambridge University Press, 2009).

[16] J. E. Krochalis and E. A. Matter, 'Manuscripts of the Liturgy', in *The Liturgy of the Medieval Church*, ed. by Thomas J. Heffernan and E. A. Matter, 2nd edn (Kalamazoo: Medieval Institute Publications, Western Michigan University, 2005), pp. 393–430 (p. 395).

[17] *Ælfric's Letter to the Monks of Eynsham*, ed. and trans. by Christopher A. Jones, Cambridge Studies in Anglo-Saxon England, 24 (Cambridge: Cambridge University Press, 1998), pp. 144–45 and 138–39.

[18] Paris, Bibliothèque Nationale, *lat*. 17436, c. 860–80. For ease of reference, I cite from *Patrologia Latina* 78, cols.

The first of the two Latin lines contained in Ælfric's 'Life of Cecilia', 'Fiat cor meum et corpus meum inmaculatum ut non confundar' ('Let my heart and my body be unstained so that I might not be put to shame'), can be found in the Compiègne Antiphoner in the chants assigned for the celebration of Cecilia's feast day. It occurs twice as an antiphon and once as a sung versal, though neither is an exact match for the Latin Ælfric quotes.[19] The second, 'Unus deus, una fides, unum baptisma' ('There is one God, one faith, one baptism'), does not appear in the Compiègne Antiphoner. It is, however, present in the Sarum Missal, which provides a late witness to the liturgical tradition.[20] The wording of the first Latin line in the Sarum text matches the Latin formulation used by Ælfric, suggesting a relationship with a common source.[21] The evidence from these two antiphoners supports the theory that Ælfric chose to include these two Latin lines in his Old English 'Life of Cecilia' because they were those that would have been repeatedly heard by his audience on the saint's day, sung with musical elaboration which would have made the Latin memorable. While I have chosen Cecilia as my example, the same case for the inclusion of Latin can be made for many of the other pieces in the *Lives of Saints*. However, neither the Compiègne or the Sarum texts provide a complete source for the Latin lines cited by Ælfric in his *Lives of Saints*. For example, the Latin line included in Ælfric's Life of Agatha, 'Mentem sanctam spontaneam, honorem deo, et patrie liberationem' ('A mind voluntarily holy, an honour to God, and deliverance to her country'; *LS* 8, line 204), appears in the chants for Agatha in the Hereford Breviary but not in the Compiègne or Sarum texts.[22] This is unsurprising because variation amongst service books is to be expected: the liturgy was not a fixed entity, and antiphoners contained patterns of chants and textual accretions which reflected localised customs. Accordingly, I am not positing any particular antiphoner as having been known by Ælfric. Rather, I am situating his choice of Latin lines within a liturgical tradition which may or may not be reflected by an individual service book.[23]

It is not only antiphoners which provide evidence that a significant proportion of the Latin quotations that Ælfric includes in his *Lives of Saints* can be explained by situating them within

---

641–850. See also R. J. Hesbert, *Corpus Antiphonalium Officii*, Rerum ecclesiasticarum documenta, series maior, 7–12, 6 vols (Rome: Herder, 1963–79). Hereafter referred to as *CAO* with an antiphon number. The association with Gregory the Great is examined in J. W. McKinnon, 'Gregorius Presul Composuit Hunc Libellum Musicae Artis', in *The Liturgy of the Medieval Church*, ed. by Heffernan and Matter, pp. 613–32. McKinnon suggests that the compilation of the book took place during the papacy of Gregory II (715–31), but that English scholars in the Carolingian court mistakenly attributed it to Gregory the Great (590–604) because of their recognition of his role in the conversion of the Anglo-Saxons (p. 632). Discussion from the point of view of Old English research is provided in Susan Rankin, 'The Liturgical Background of the Old English Advent Lyrics: A Reappraisal', in *Learning and Literature*, ed. by Lapidge and Gneuss, pp. 317–40 (319–20).

[19] The antiphon is 'Fiat domine cor meum et corpus meum inmaculatum ut non confundar' (*Patrologia Latina* 78, cols. 816A, 816B), but has the word 'domine' which is not in Ælfric's Latin. The versal is 'Fiat cor meum inmaculatum ut non confundar' (*Patrologia Latina* col. 817A), omitting 'et corpus' which is found in both Ælfric and the preceding antiphon. As noted above in footnote 6, the wording of the Vulgate does not match that used by Ælfric.

[20] *Breviarum ad usum insignis ecclesiae Sarum*, ed. by F. Procter and C. Wordsworth, 3 vols (Cambridge: Almae Matris Academiae, 1886), III, 1083.

[21] *Sarum*, ed. by Procter and Wordsworth, III, 1080 (response); iii. 1082 (antiphon).

[22] *The Hereford Breviary, edited from the Rouen edition of 1505, with collation of Manuscripts*, ed. by Walter Howard Frere and Langton E. G. Brown, Publications of the Henry Bradshaw Society, 26, 40, 46, 3 vols (London: Henry Bradshaw Society, 1911), II, 110. *CAO* 3746.

[23] It should be noted, however, that there is some correspondence between the chants listed by Ælfric in his 'Letter to the Monks of Eynsham' and those in the Compiègne Antiphoner; see J. R. Hall, 'Some Liturgical Notes on Ælfric's Letter to the Monks of Eynsham', *Downside Review*, 93 (1975), 297–303 (p. 299).

a liturgical context. The Book of Psalms also provides important support for this idea because it is the source for just over a third of the Latin lines that Ælfric cites in the *Lives of Saints*. As noted earlier, the Book of Psalms would have been familiar to monks through the daily cycle of recitation. The particular verses that Ælfric selected from the Psalms to include in Latin in his saints' lives, however, are often of more direct relevance to the liturgy than this because they are those which played a central part in the services. For instance, in his 'Life of George', Ælfric has George defiantly proclaim Psalm 69 .2 when strapped to a wheel, about to be tortured by the Emperor Datian: 'Deus in adiutorium meum intende; domine, ad adiuuandum me festina' ('O God, come to my assistance; O Lord, make haste to help me': *LS* 14, line 90). The request for urgent divine assistance fits the narrative well enough, but the reason that Ælfric opts to have George speak in Latin, rather than just Old English, is because Psalm 69. 2 would have been known to the monks in his audience because it was chanted as the opening for each of the monastic hours.[24] Not only that, but as we see from Ælfric's directions in the 'Letter to the Monks of Eynsham' (§4, §26, and §47), this verse was prominent at other sections of the liturgy too. On the surface, the decision to include Psalm 69. 2 in Latin in his 'Life of George' provides an opportunity to explain the meaning of this familiar Latin formula. Ælfric may well have intended to do more than that, however, because putting the oft-chanted words in George's mouth creates an associative identification between the saint and the daily routines of the monks. With an awareness of this associative process, we can return to Ælfric's portrayal of Cecilia at her wedding feast: 'Þa betwux þam sangum and þam singalum dreamum, sang Cecilia symle þus Gode, "*Fiat cor meum et corpus meum inmaculatum ut non confundar*" [...] And sang symle swa.' ('Then in the midst of the songs and the constant melodies, Cecilia sang continually to God in this way, "*Let my heart and my body be unstained so that I might not be put to shame*" [...] And she always sang in this way'). The repetition of the adverb 'symle' ('continually, always') highlights Cecilia's constant devotion to prayer, providing both mirror and paradigm for the monks with their unending regime of chants.

Not every one of Ælfric's *Lives of Saints* includes Latin which relates to the liturgy. Noteworthy examples of this absence of Latin liturgical material are Ælfric's lives of Agnes and Martin: both of these saints had a set of antiphons associated with their feast days and so it is surprising that Ælfric's does not incorporate this. What this absence of Latin may suggest is that Ælfric's did not have at his disposal liturgical chants for these saints, offering us a potential window into the content of his antiphoner. Along similar lines, it seems possible that the reason that there is no liturgical Latin quotation in Ælfric's lives of saints Æthelthryth, Swithun, and Oswald is because these three saints were comparatively recent, and from England, and so did not have an established Latin liturgy associated with them.[25] In this regard, one may note Ælfric's comment in the 'Letter to the Monks of Eynsham' that the correct chants should be sung for the feasts of all the saints throughout the year, but if these are not available, then other appropriate ones could be adapted in line with their usual practice (§73). Clearly, it

---

[24] A. Hughes, *Medieval Manuscripts for Mass and Office: A Guide to their Organization and Terminology* (Toronto: University of Toronto Press, 1982), §403 and §407.

[25] As regards their English provenance, note Ælfric's defensive tone at the end of his 'Life of Edmund' (*LS* 32, lines 259–263): 'Nis Angelcynn bedæled Drihtnes halgena, þonne on Englalanda licgaþ swilce halgan swylce þæs halga cyning is, and Cuþberht se eadiga, and sancte Æþeldryð on Elig, and eac hire swustor, ansunde on lichaman, geleafan to trymminge' ('The English nation is not deprived of the Lord's saints, since in the English land lie such saints as this holy king, and the blessed Cuthbert, and Saint Æthelthryth in Ely, and also her sister, incorrupt in body, for the confirmation of the faith.')

was not uncommon for the monks to find that they did not have chants for the saints being commemorated. Even so, setting aside the anomalies, there appears to be sufficient evidence to point to a link between the Latin lines in the *Lives of Saints* and the liturgy, with the Latin lines Ælfric quotes being those which would have been heard in the antiphonal chants for the saints' day in question. By including the Latin in his Old English adaptations, Ælfric points to the link between the narratives of the saints' lines and the services commemorating them.

The Cotton-Corpus legendary

Having argued that the liturgy served as inspiration and source for the Latin that Ælfric's includes in his saints' lives, it seems appropriate to consider the question of the source materials that he drew upon for his *Lives of Saints*. As Patrick Zettel demonstrated, the Cotton-Corpus Legendary — or, to be more precise, something similar to it in scope and content — is likely to have served as the Latin source for many of Ælfric's saints' lives.[26] Accordingly, when Ælfric quotes lines in Latin in his *Lives of Saints* one might expect the Latin wording to match that of the Cotton-Corpus Legendary source text. For the lives of Cecilia and Agatha, the Cotton-Corpus Legendary contains a good match. This is not, however, always the case: in the 'Life of Julian and Basilissa' the Cotton-Corpus Legendary has Psalm 67. 29 as 'Confirma hoc deus, quod operaris in nobis' ('O God confirm what you have wrought in us') whereas Ælfric's Latin is 'Confirma hoc deus, quod operatus es in nobis'. Ælfric's version of this psalm is that found in the liturgy (e.g. *CAO* 1873 and 7990) and it would seem that he deliberately chose the liturgical (non-Vulgate) form over that found in his source. In light of this, one may conclude that when there is agreement between the Latin lines quoted by Ælfric and those found in the Cotton-Corpus Legendary (as with Cecilia and Agatha), it is because the Cotton-Corpus Legendary is using the form which Ælfric knew from the liturgy. This does not challenge the primacy of the Cotton-Corpus Legendary as Ælfric's source for his *Lives of Saints*, but opens up a new avenue of research when considering his treatment of his source materials.

Latin in the *Homilies*

The use of Latin in Ælfric's homilies is often more extensive than in the *Lives of Saints*. In a number of the *Catholic Homilies*, for example, Ælfric quotes many lines of Latin taken from the gospel reading that the homily discusses, dissecting and expounding the meaning of that Latin line by line. The inclusion of Latin becomes a more frequent feature in Ælfric's later homilies, leading Malcolm Godden to argue that Ælfric's increased inclusion of biblical quotations in Latin demonstrates that Ælfric anticipated a more sophisticated audience for the Second Series of *Catholic Homilies* than for the First Series. We can even see this process in action, for when revising the Second Series of homilies, Ælfric appears to add Latin versions of biblical verses in two places which originally only had his Old English rendering.[27] In the homilies written towards the end of Ælfric's career, quotation in Latin became even more common. Despite this general trend, there is still much variation between individual homilies.

---

[26] Patrick H. Zettel, 'Ælfric's Hagiographic Sources and the Latin Legendary Preserved in B. L. Ms. Cotton Nero Ei + C.C.C.C. Ms. 9 and Other Manuscripts' (unpublished doctoral thesis, Oxford, 1979), p. 43; Patrick H. Zettel, 'Saints' Lives in Old English: Latin Manuscripts and Vernacular Accounts: Ælfric', *Peritia*, 1 (1982), 17–37.

[27] Godden, 'The Development of Ælfric's Second Series of *Catholic Homilies*', p. 216.

Some homilies contain several quotations in Latin (e.g. *CH* 1, 19; *CH* 2, 20; *CH* 2, 22; and *CH* 2, 24), while others — even those judged to be composed toward the end of Ælfric's career — do not contain any Latin at all, aside from a rubric assigning the liturgical date (e.g. *CH* 1, 29; *CH* 2, 33; and *SH* 12). In some ways this variation is not unexpected because the homilies encompass a variety of genres, and vary between being didactic, exegetical, and hagiographic. The heterogenous nature of the homilies makes them a particularly productive corpus to examine through the lens of the Latin liturgical cycle.

As with the *Lives of Saints*, the texts of the liturgy provide an explanation not only for Ælfric's inclusion of many of the Latin lines in his homilies, but also for their wording. For example, in his homily on the Nativity of Christ, Ælfric uses the liturgical Latin form 'gloria in excelsis deo' in preference to the Vulgate's 'gloria in altissimis deo':

> Þa færlice æfter þæs engles spræce wearð gesewen micel meniu heofenlices werodes. god heriendra and syngendra: '*Gloria in excelsis deo. et in terra pax hominibus bone uoluntatis*'; þæt is on urum gereorde: 'Sy wuldor gode on heannyssum. and on eorðan sib mannum. þam ðe beoð godes willan. and þa englas þa gewiton of heora gesihðe to heofonum.'[28]
>
> Then suddenly after the angel's speech, there was seen a great multitude of the heavenly host, praising God and singing '*Glory in the highest to God. And on earth peace to men of good will*'; that is in our language 'Glory to God in the highest and peace to men who are of good will.' And the angels then departed from their sight to heaven.

The 'Gloria', as the hymn is frequently called, had a prominent part in the liturgy, and it makes sense for Ælfric to cite it in its familiar liturgical form — as it would be sung and heard — in order to avoid confusion upon the part of the audience for his homily.[29] An Old English homily on this topic provides an ideal opportunity to supply the narrative context for the frequently-repeated 'Gloria' chant, and the liturgical prominence of the 'Gloria' explains Ælfric's inclusion of the line in Latin, twice, in his homily on the Nativity of Christ.[30] Ælfric is consistent in his use of this non-Vulgate wording, and thus we see him quote the 'Gloria' in this form when addressing his monks in his 'Letter to the Monks of Eynsham' (e.g. §16, §22, §26, and §52) and also throughout his homilies.[31]

A significant proportion of Ælfric's exegetical homilies open with a Latin quotation. These Latin openings are often very brief, sometimes no more than a few words, and have not attracted sustained scholarly interest because it has been assumed that the Latin that Ælfric includes is simply a small extract taken from the gospel reading of the day. That assumption is lent credence by Ælfric establishing the connection between a particular homily and the gospel text with linking phrases such as 'þe nu geræd wæs' ('which was now read') and 'on ðisum godspelle þe we nu gehierdon' ('in this gospel which we now heard').[32] These phrases clearly indicate that the homily is designed to be read directly after the daily reading from the gospel to which it refers. A second, related scholarly assumption has been that the Latin Ælfric quotes is taken from the Vulgate. John C. Pope, for example, asserts that 'Ælfric normally quotes the

---

[28] *CH* 1, 2. 29, 129–30. My emphasis. See Malcolm Godden, *Ælfric's Catholic Homilies: Introduction, Commentary and Glossary*, Early English Text Society, s. s., 18 (London: Oxford University Press, 2000), p. 16. The biblical verse is Luke 2. 14.
[29] The 'Gloria' occurs frequently in the antiphoner, e.g. *CAO* 2946 and *CAO* 6858a.
[30] The second instance is omitted in CUL Gg. 3. 28, which only has the verse in Old English on the first occasion.
[31] See, for example, *CH* 1, 2. 29, 129–30; *CH* 1, 38. 113–15; *CH* 2, 5. 233, 255, 281.
[32] *CH* 1, 17. 3 and *CH* 1, 10. 3. See also, *CH* 1, 11. 3, and many further examples.

Vulgate' and that Ælfric's 'pericopes and other extended translations from the gospels clearly follow the Vulgate, though one cannot always choose among the minor variants.'[33]

When comparing the Latin that Ælfric cites in his homilies with the Vulgate, it becomes apparent that some of the passages match reasonably well, but there are a number which display significant levels of variation. The examples below demonstrate the nature of this divergence:

> 1) postquam impleti sunt dies purgationis MARIAE. et Reliqua;
>
> (*CH* 1, 9. 3, 'Purificatione Santctae Mariae': 'After the days of the purification of Mary.')
> et postquam impleti sunt dies purgationis eius secundum legem Mosi tulerunt illum in Hierusalem ut sisterent eum Domino (Luke 2. 22: 'And after the days of her purification, according to the law of Moses, were accomplished, they carried him to Jerusalem, to present him to the Lord'.)
>
> 2) Cum turba plurima conueniret ad Iesum. Et reliqua
>
> (*CH* 2, 6. 1, 'Dominica in Sexagesima': 'When a very great multitude was gathered to Jesus, and the remainder.')
> cum autem turba plurima conveniret et de civitatibus properarent ad eum dixit per similitudinem (Luke 8. 4: 'And when a very great multitude was gathered together, and hastened out of the cities unto him, he spoke by a similitude.')
>
> 3) Amen, dico uobis, nisi abundauerit, et reliqua (*SH* 15, 'Dominica VII Post Pentecosten', line 0: 'Amen, I say to you, unless abound, and the remainder.')
> dico enim vobis quia nisi abundaverit iustitia vestra plus quam scribarum et Pharisaeorum non intrabitis in regnum caelorum (Matthew 5. 20: 'For I tell you, that unless your justice abound more than that of the scribes and Pharisees, you shall not enter into the kingdom of heaven.')
>
> 4) Ex quo omnia, per quem omnia, in quo omnia; ipsi gloria in secula (*SH* 21, 'De Falsis Diis', lines 4–5: 'From him are all things, and through him are all things, and in him are all things; to him be glory forever.')
> quoniam ex ipso et per ipsum et in ipso omnia ipsi gloria in saecula (Romans 11. 36: 'For of him, and by him, and in him, are all things: to him be glory for ever.')

In the first example above, Ælfric's Latin is close to that found in the Vulgate, with the only (noteworthy) difference being the presence of 'Mariae'. The second example also presents a reasonable match between Ælfric's text and the Vulgate; the absence of the Vulgate's 'autem' from Ælfric's version does not constitute enough of a divergence to suspect a non–Vulgate origin. As with the first example, there is the addition of a named indirect object ('ad Jesum') which is not present in the Vulgate. The third example has the additional word 'Amen' and omits the Vulgate's 'enim', both of which could be seen as within the range of textual variation that is found in texts that are derived from the Vulgate. The final example, from Ælfric's homily 'De Falsis Diis', exhibits the greatest differences between Ælfric's Latin text and the Vulgate and is suggestive of a non–Vulgate source text. In his edition of 'De Falsis Diis', Pope evinces surprise at Ælfric's departure from what he regards as the primacy of the Vulgate text and locates equivalent Latin wording in Augustine's *De Vera Religione* and *De Doctrina Christiana*.[34] However, Pope remains sceptical that either of these works of Augustine served

---

[33] *Supplementary Homilies*, ed. by Pope, pp. 713 and 152. This view is accepted by James E. Cross, 'The Literate Anglo-Saxon: On Sources and Disseminations', *Proceedings of the British Academy*, 58 (1972), 67–100 (p. 89), who likewise argues for the primacy of the Vulgate, though he notes the desirability of looking for Old Latin influences.

[34] It is not unusual for Augustine to quote older Latin, pre–Vulgate forms of the Bible in his writings.

as a direct source for Ælfric, noting that he cannot help suspecting that Ælfric lifted the entire Latin opening to 'De Falsis Diis' from a Latin sermon of the Augustinian era but that he is unable find a text to support this hypothesis.[35]

Comparison of Ælfric's Latin citations with the Vulgate text leads to two findings. First, although the wording of Ælfric's Latin quotations is often close to the Vulgate, it nonetheless contains minor differences, with these differences sometimes being of enough significance to suggest a non–Vulgate source. Secondly, a number of the Latin verses that Ælfric quotes have been altered (e.g. by adding a subject or an object to the sentence) in order to clarify their sense outside of the context of the biblical narrative from which they have been extracted. After examining potential biblical sources, such as Vulgate texts and older Latin bibles, it is clear that there is no precise match with the wording of Ælfric's Latin and that this divergence cannot be explained away as the result of variation amongst Latin bibles. When looking at liturgical material, however, Ælfric's Latin formulas can be found. For each of the examples cited above, material can be located in the antiphonaries which exactly matches that quoted by Ælfric:

> 1) postquam impleti sunt dies purgationis MARIAE. et Reliqua; (*CH* 1, 9. 3, 'Purificatione Santctae Mariae': 'After the days of the purification of Mary, and the remainder.')
>
> Postquam impleti sunt dies purgationis Mariae tulerunt illum in Jerusalem ut sisterent eum domino (*CAO* 7307a, 'Purificatio Mariae': 'After the days of the purification of Mary were fulfilled, they brought him to Jerusalem, to present him to the Lord.)
>
> 2) Cum turba plurima conueniret ad Iesum. Et reliqua (*CH* 2, 6. 1, 'Dominica in Sexagesima': 'When a very great multitude was gathered to Jesus, and the remainder.')
>
> Cum turba plurima conveniret ad Jesum et de civitatibus properarent ad eum dixit per similitudinem exiit qui seminat seminare semen suum (*CAO* 2040, 'Dom. Sexagesimae': 'When a very great multitude was gathered to Jesus and hastened out of the cities, He spoke by a similitude: 'the sower went out to sow his seed'.)
>
> 3) Amen, dico uobis, nisi abundauerit, et reliqua (*SH* 15, 'Dominica VII Post Pentecosten', line 0: 'Amen, I say to you, unless abound, and the remainder.')
>
> Amen dico vobis nisi abundaverit justitia vestra plus quam scribarum et pharisaeorum non intrabitis in regnum caelorum alleluia (*CAO* 1379, 'Dom. 7 Post Pent.': 'Amen. I say to you unless your justice abound more than that of the Scribes and Pharisees, you shall not enter into the kingdom of heaven. Halleluyah.')
>
> 4) Ex quo omnia, per quem omnia, in quo omnia; ipsi gloria in secula (*SH* 21, 'De Falsis Diis', lines 4–5,: 'From him are all things, and through him are all things, and in him are all things; to him be glory forever.')
>
> Ex quo omnia per quem omnia in quo omnia ipsi gloria in saecula (*CAO* 2751, 'De Trinitate': 'From him are all things, and through him are all things, and in him are all things; to him be glory forever.')

Given this exact match in wording, there seems no doubt that Ælfric is quoting his Latin openings to the homilies from an antiphoner. Each of the gospel readings would have been accompanied by an appropriate antiphon or response, and it is these which Ælfric repeats, in Latin, in his homilies. This is not simply a question of identifying a source, however; the importance of this is recognising that Ælfric deliberately quotes from the antiphoner in order to reinforce the relationship between the liturgy sung in the service and his homily which is read after it. Having established that the Latin openings to the homilies are directly drawn from the liturgical chants which accompanied the readings from the gospels, it becomes clear

---

[35] *Supplementary Homilies*, ed. by Pope, p. 713.

that Ælfric consistently and consciously introduces material of a non–Vulgate, older Latin, origin into his homilies. While the antiphons are often of non–Vulgate origin, however, it does not necessarily follow that the readings from the biblical texts themselves were non–Vulgate. Accordingly, even though antiphonal chants may be cited in older Latin forms in the openings to Ælfric's homilies, the main body of his homilies often rely upon the Vulgate.[36]

Questions of audience

Finally, I would like to address the question of whether the presence of Latin citations offers sufficient evidence to justify assumptions that the *Lives* are aimed at a more educated audience, learned in Latin. Ælfric was trained at Winchester in a monastic setting which cared also for the laity, and so he often writes with a mixed congregation in mind.[37] If the inclusion of quotations in Latin had been intended for a 'learned' few, the Old English translations which accompany each Latin line would have been redundant. Rather, Ælfric sets his sights upon those who might hear the responses sung in Latin but not necessarily understand their meaning or their relevance to the saints' lives being celebrated. As argued above, Ælfric includes the Latin in his Old English adaptations of these lives in order to provide the background information and ensure that the sung responses are more clearly understood. Through such explanation, he is able to enhance the experience of all those participating in services and add to the significance of the recital of the liturgy.

Conclusion

In this paper I have pointed to some of the ways in which an understanding of Ælfric's educative project can be teased out from a close study of his inclusion of Latin quotations when these are viewed in the wider context of the medieval Latin liturgical cycle. Ælfric chose to include Latin verses in his Old English *Lives of Saints* and homilies that would have been familiar to his audience from the antiphons and responses in the liturgy. Not every Latin quotation can be explained in this way, but what is clear is that we have not yet uncovered the full significance of Ælfric's linguistic choices and there is still scope for a careful reconsideration of the function of Latin quotation in Ælfric's writings. It may be possible, and I propose this somewhat tentatively, to reconstruct the antiphoner that Ælfric had before him (or recalled from memory) when composing his homilies. The evidence for the homilies is much stronger than that for the *Lives of Saints* and it is probable that this is because the antiphons associated with the saints' lives were not so firmly established at that time or, at least, Ælfric did not have access to them in his antiphoner.

---

[36] Pope argues that Ælfric 'presumably turned to his own copy of the Latin Bible' when translating extended sections (*Supplementary Homilies*, p. 152). The presence of quotations in Latin makes it much easier to distinguish between variant Latin sources, of course. When our sole evidence for those Latin sources are Ælfric's translations into Old English, then the situation is not as clear cut.

[37] Mary Clayton, 'Homiliaries and Preaching in Anglo-Saxon England', *Peritia*, 4 (1985), 207–42.

Looming Danger and Dangerous Looms: Violence and Weaving in Exeter Book *Riddle 56*

Megan Cavell

Violence in the Exeter Book riddles is not a new topic. Many discussions of these fascinating texts focus on the way in which commonplace objects are personified and then attacked, bound, mutilated and/or killed.[1] This violence, which is both carried out by humans and at the same time frequently punctuated by expressions of human empathy for the wounded objects, has been explained as acceptable because it occurs in the safe, playful and inverted world of the riddle.[2] Indeed, Ruth Wehlau notes that, as with the saints' lives, '[p]art of the pleasure in reading the riddles comes from the idea of violence as spectacle, combined with our knowledge that the violence is confined to the words'.[3] The loom riddle,[4] which is *Riddle 56* according to the numbering in the Anglo-Saxon Poetic Records (hereafter ASPR),[5] is one of these texts, and the violent imagery here is particularly problematic because it characterizes the construction

---

[1] See, for example, Dieter Bitterli, *Say What I Am Called: The Old English Riddles of the Exeter Book and the Anglo-Latin Riddle Tradition* (Toronto: University of Toronto Press, 2009); Jerome Denno, 'Oppression and Voice in the Anglo-Saxon Riddles', *Papers Presented at the 35th International Congress on Medieval Studies, 2000* <http://www2.kenyon.edu/AngloSaxonRiddles/Denno.htm> [accessed 19 January 2011]; Ruth Wehlau, *'The Riddle of Creation': Metaphor Structures in Old English Poetry*, Studies in Humanities: Literature-Politics-Society (New York: Peter Lang, 1997), pp. 102–5; Jonathan Wilcox, ' "Tell Me What I Am": The Old English Riddles', in *Readings in Medieval Texts: Interpreting Old and Middle English Literature*, ed. by David F. Johnson and Elaine M. Treharne (Oxford: Oxford University Press, 2005), pp. 46–59.

[2] See, in particular, Edward B. Irving, Jr., 'Heroic Experience in the Old English Riddles', in *Old English Shorter Poems*, ed. by Katherine O'Brien O'Keeffe (New York: Garland, 1994), pp. 199–212 (p. 199); Marie Nelson, 'Four Social Functions of the Exeter Book Riddles', *Neophilologus*, 75 (1991), 445–50; Elinor Teele, 'The Heroic Tradition in the Old English Riddles' (unpublished doctoral thesis, University of Cambridge, 2004), pp. 205 and 226.

[3] Wehlau, p. 105.

[4] The major authorities on this riddle's solution are Frederick Tupper, Jr., whose *Riddles of the Exeter Book* (Boston: Ginn, 1910), pp. 192–93 offers the solution 'web and loom', which George Philip Krapp and Elliott van Kirk Dobbie support in their edition of *The Exeter Book*, Anglo-Saxon Poetic Records, 3 (New York: Columbia University Press, 1936), p. 350. Craig Williamson similarly includes the solution 'web and loom' in his *Old English Riddles of The Exeter Book* (Chapel Hill: University of North Carolina Press, 1977), p. 305, and Bernard J. Muir defers to the solutions of Williamson and Donald K. Fry in his own edition, *The Exeter Anthology of Old English Poetry*, 2 vols (Exeter: University of Exeter Press, 1994), ii, p. 575. Fry's article, 'Exeter Book Riddle Solutions,' *Old English Newsletter*, 15.1 (1981), pp. 22–33 (p. 24), lists other proposed solutions including 'lathe', 'flail' and 'execution', but 'loom' still maintains the highest level of support at the time of his survey of riddle solutions.

[5] There are a variety of approaches to numbering the Exeter Book riddles, and the loom riddle in particular ranges between number 54 and 57 depending on the editor. This paper uses the numbering assigned by the ASPR,

of an object that was beneficial to humans — that is, cloth. From the perspective of textiles research, this violence is off-putting — cloth usually plays a positive role because it is essential to human culture and since 'its constituent fibers can evoke ideas of connectedness or tying', it is frequently employed as a metaphor for society.[6] However, such an approach of construction-through-destruction is wholly appropriate to the world of riddles, which show how the raw material in nature is turned into the 'cooked' objects of culture:

> The riddles not only present objects in anthropomorphic guise; they also arrange them in anthropocentric systems of order. Virtually everything that they name has a function. What the riddles prize above all is the way things turn to the welfare of humankind. Rarely is the 'raw' stuff of nature introduced (a deer's antlers, an ox's hide) without its being brought into relation to the 'cooked' elements of culture (a pair of inkwells, a set of leather goods). The riddles thus domesticate the elements of nature and turn them to human use.[7]

However, even with this raw-cooked or living-dead opposition recognized as part of the riddling tradition, the loom riddle remains a complicated text. Both the loom and the fabric being woven upon it are 'cooked', manmade artifacts, indicating that the violence inherent in the construction-from-destruction motif is working differently here. Given this context, it seems time for a fresh reading of *Riddle 56*, which scholarship has, until now, generally only addressed in passing.[8]

In focusing on the violent imagery of the loom riddle, the following discussion endeavours to offer a more comprehensive reading of the riddle and pose some new questions. Accepting that violence is an important part of the riddling genre, as outlined above, this paper will not look at *why* violence is associated with weaving, but rather at how this association functions and what this means for our interpretation of the riddle at large. By arguing that this association functions primarily through the poem's use of heroic imagery — with the violence being related to warfare, torture and execution — I shall demonstrate how the loom riddle sets itself apart from many other domestic riddles. While this may initially strike the reader as odd, I shall further outline the way in which the use of this heroic imagery emphasises the high status of crafted objects, in which category cloth is quite firmly situated. With the recognition of the importance of the craftsman in Old English poetry, the association between heroic violence and weaving becomes all the more appropriate.

Turning first to the poem itself, the loom riddle reads:

> Ic wæs þær inne   þær ic ane geseah
> winnende wiht   wido bennegean,

---

from which all citations, unless otherwise stated, are taken. Muir's edition maintains ASPR numbering, and Williamson's edition of the riddles numbers this *Riddle 54*.

[6] A. Weiner, and Jane Schneider, *Cloth and Human Experience* (Washington: Smithsonian Institution Press, 1989), p. 2.

[7] John D. Niles, *Old English Enigmatic Poems and the Play of the Texts*, Studies in the Early Middle Ages, 13 (Turnhout: Brepols, 2006), p. 54. Niles employs the terminology of Claude Lévi-Strauss's *The Raw and the Cooked*, trans. by John and Doreen Weightman (London: Cape, 1970; repr. Chicago: University of Chicago Press, 1990), originally published as *Le cru et le cuit* (Paris: Plon, 1964). This anthropological study views cooking as a cultural process and outlines the way in which mythological depictions of the raw and the cooked correspond to a nature/culture binary.

[8] There are no lengthy discussions devoted entirely to *Riddle 56*, although one article does refer to it within the context of other loom riddles and the actual mechanism of the warp-weighted loom: Erika von Erhardt-Siebold, 'The Old English Loom Riddles', in *Philologica: The Malone Anniversary Studies*, ed. by Thomas A. Kirkby and Henry Bosley Woolf (Baltimore: Johns Hopkins Press, 1949), pp. 9–17. Other discussions of this riddle occur in editions of the text and in passing references in articles and books. Teele devotes several pages to heroic echoes and analogues in the poem (pp. 153–55).

holt hweorfende;   heaþoglemma feng,
deopra dolga.   Daroþas wæron
weo þære wihte,   ond se wudu searwum
fæste gebunden.   Hyre fota wæs
biidfæst oþer,   oþer bisgo dreag,
leolc on lyfte,   hwilum londe neah.
Treow wæs getenge   þam þær torhtan stod
leafum bihongen.   Ic lafe geseah
minum hlaforde,   þær hæleð druncon,
þara flana,   on flet beran.[9]

I was inside there where I saw a wooden object wounding a certain struggling creature, the wood turning;[10] it received battle-wounds,[11] deep gashes. Darts were woeful to that creature, and the wood skillfully bound fast. One of its feet was held fixed, the other endured affliction, leapt into the air, sometimes near the land. A tree, hung about by leaves, was near to that bright thing [which] stood there, I saw the leavings of those arrows, carried out onto the floor to my lord, where the warriors drank.

It is fair to say that for a modern reader, a cursory glance at *Riddle 56* would be unlikely to yield the solution 'loom', or 'web and loom', which I shall sketch out below. That the imagery of a struggling creature suffering from battle-wounds and deep gashes while being bound fast beside a tree does not immediately bring weaving to mind is partly indicative of the poem's removal from its historical context — a context in which looms played a much more important role than they do in modern life. One of the looms in use at this time, with archaeological evidence supporting its existence in Anglo-Saxon contexts, was the vertical, warp-weighted loom.[12] This type of loom was used in many parts of medieval Europe, and survived in some areas of modern Scandinavia.[13] Marta Hoffmann, who surveyed the warp-

---

[9] Krapp and Dobbie, p. 208 (with modifications explained below). Unless otherwise stated, all translations are my own. The ASPR edition makes several emendations to the manuscript reading of the riddle. In line 7, the MS reads 'biid fæft', which Krapp and Dobbie, Williamson (p. 101) and Muir (p. 328) all emend to 'biidfæst'. In line 12, the MS reads 'flan', which Krapp and Dobbie emend to 'flana', arguing that '*þara flana*, followed by a noun parallel to *lafe*, seems more probable here' than previous emendations (p. 350). This prompts them to supply the word 'geweorc', which does not appear in the MS. Williamson emends to 'flana' (p. 101), maintaining that the genitive is governed by 'lafe', which frequently takes the genitive in the riddles and thus does not require a parallel accusative noun (p. 307). Muir similarly emends to 'flana' (I, 328), and so this is the reading that I have adopted.

[10] The syntax of the first two and a half lines is fairly ambiguous because of the nature of the reported vision. Both the subject of the infinitive verb 'bennegean' ('to wound') and the object being wounded are potentially in the accusative. This is further complicated by the use of apposition, making it unclear which terms refer to the object that is wounding and which to that being wounded. Williamson reads 'wido' and 'holt hweorfende' as appositives (p. 306), and Bosworth and Toller take these as the subject, making the 'ane' and 'winnende wiht' the object, as I have attempted to show in my translation. See Joseph Bosworth and T. Northcote Toller, *An Anglo-Saxon Dictionary* (Oxford: Oxford University Press, 1898), *Supplement* by T. Northcote Toller (Oxford: Oxford University Press, 1921; repr. London: Lowe and Brydone Ltd., 1966), digital edition (Prague: Faculty of Arts, Charles University, 2010), s.v. *bennian* <http://bosworth.ff.cuni.cz/> [accessed 5 July 2011].

[11] The term 'heaþuglemm' is a *hapax legomenon*, as is the second component of the compound, 'glemm', which appears in Wulfstan's homily *Her Ongynð be Cristendome* (see Dorothy Bethurum, *The Homilies of Wulfstan* (Oxford: Clarendon Press, 1957), pp. 200–10 (p. 202, l. 45)). For 'glemm', the *Dictionary of Old English* notes some ambiguity with regard to the definition, offering '? stain, ? wound': *The Dictionary of Old English: A-G*, ed. by Angus Cameron, Ashley Crandell Amos and Antonette di Paolo Healey (Toronto: Dictionary of Old English Project, University of Toronto, 2008) [on CD], s.v. For 'heaþuglemm', Bosworth and Toller, perhaps taking their cue from the first element, offer 'a wound got in fight' with no reference to difficulties defining the term.

[12] Gale R. Owen-Crocker, *Dress in Anglo-Saxon England*, rev. edn (Woodbridge: Boydell, 2004), p. 287.

[13] Marta Hoffmann, *The Warp-Weighted Loom: Studies in the History and Technology of an Ancient Implement*, Studia Norvegica, 14 (Oslo: Universitetsforlaget, 1964), p. 6.

weighted loom's use and distribution, argued that this type of loom 'has remained practically unchanged from the earliest times down to the present. It is the oldest loom known to have been used in Europe, and it is of this loom and its products that we find traces in the Swiss Neolithic Age'.[14] Hoffmann also offers a straight-forward description of weaving, stating:

> The basic characteristic of weaving is that two systems of threads cross each other at right angles: one — the warp — is stretched taut, while the other — the weft — is introduced as the work proceeds, and is bound in place by the warp threads.[15]

Already, we can see how the stretching of one system of threads and the moving and binding of another relates to the riddle's description of this bound and struggling creature.

In order to fully contextualize this riddle, an explanation of the mechanism of the warp-weighted loom is necessary (see Figure 1). The following description of this piece of equipment relies heavily on Gale Owen-Crocker's research on textiles presented in *Dress in Anglo-Saxon England*.[16] The warp-weighted loom consisted of two uprights with a horizontal beam across the top, and would have rested against the wall or roof so the uprights were tilted. Warp threads were attached to the top beam, and kept taut with weights attached at the bottom. Half of the threads would be pulled in front of and half placed behind the shed rod, a cross bar fixed between the uprights and frequently situated toward the bottom of the loom. Sitting in brackets attached to the uprights was the heddle rod, which was movable, attached only to the warp threads at the back of the loom. When the heddle rod was pulled away from the loom, the weaver could move the back threads forward and change the shed, the space between the warp threads through which the weft threads were passed. The warp threads relate to the poem's description of the struggling creature's bound foot and jumping foot: of the two rows of warp threads, one remains in place while the second row moves with the change of shed.[17] The weft threads could be passed through the shed by means of a needle or a shuttle, and Erika von Erhardt-Siebold argues that the piece of wood which wounds the web in the riddle — and the battle scars which result — refer to one of these implements.[18] The threads of the fabric were straightened with bone or wood picks when they clung together and, because the weft would be left quite loose in order to stop it from pulling too tight and causing the cloth to contract, it would have to be beaten upwards with a sword-shaped beater. The fabric picks and sword beater also arguably appear in the riddle, in the reference to the darts that wound the creature.[19] As for the nearby tree, hung about by leaves, this is likely the distaff standing near the loom, whose wool or flax would have gone in to the making of the web.[20] Finally, the 'laf', the leavings which are carried to the lord in the hall, refers to the finished cloth, the struggling web having now been fully subdued.

Looms like these were essential parts of Anglo-Saxon life, since the work of clothing the family through spinning and weaving was done at the household level.[21] The loom would of course be an obvious candidate for the riddling genre because the riddles so often find their

---

[14] Hoffmann, p. 5.
[15] Hoffmann, p. 5.
[16] Owen-Crocker. See in particular pp. 286–91.
[17] Erhardt-Siebold, p. 15; and Williamson, p. 307.
[18] Erhardt-Siebold, p. 15.
[19] Erhardt-Siebold, p. 15; F. H. Whitman, *Old English Riddles* (Ottawa: Canadian Federation for the Humanities, 1982), p. 140.
[20] Erhardt-Siebold, p. 15.
[21] Penelope Walton Rogers, *Cloth and Clothing in Early Anglo-Saxon England, AD 450–700*, CBA Research Report, 145 (York: Council for British Archaeology, 2007), p. 47.

Figure 1: A Faroese warp-weighted loom in the Copenhagen Museum. Taken from Oscar Montelius, *Civilisation of Sweden in Heathen Times*, trans. by the Rev. F. H. Woods, 2nd edn (London: Macmillan, 1888), p. 160, via H. Ling Roth, *Ancient Egyptian and Greek Looms* (Halifax: Bankfield Museum, 1913), p. 34 (as it appears on the Project Gutenberg website, <http://www.gutenberg.org/files/25731/25731-h/25731-h.htm> [accessed 1 June 2011]).

subject matter in the commonplace.[22] Furthermore, as riddle theory makes clear, it is the function of riddles to play with the limitations and parameters of the riddler's society.[23] In approaching the question of how the violent association is functioning in *Riddle 56*, it is useful to ask what in the riddler's society is being played with here.

Many domestic riddles play with the concept of gender, and so we may use this as an starting point, and one which seems fairly obvious given that weaving was women's work in the medieval period.[24] Thus, some have read this poem as an inversion of two types of work

---

[22] There are, for example, several riddles referring to products, tools and animals associated with agriculture, including *21* (plough), *34* (rake), *42* (cock and hen), *52* (flail), *82* (harrow), the ox/bull riddles (*12*, *38* and *72*) and the onion riddles (*25* and *65*). Similarly, several refer to domestic objects and food/drink, such as *27* (mead), *45* (bread dough), *49* (oven), *54* (churn), *58* (well sweep), *81* (weathercock), the bellows riddles (*37* and *87*) and the key(-hole) riddles (*44* and *91*). This list is meant to be representative rather than exhaustive, and so I have not included riddles with contested meanings.

[23] Wilcox, p. 58; Roger D. Abrahams, 'The Literary Study of the Riddle', *Texas Studies in Literature and Language*, 14 (1972), 177–97 (p. 182).

[24] The major discussions of Anglo-Saxon weaving all place this activity within the realm of women. While some, like Owen-Crocker and Walton Rogers, are more concerned with the technology and process itself, many discussions of weaving approach this task through the lens of gender studies and women's roles. The notable studies here are Christine Fell's *Women in Anglo-Saxon England* (London: British Museum Publications, 1984) and Jane

generally divided by gender.²⁵ With weaving being the work of women and battle the work of men in the Anglo-Saxon period, the fact that these two spheres of work are mapped onto one another is very interesting. However, while this is a valid line of inquiry, it is also important to note that the weavers and their gender are not actually referred to in this text, unlike in some riddles where women are clearly present and involved in domestic labour. Notable in this context are *Riddles 25* and *45*, solved as 'onion' and 'bread dough'.²⁶ In these poems, two of the 'obscene' riddles of the Exeter Book, women are presented as rather fearless sexual aggressors.²⁷ Their physical appearances, class, personalities and actions are all described. The appearance of the woman in *Riddle 25* is indicated by the terms 'ful cyrtenu' ('very pretty'; 6a) and 'wundenlocc' ('curly-haired'; 11a).²⁸ Her class is explicitly mentioned when she is referred to as a 'ceorles dohtor' ('free man's daughter'; 6b), while *Riddle 45* depicts instead a 'bryd' ('bride'; 3b) who is a 'þeodnes dohtor' ('ruler's daughter'; 5b). Both women are proud-minded or -hearted, one 'modwlonc' (*Riddle 25* 7a) and the other 'hygewlonc' (*Riddle 45* 4a). While *Riddle 45* is much shorter and does not refer explicitly to the woman's appearance, her clothing is implied by the term 'hrægle' (4b), which is both a cloth used to cover the bread

---

Chance's *Woman as Hero in Old English Literature* (Syracuse: Syracuse University Press, 1986), both of which have been very influential. Similarly, Michael Enright's *Lady with a Mead Cup: Ritual, Prophecy and Lordship in the European Warband from La Tène to the Viking Age* (Dublin: Four Courts Press, 1996) and Maren Clegg Hyer's 'Textiles and Textile Imagery in Old English' (unpublished doctoral thesis, University of Toronto, 1998) have a strong focus on the role of women as literal or metaphorical weavers. For an archaeological perspective, see Nick Stoodley, *The Spindle and the Spear: A Critical Enquiry into the Construction and Meaning of Gender in the Early Anglo-Saxon Burial Rite*, British Archaeological Reports, British Series, 288 (Oxford: Hedges/Archaeopress, 1999). This study's analysis of data from Anglo-Saxon burials finds that weaving tools were primarily female grave goods (esp. pp. 31, 33, 75 and 136).

25 See, for example, Russell G. Poole, *Viking Poems on War and Peace: A Study in Skaldic Narrative*, Toronto Medieval Texts and Translations, 8 (Toronto: University of Toronto Press, 1991), pp. 138–40.

26 Krapp and Dobbie, pp. 193 and 205.

27 Edith Whitehurst Williams, 'What's So New about the Sexual Revolution?: Some Comments on Anglo-Saxon Attitudes toward Sexuality in Women Based on Four *Exeter Book* Riddles', *Texas Quarterly*, 18 (1975), 46–55 (p. 48).

28 There is some debate as to the nature of 'wundenlocc', a term which occurs four times in Old English poetry: once here and three times in *Judith* at lines 77b, 103b and 325a, where it twice describes the heroine herself and once the rest of the Hebrew nation. It is unclear whether these twisted locks are curly or braided, with editors, dictionaries and commentators frequently coming to different conclusions. For those who support the 'curly-haired' reading, see Williamson, p. 464; John P. Hermann, *Allegories of War: Language and Violence in Old English Poetry* (Ann Arbor: University of Michigan Press, 1989), pp. 191–92; and Susan Kim, 'Bloody Signs: Circumcision and Pregnancy in the Old English Judith', *Exemplaria*, 11 (Fall 1999), 285–307. For those who support the 'braided hair' reading, see Bosworth and Toller, s.v.; J. R. Clark Hall, *A Concise Anglo-Saxon Dictionary*, 4th edn (Toronto: University Press, 1960), s.v.; and Teele, p. 132. Several offer both readings, such as *Judith*, ed. by Mark S. Griffith, Exeter Medieval English Texts and Studies (Exeter: The University of Exeter Press, 1997), p. 222; and Tupper, p. 125. I am inclined to support the 'curly-haired' theory for two reasons. Firstly, since the term most frequently describes Judith and other Hebrew figures, we may read curly hair as a more appropriate distinguishing feature of a cultural group than bound or braided hair would be, as Hermann notes (p. 191), especially given that Anglo-Saxon women also bound their hair (see Gale R. Owen-Crocker, 'Women's Costume in the Tenth and Eleventh Centuries and Textile Production in Anglo-Saxon England', in *The Archaeology of Anglo-Saxon England: Basic Readings*, ed. by Catherine E. Karkov (New York: Garland, 1999), pp. 423–85 (esp. pp. 435–7)). Secondly, the simplices 'wunden' and 'loccas' appear together in line 104 of *Riddle 40* (Creation), and the corresponding lines of Aldhelm's Latin version of this riddle (*Enigma 101, De creatura*) clearly refer to curls (see in particular lines 44–7 in *Through a Gloss Darkly: Aldhelm's Riddles in the British Library MS Royal 12.C. xxii*, ed. by Nancy Porter Stork, Pontifical Institute of Mediaeval Studies, Studies and Texts, 98 (Toronto: Pontifical Institute of Mediaeval Studies, 1990), p. 233). If we take the Latin into consideration when translating the Old English, it would seem that, in this riddle at least, the 'wundne loccas' are curls rather than braided locks.

dough and a garment that hides the sexual encounter. Furthermore, the use of 'gripan' ('to grip'; *Riddle 25* 7b) and 'grapian' ('to seize'; *Riddle 45* 3b), focuses attention on the women's hands, a somewhat violent tool of seduction according to the double entendre-reading, or of domestic labour according to the solutions 'onion' and 'bread dough'.

The highly gendered and sexualized approach to women and their work evident in these two riddles could easily have been applied to weaving in *Riddle 56*, but it is not. In its approach to the labour of weaving, *Riddle 56* maintains a greater focus on the construction of cloth itself rather than the weavers. Indeed, this trend can be read across the Old English poetic corpus at large. There is only one instance in the poetry where the textile-maker is the focus, and this is actually a reference to embroidery, rather than to weaving. This is, of course, the famous passage in *Maxims I*, which asserts: 'Fæmne æt hyre bordan geriseð' ('a woman belongs at her embroidery'; 63b).[29] However, all of the references to actual weaving or woven objects focus upon the object rather than the creator of the object.[30] Such an emphasis on the product rather than the producer sets Old English poetry as distinct from other medieval representations of weaving, such as the supernatural women who weave a bloody banner in the Old Norse *Darraðarljóð*,[31] a poem which is often read in conjunction with this riddle.[32] This is a very important distinction, and one which creates problems for those who would use this poem as evidence in broader discussions of gender and work.

Returning to the question of what in the riddler's society is being inverted and played with here, we can now safely say that it does not appear to be gender. Other popular areas for the riddles to probe include class, which provides another possible approach to the use of violent imagery in the poem. Riddles dealing with domestic chores often include imagery of forced servitude, such as the enslaved plough of *Riddle 21*[33] which is 'bunden cræfte' ('skillfully bound'; 7b) and driven along with spikes piercing its back and head (11–13a), or the fettered prisoners steered by a slave-woman in *Riddle 52*, often solved as 'flail'. Indeed, the ox/bull riddles all allude to binding and slavery at some point, with *Riddle 72* describing the ox as 'bunden under beame' ('bound under a beam'; 13a) where it endures work ('weorc þrowade'; 14b). That this forced servitude involves being subjected to violence is clear in the final lines (15b–18):

> Oft mec isern scod
> sare on sidan; ic swigade,
> næfre meldade monna ængum
> gif me ordstæpe egle wæron.

> Often iron injured me, sore on my sides; I kept silent, never proclaimed to any of men if the spear-stabs were painful.

---

[29] T. A. Shippey, *Poems of Wisdom and Learning in Old English* (Cambridge: Brewer, 1976), p. 66.

[30] This statement applies to the production of objects and artifacts. I should emphasize that I am excluding metaphorical weaving because there are several instances where Old English poetry refers to weavers of abstract concepts, including words (*Elene* 1237a), fate (*Guthlac B* 1351a; *The Riming Poem* 70a) and peace (*Beowulf* 1942a; *Elene* 88a; *Widsið* 6a). The focus in these instances is on concepts rather than objects, and yet the concepts are similarly attributed with value. However, as I argue elsewhere, gender is not necessarily implied in any of these contexts. For more on this see my forthcoming 'Representations of Weaving and Binding in Old English Poetry' (unpublished doctoral thesis, University of Cambridge).

[31] For a recent edition, see Poole, pp. 116–18.

[32] The first to make this connection is F. Dietrich, 'Die Räthsel des Exeterbuchs: Würdigung, Lösung und Herstellung', *Zeitschrift für Deutsches Altertum*, 11 (1859), 448–90 (p. 476). For other discussions, see Poole, pp. 138–39; Teele, p. 153; Hyer, p. 139; and Karen Bek-Pedersen, 'Are the Spinning Nornir Just a Yarn?', *Viking and Medieval Scandinavia*, 3 (2007), 1–10.

[33] Krapp and Dobbie, p. 191.

Looming Danger and Dangerous Looms

This association between beasts of burden and slavery seems appropriate, especially considering slaves would have had close contact with these animals. Indeed, David Pelteret maintains that ploughing was the most common job for male slaves in Anglo-Saxon England.[34] However, while there is much binding and violence, there are no prisoners or slaves at work in *Riddle 56*. Thus, once again the answer appears to be no: the loom riddle does not deal with class or servitude; this seems to be an attribute of agricultural riddles instead.

The sexual violence employed by women working in the domestic sphere and the violence of slavery imposed upon objects used in agriculture, at a basic level, are both linked with food growth and production. While it would seem to make sense for weaving, as a similar widespread domestic chore, to be associated through shared imagery with this food production, and while all of our modern conceptions of medieval women's work would encourage us to see this connection, this is simply not the case. The violence in *Riddle 56* has nothing to do with gender or class. Instead, weaving is depicted in terms of battle, torture and execution, and the association seems to be with heroic literature.

Two of the battle words that associate the riddle's imagery with martial violence are the 'heaþoglemma' ('battle-wounds'; 3b) and 'deopra dolga' ('deep gashes'; 4a) caused by the wooden object in line 2. As noted above, these probably refer to the piercings of the shuttle through the web's body, but as wounds they are associated with battle through the first element of the first compound. While the term 'heaþuglemm' only appears in this riddle, compounds beginning with *heaþu-* are very common in heroic discourse. A search of the *Dictionary of Old English Corpus* reveals sixty-three compounds in poetry with *heaþu-*[35] as the first component, the vast majority of which occur in *Beowulf*. Eight of these are proper names and the rest adjectives or nouns that can be placed within the realm of heroic diction, given their concern with battle.[36] The wounds described here may, in a poetic context, also hold associations with religious tribulation and martyrdom. There are fifteen other instances of the term *dolg* ('wound') and the related past participle, *gedolgod* ('wounded') in Old English poetry, ten of which describe Christ's crucifixion and the torture of saints.[37] Of the remaining five, two of them refer to violence done upon evil figures in *Judith* (107a) and *Beowulf* (817a) and two refer to battle wounds and medical ailments.[38] The final instance is ambiguous because it occurs in the unsolved *Riddle 53* (6a), in a description of a tree that has been mutilated and enslaved for human use. Several solutions have been offered for the riddle, including 'battering ram',[39] which would indicate that the connotations are martial ones. However, it has also been solved as 'cross' and 'gallows',[40] in which case the use of this term could be a reference to the torture

---

[34] David Pelteret, *Slavery in Early Mediaeval England: From the Reign of Alfred Until the Twelfth Century*, Studies in Anglo-Saxon History, 7 (Woodbridge: Boydell, 1995), p. 117.

[35] Variant spellings include: *heaðu-*, *heaþo-* and *heaðo-*.

[36] The most common second components are *-wielm* ('burning'; *Elene* 579a, 1305a; *Beowulf* 82b, 2819a; *Genesis B* 324a; *Exodus* 148a; *Andreas* 1542a), *-rinc* ('warrior'; *The Metres of Boethius* (Metre 9) 45a; *Judith* 179a, 212b; *Exodus* 241a; *Beowulf* 370a, 2466a) and *-rof* ('brave'; *The Menologium* 14a; *The Phoenix* 228a; *Beowulf* 381a, 864a, 2191a). Interestingly, *heaþuwylm* is frequently applied to descriptions of hell, while *heaþurinc* and *heaþurof* are generally more straightforward descriptions of brave fighters.

[37] See *Christ III* (1107b, 1206b, 1454a), *The Dream of the Rood* (46b), *Riddle 59* (chalice) (11a) and *Andreas* (942a, 1244a, 1397a, 1406a, 1475a).

[38] See *Riddle 5* (shield) (13a) and the *Metrical Charm, Wið Wæterælfadle* ('Against Water-Elf Disease'; 12a).

[39] Fry lists other solutions including 'spear', 'phallus' and 'cross', but notes that 'battering ram' has the most support (p. 24). This is the solution that Krapp and Dobbie (pp. 348–39) and Williamson (p. 297) list.

[40] F. H. Whitman solves the riddle as 'cross' in his 'Significant Motifs in Riddle 53', *Medium Ævum*, 46 (1977), 1–11; and Jonathan Wilcox puts forward a strong case for 'gallows' in 'New Solutions to Old English Riddles:

and execution of martyrs and the crucifixion of Christ. The higher quantity of occurrences in religious contexts would seem to suggest that, although the term could be applied to other contexts (and frequently was in prose, of course), as poetic diction, it also frequently carried religious connotations.

Indications of torture may also be read in the description of the weighted warp-threads: 'Hyre fota wæs / biidfæst oþer, oþer bisgo dreag' ('One of its feet was held fixed, the other endured affliction'; 6b-7). The phrase 'bisgo dreag', can mean either 'endured affliction' or 'worked busily',[41] and thus points to a double meaning at work here. The 'affliction' sense of the term *bysgu* notably appears also in *Juliana* (625b), *Guthlac A* (714b) and *Beowulf* (281a), and of course other affliction terms are prevalent in the torture scenes of saints and martyrs in Old English. Obviously affliction can equally be endured in battle, indicating that the imagery here is once again applicable to both war and martyrdom.

Another place where the imagined struggle arguably carries connotations of both warfare and torture is in lines 4b–6a, where

> [...] Daroþas wæron
> weo þære wihte, ond se wudu searwum
> fæste gebunden
>
> Darts were woeful to that creature, and the wood skillfully bound fast.

As discussed above, these darts seem to be either the fabric picks or possibly the points of a toothed weaver's beater.[42] Such beaters were similar to swords in form, and there is at least one find of a beater having been refashioned out of a pattern-welded sword, as well as others possibly fashioned from spear-heads.[43] Thus, the association between the weaver's beater and weapons links the imagery to warfare and heroic diction. In this particular passage, the wood that is bound fast relates to the bound construction of the loom. Not only is the wood a bound object, but it is also doing the binding, as it holds the creature fast. Hence, both the loom and the fabric are bound, in their construction and in their servitude to humans. This multi-layered binding of construction and service is, of course, common in other riddles, and several of the armament riddles employ references to binding to emphasize their situation. *Riddle 23* (bow),[44] for example, ends with the statement 'nelle ic unbunden ænigum hyran / nymþe searosæled' ('unbound I will not obey anyone unless skillfully tied'; 15–16). The indication here, as with the loom riddle, is both one of service to the bow's human owner and of its construction, in that a bow must be properly strung in order to function properly.

The nature of the riddles makes them some of the most useful Old English poetic texts for discussions of material culture. And, indeed, if we look at other large wooden constructions known to the Anglo-Saxons, we find that the imagery of violence in *Riddle 56* is heightened. Niles draws attention to the loom as a type of *hengen* ('cross-rack').[45] He notes 'the physical resemblance of a *hengen* that is used to hang or stretch criminals to a *hengen* that is used to support the weaving apparatus of a loom', remarking that one of Ælfric's homilies joins

---

Riddles 17 and 53', *Philological Quarterly*, 69 (1990), 393–408.

[41] The *DOE* offers the following definitions for *bysgu*: 'activity, occupation; work, toil, labour' (s.v., sense 1.) and 'affliction, trouble, anxiety, care' (s.v., sense 2.). For *dreogan*'s connotations of suffering and endurance, see senses A.2.a. 'to endure, suffer; *deaþ*(-*cwale*) *dreogan* "to die" ' and B.2. 'to suffer'. For its connotations of labour, see senses A.1. 'to do, perform, work, carry out' and B.1.b. '*dreogan unstille / bysig* "to be busy" ', which the *DOE* gives as the main sense of this particular passage.

[42] Erhardt-Siebold, p. 15.
[43] Owen-Crocker, p. 276.
[44] Krapp and Dobbie, p. 192
[45] Niles, p. 81.

imagery of weaving with that of a torture device.⁴⁶ The relevant passage from the *Homilies of Ælfric* reads:

> Ða het Aurelianus on hengenne afæstnien
> þone halgan wer, and aðenian his lima
> swa swa man webb tyht; ac he nan word ne gecwæð.⁴⁷
>
> Then Aurelianus commanded that the holy man be fastened to a rack and that his limbs be drawn out just as one stretches the weft; but he did not say a word.

This example lends credence to the torture reading of the loom riddle, as does the description of the harmful wooden object in terms of 'holt hweorfende' ('the wood turning'; 3a), which could imply the stretching out of its victim. Niles indicates that the Anglo-Saxons clearly had knowledge of the rack because elsewhere Ælfric refers to the rack used to torture St. Vincent as a 'hengen', a structure which is different from the gallows to which he is later moved:⁴⁸ 'ahoð hine on þære hengene, and hetelice astreccað ealle his lima, þæt þa liþa him togaan!'⁴⁹ ('hang him on the rack, and violently stretch out all his limbs so that his joints are separated!'). The rack's ability to tear limbs as outlined here could be reflected in *Riddle 56*'s description of the struggling creature's wounds.

In addition to the possibility that the poem refers to a torture device, we may equally read the constructed object in the context of a gallows. Andrew Reynolds argues that execution cemeteries 'are characterised by untidy, and in many cases excessively violent' deaths either by beheading or by hanging, which was the most common method of execution.⁵⁰ Furthermore, there is archaeological evidence for a two-post gallows at several execution sites including Sutton Hoo in Suffolk and South Acre in Norfolk,⁵¹ as well as pictorial evidence for such two-post constructions in the Anglo-Saxon illustrated Hexateuch, where the gallows' uprights and crossbeam resemble a warp-weighted loom.⁵²

The gallows is, of course, also frequently referred to in Old English literature, not the least in descriptions of martyrdom. If we read the poem as linked to the torture of religious heroes, as evidenced by the diction of the *milites Christi* and by the *hengen* passages in Ælfric discussed above, then the gallows is a fitting construction to consider. Of course, stoic acceptance in the face of tribulation, imprisonment and torture are all common elements in the Old English poetic saints' lives, notably, *Guthlac*, *Andreas* and *Juliana*. This stoicism is something the saints have in common with other Old English heroes,⁵³ which suggests parallels between the two genres, as well as between secular warriors and *milites Christi*. Another commonly drawn upon example is the martial diction of *The Dream of the Rood*,⁵⁴ as applied to both Christ

---

[46] Niles, pp. 81–82.
[47] Ælfric, *Homilies of Ælfric: A Supplementary Collection*, ed. by John C. Pope, Early English Text Society, o. s., 259–60, 2 vols (Oxford: Oxford University Press, 1967), II, 745.
[48] Niles, p. 74.
[49] Ælfric, *Ælfric's Catholic Homilies, The Second Series: Text*, ed. by Malcolm Godden, Early English Text Society, s. s., 5 (London: Oxford University Press, 1979), p. 146.
[50] Andrew Reynolds, 'Executions and Hard Anglo-Saxon Justice', *British Archaeology*, 31 (1998), 8–9 (p. 8).
[51] Reynolds, p. 9.
[52] Niles, p. 71. The picture in the Hexateuch (London, British Library, Cotton MSS, Claudius B IV) occurs at folio 59.
[53] Thomas D. Hill, 'The Unchanging Hero: A Stoic Maxim in *The Wanderer* and its Contexts', *Studies in Philology*, 101 (2004), 233–49 (p. 236).
[54] *The Vercelli Book*, ed. by George Philip Krapp, ASPR, 2 (New York: Columbia University Press, 1932), pp. 61–5.

and the cross,[55] which aligns the religious hero with an undeserved violent death upon the gallows. The cross is referred to as a *gealga* ('gallows') on three occasions, twice as a simplex (10b, 40b) and once as the first element in the compound 'gealgtreow' ('gallows-tree'; 146a), and is depicted as taking on the suffering of Christ (46-51a), who is eager to redeem mankind through his crucifixion (41). As demonstrated by the violent descriptions of Christ's death on the gallows as well as by archaeological evidence and prose descriptions of torture, it is safe to say that Anglo-Saxons writers were certainly aware of the potentially painful outcomes of judicial punishment. Indeed, we need only look at the extant law codes to find a trail of missing fingers, hands, eyes and noses, which marked the committing of a crime upon the human body.[56]

Thus, the wounds and violence of *Riddle 56* may be situated within a number of contexts — battle, torture and execution — all linked by their inherent violence. This violence is, furthermore, associated with heroic depictions in Old English poetry, whether of actual fighters or of Christ and his martyrs. Indeed, even executions of non-religious figures find their way into heroic poetry, such as the passage from *Beowulf* that depicts a father lamenting his son who has been hanged as a criminal (2444–59). Furthermore, the gallows is included in a long list of violent deaths and maimings available to humans in *The Fortunes of Men* (33–42). Because that gallows-death is accompanied by a description of the raven, one of the beasts of battle, it is arguably placed in a context of war and battle-related violence, acting as a further reminder that, as Adrien Bonjour put it, 'death is foreordained for every man on earth'.[57] Given all of this, we can see that drawing parallels between the common domestic task of weaving and imagery of violence through battle, torture and execution causes the riddle to transgress boundaries of genre and register, moving it from the quotidian realm to the heroic.

Finally, in case the violent encounter itself is too ambiguous, the last two and a half lines of the poem tie the riddle firmly to the heroic world of lord and retinue:

> [...] Ic lafe geseah
> minum hlaforde,   þær hæleð druncon,
> þara flana,[58]   on flet beran
>
> I saw the leavings of those arrows, carried out on the floor to my lord, where the warriors drank.

The images presented in these lines are interspersed, but remain clear examples of heroic diction. Each half-line contains at least one term relevant to heroic poetry, and all together they draw the picture of a hall-setting quite thoroughly. *Hlaford* ('lord') is, of course, used commonly in Old English poetry, occurring sixty-three times in total. While it may be used in religious contexts as well as of worldly lords, in conjunction with the rest of the terms, it is

---

[55] See particularly lines 33b–47 where Christ is described in terms of a hero: 'efstan elne mycle' ('he hastened with great courage'; 34a), 'strang ond stiðmod' ('strong and resolute'; 40a), 'modig on manigra gesyhðe' ('brave in the sight of many'; 41a) and the cross as his faithful, unbending retainer: 'þær ic þa ne dorste ofer dryhtnes word / bugan oððe berstan' ('I did not then dare there, against the word of the Lord, to bend or burst'; 35-36a), 'Ealle ic mihte / feondas gefyllan, hwæðre ic fæste stod' ('I was able to fell all those enemies, yet I stood fast'; 37b-38), 'Ne dorste ic hwæðre bugan to eorðan, / feallan to foldan sceatum, ac ic sceolde fæste standan' ('yet I did not dare to bend to the earth, to fall to the corners of the earth, but I had to stand fast'; 42a-43), 'hyldan me ne dorste' ('I did not dare to bend myself'; 45b).

[56] For a detailed discussion of this legal context of mutilation and torture in Old English literature, see Katherine O'Brien O'Keeffe, 'Body and Law in Late Anglo-Saxon England', *Anglo-Saxon England*, 27 (1998), 209–32.

[57] Adrien Bonjour, 'Beowulf and the Beasts of Battle', *Proceedings of the Modern Languages Association*, 72 (1957), 563–73 (p. 566).

[58] See note 9 above.

placed within the heroic realm. *Flan* ('arrow') rather obviously finds its place in heroic diction because it is a weapon-term, as is *laf* ('leavings, remnant'), when used of swords — although here it literally refers to the finished web. *Laf* occurs frequently in verse, either as a simplex or as the second element in a compound. According to Phyllis Portnoy, the two most common uses of *laf* are 'survivor', at about 34% of instances, followed by 'sword' at 29%.[59] *Beowulf* once again dominates the poetic uses, followed by *Genesis A*.[60]

In addition to these weapon terms, the hall is evoked in the formulaic description of men drinking. This formula, 'þær hæleð druncon', in line 11b also occurs in line 1b in *Riddle 55*, the poem directly preceding the loom riddle in The Exeter Book. *Riddle 55*, a poem similarly inflected with heroic imagery, is one of the riddles whose solution has not yet achieved scholarly consensus. Suggestions include 'shield', 'scabbard', 'harp', 'cross', 'gallows', 'swordrack', 'tetraktys' and 'swordbox', with 'cross' and 'swordrack' maintaining the most support.[61] More recently, the solution of 'mead barrel' or 'drinking bowl' has been suggested.[62] However, Niles has argued against this suggestion because, in his opinion, bowls and barrels are too different from the gallows referred to in the poem.[63] Furthermore, he questions how these objects tie in with the riddle's description of the object offering weapons to its lord.[64] The solution which Niles himself offers is perhaps more in line with scholarly trend: *wæpen-hengen* ('weapon-rack').[65] If this were a two-post structure, like the warp-weighted loom, then we have both an explanation for the similarities between the two poems and also the reference to the gallows: when hung with a mail-coat, this object could resemble both.[66] In addition to the formulaic reference to men drinking in *Riddle 56*, *flet* is also a term consistent with the heroic imagery of the hall. It occurs no less than fifteen times in *Beowulf*, sometimes as a simplex and sometimes as the first element of a compound. As well as its frequent use in heroic contexts, the entire half-line 'on flet beran' is also a formula repeated in *Riddle 55* (2a). It would seem that these two riddles are bound together by their imagery of a person bearing an object onto the hall floor where the warriors drink.

Thus, one set of images — the lord and retinue drinking on the floor of the mead-hall — appears to be depicted in the positive light of celebration and camaraderie, as is typical of this sort of scene. However, the second set of images — the leavings and the work of arrows which are carried out onto the mead-hall floor — is not as easy to interpret. Is this a victorious presentation of a defeated foe? Is the *laf*, the remains of the struggling creature, a token of the battle, like the swords so often named by this term in heroic poetry? Or is this a loss for the

---

[59] Phyllis Carole Portnoy, 'The Riddle of the Remnant: Solving OE Laf', *Papers Presented at the 35th International Congress on Medieval Studies, 2000* <http://www2.kenyon.edu/AngloSaxonRiddles/Portnoy.htm> [accessed 19 January 2011].

[60] *Beowulf* contains thirteen instances of the term *laf* (455b, 795b, 1032a, 1488b, 1688a, 2036b, 2191b, 2563b, 2611b, 2628b, 2829b, 2936b, 3160b), while *Genesis A* has five (1343a, 1496b, 1549b, 2005b, 2019a).

[61] Fry, p. 24. Krapp and Dobbie favour 'swordrack' (p. 350), while Williamson (p. 300) remains uncertain, offering the guess 'that the creature is an ornamented sword box and that somehow (either by an unknown wordplay or because of some unknown similarity of function or design) the box is being compared to a gallows or rood in the riddle' (p. 301). Tupper argues that it refers to any vertical pole that contains a crossbeam, a solution which simultaneously explains the imagery of the cross, the gallows and the swordrack (p. 189).

[62] Keith P. Taylor, 'Mazers, Mead, and the Wolf's-head-tree: A Reconsideration of Old English Riddle 55', *Journal of English and Germanic Philology*, 94 (1995), 497–512.

[63] Niles, p. 69.

[64] Niles, p. 70.

[65] Niles, p. 75.

[66] Niles, p. 84.

war-band?: the *laf* could just as easily be referring to a companion, just as Beowulf refers to Wiglaf as the final remnant of their tribe in his last speech: 'þu eart endelaf usses cynnes, / Wægmundinga' ('you are the final remnant of our kin, of the Wæmundings'; 2813–14a).[67]

Given this analysis, it seems fair to say that the imagery of the loom riddle is quite clearly concerned with the heroic, and the violence depicted carries associations of battle, torture and execution. That being said, this connection is initially surprising given that most of the riddles describing objects through heroic imagery can be associated with battle in some way. The obvious example is the sword of *Riddle 20*, but also the bow of *Riddle 23*, and the horns of *Riddles 14* and *80*. The use of heroic imagery in all of these is appropriate because the objects are artifacts that would be used by noble warriors. But the loom is an object used by women, and not just noblewomen — its use is universal. Furthermore, there is a parallel association between weaving and war in *Riddle 35* (mail-coat). This riddle exists not only as a part of the Exeter Book collection, but also as the Northumbrian *Leiden Riddle*, both of which are versions of a translation of Aldhelm's Latin *Enigma 32, De lorica*.[68] This poem is a first-person description of a mail-coat, which identifies itself in the negative:

> Mec se wæta wong, wundrum freorig,
> of his innaþe ærist cende.
> Ne wat ic mec beworhtne wulle flysum,
> hærum þurh heahcræft, hygeþoncum min.
> Wundene me ne beoð wefle, ne ic wearp hafu,
> ne þurh þreata geþræcu þræd me ne hlimmeð,
> ne æt me hrutende hrisil scriþeð,
> ne mec ohwonan sceal am cnyssan.
> Wyrmas mec ne awæfan wyrda cræftum,
> þa þe geolo godwebb geatwum frætwað.
> Wile mec mon hwæþre seþeah wide ofer eorþan
> hatan for hæleþum hyhtlic gewæde.
> Saga soðcwidum, searoþoncum gleaw,
> wordum wisfæst, hwæt þis gewæde sy.

> The wet plain, wonderfully cold, bore me out of its womb. I know in my mind I was not wrought of wool from fleeces, with hair through great skill. I am not wound about with a weft, nor do I have a warp, nor does thread resound in me through threatening attack, nor does a whirring shuttle glide upon me, nor must the beater strike me anywhere. The worms which adorn fine yellow cloth with trappings did not weave me together with the skills of the fates. Nevertheless widely over the earth someone calls me a joyful garment for warriors. Say with true words, clever with skilful thoughts, with very wise words, what this garment is.

The association in *Riddle 35* is the flipside of that in *Riddle 56*: here we have an object of war described in relation to the domestic task of weaving, whereas in *Riddle 56* we have an implement of weaving described in relation to war and violence. The crucial question, then, is why the loom and the act of weaving upon it are so associated with heroic violence.

If we look at where weaving, binding and braiding terms are applied in the larger context of Old English poetry we find that this association is actually not so strange. When construction

---

[67] *Klaeber's Beowulf*, ed. by Robert D. Fulk, Robert E. Bjork and John D. Niles, 4th edn (Toronto: University of Toronto Press, 2008).

[68] The text of *Riddle 35* is taken from Krapp and Dobbie, p. 198. For an edition of the *Leiden Riddle*, see Elliott van Kirk Dobbie's *The Minor Poems*, ASPR, 6 (New York: Columbia University Press, 1942), p. 109. For *De lorica*, see Stork, p. 139.

through weaving and binding is applied to objects, they are invariably objects of high status. Examples include religious cloths, like the temple veil that is torn during the crucifixion in *Christ III* (1134b), as well as tapestries and banners, like those on the walls of Heorot after Beowulf has defeated Grendel (994b–6). Halls are also frequently described as having been constructed from bound timbers, with the formulaic system *x-bendum fæst* used in *Beowulf* no less than six times (722a, 998b, 1878b, 1918a, 2086b, 3072b) and also once in *Guthlac B* (955b). Expensive metal-work is similarly woven, bound or braided, and this includes everything from interwoven mail-coats, to wire-wound swords and helmets, and even the jewel encrusted gates of Paradise in *Christ I* (308b–310a). When used abstractly, weaving and binding are applied to the creation of the world, fate, magic and even language where words are woven into poetry.[69] These weaving and binding terms are powerful, and they are associated with acts of great artistry. Such an appreciation of the artistry that went into weaving fabric of quality is not unlike that attributed to the smith, a highly esteemed figure in Old English poetry, and one whose own work is elsewhere imagined in relation to textile-production: 'on him byrne scan, / searonet seowed smiþes orþancum' ('a mail-coat shone on him, an armour-net sewn by the skills of the smith'; *Beowulf* 405b–6). Thus, because weaving and binding are used of artistic construction in general, and because this construction is already associated with high status, it is appropriate that weaving should be placed in a heroic register in the poem. There seems in fact to be a great deal of logic to the inversions of riddles.

A final note of emphasis should be placed on the way in which the loom riddle carves out a space for the creative aspects of a domestic chore within the ethic of the war-band and the mead-hall. The craftsman is, of course, just as essential to the lord and to the war-band as he or she is to the household because noblemen, like farmers, need to be clothed and armed with the implements of their trade. And, of course, God, as the creator of the world, is the ultimate craftsman, as Wehlau emphasizes:

> The supreme architect is God, who is often called *meotod* (measurer') and *scyppend* ('shaper'). These terms are so commonly used as to be barely noticeable. Nevertheless, they make clear the predominant metaphors underlying Anglo-Saxon concepts of Creation, and these metaphors are concerned with artistic skills.[70]

Thus, in creating objects through the weaving and binding together of elements, humans both emulate God's example and, perhaps more controversially, imagine God in their own image.

---

[69] See note 30 above.
[70] Wehlau, p. 16. See also Kathryn Hume, 'The Concept of the Hall in Old English Poetry', *Anglo-Saxon England*, 3 (1974), 63–74 (p. 74), where she discusses descriptions of heaven and hell as influenced by the idea-complex of the 'hall' and 'anti-hall'.

The Nun's Priest's Identity and the Purpose of his Tale

Carol F. Heffernan

This article reconsiders the matter of the identity of the Nun's Priest and the purpose of the tale he tells. The priest enters *The Canterbury Tales* after the famous portrait of the Prioress in the *General Prologue* where we read, 'Another Nonne with hire hadde she, / That was hir chapeleyne, and preestes thre' (163–64).[1] The lines are problematical. As we are reminded by Florence Ridley, there is the matter of the pilgrim-count: 'if three priests accompany the Prioress, the number of pilgrims listed in the GP is thirty-one; if Chaucer meant the Prioress to have but one attendant priest, the total is twenty-nine.'[2] The pilgrim count is definitely fuzzy business. The words 'As I lay' (*General Prologue*, l. 20) indicate that Chaucer is already comfortably set up in the Tabard Inn when the 29 pilgrims arrive as night falls. Does that mean we should think of him as pilgrim number 30? Furthermore the use of 'wel' before the number 29 seems to be a modifier indicating 'about' or 'as many as' or 'nearly' ('At nyght was come into that hostelrye / Wel nyne and twenty'; *General Prologue*, ll. 23–24). Perhaps the pilgrim count from the very outset was never meant to be precise. There are also textual issues. The views among textualists descend from the influential librarian of the British Museum, Henry Bradshaw, who maintained that Chaucer left the line unfinished after the word *chapeleyne*, and Edith Rickert, who argued that 'and the preest is thre' was later inserted (and then later miscopied so that 'preest is' became 'preestis'), leaving one priest who also served as chaplain.[3] The marginal notation in both the Hengwrt and Ellesmere manuscripts, the most reliable of the manuscripts of *The Canterbury Tales*, however, reads 'Nonne Chapelayne.' It does appear, moreover, that Chaucer meant *three* when he said *three*. Even though the *General Prologue* tells us twenty-nine pilgrims met in the Tabard Inn, there is no evidence of revision in the manuscripts of *The Canterbury Tales* of the number of priests in attendance to the Prioress. Chaucer could have changed the number if he wanted to, for as Helen Cooper points out in a discussion of the *General Prologue*, 'there is at least a possibility that some parts were written or adapted when the writing of the tales was well advanced.'[4]

---

[1] All quotations of Chaucer are from *The Riverside Chaucer*, ed. by Larry D. Benson, 3rd edn (Boston: Houghton Mifflin, 1987).

[2] Florence Ridley's note to 'preestes thre' in her explanatory notes to *The General Prologue* portraits of the Second Nun and the Nun's Priest, *The Riverside Chaucer*, p. 806.

[3] *The Text of 'The Canterbury Tales' Studied on the Basis of Known Manuscripts*, ed. by John M. Manly and Edith Rickert, 8 vols (Chicago: University of Chicago Press, 1940), ii, p. 428. Cited by Ridley, p. 806.

[4] Helen Cooper, *The Canterbury Tales*, 2nd edn, Oxford Guides to Chaucer (Oxford: Oxford University Press, 1996), p. 27.

The Nun's Priest's Identity and the Purpose of his Tale

Scholars have tended to regard the priest as part of the Prioress's entourage, whether alone or one of three priests, acting as a protector or confessor of the Prioress and the second nun. John Manly, working from an historical perspective, associated the Prioress with the small convent of St. Leonard's and made a case for the priest as the local parish priest — Manly rejected 'preestes thre' — who served as father-confessor of the convent.[5] Robert Lumiansky thought the Priest was 'weak in body and fawning in manner', an antifeminist unhappy at 'being under the "petticoat rule" of the Prioress'.[6] Charles Owen concurred, viewing the Priest as suffering 'the inner conflict of the misogynist employed by a woman'.[7] Developing these positions, Arthur Broes argued that the rooster, Chauntecleer, in the *Nun's Priest's Tale* 'is nothing less than the thinly disguised animal counterpart of the Priest ... through which he can criticize women and enjoy dominance over them'.[8]

No one, as far as I know, has suggested that the priest was left without a specific portrait in the *General Prologue* because Chaucer had conflated him with one of the three clergymen-pilgrims whose full portraits followed shortly after that of the Prioress: that is, the Clerk. That association, I suggest, sheds added light on the purpose of the tale told by the Nun's Priest. Furthermore, by giving his tale such an anonymous title, Chaucer could keep his options open.

The identity of the Nun's Priest

Of the four portraits following immediately after that of the Prioress in the *General Prologue*, two are definitely of priests (the Monk, ll. 165–207 and the Friar, ll. 208–69), one could be that of a priest (the Clerk, ll. 285–308),[9] and the remaining fourth is a portrait of a merchant (ll. 270–84) so brief at 14 lines as to be almost invisible among 42 lines of monk, 61 lines of friar, and 23 lines of clerk. These three might be the 'preestes thre' who form an entourage around the Prioress and her attendant nun rather than some separate, undescribed, additional priests (or priest). The order of description invites the reader to see the Prioress, second nun, Monk, Friar, Merchant, and Clerk moving near one another on the road to Canterbury. The lecherousness suggested in the Friar's portrait together with the physicality of the Monk-horseman's portrait make it easy, moreover, to imagine that these two priests would be only too ready to ride in close proximity to the Prioress with her glittering good looks. As for the

---

[5] *Canterbury Tales*, ed. by John M. Manly (New York: Holt, 1928), p. 509.

[6] Robert M. Lumiansky, 'The Nun's Priest in "The Canterbury Tales" ', *Publications of the Modern Language Association*, 68 (1953), 896–906 (p. 902).

[7] Charles A. Owen, Jr., 'Crucial Passages in Five of *The Canterbury Tales*', in *Chaucer: Modern Essays in Criticism*, ed. by Edward Wagenknecht (New York: Oxford University Press, 1959), p. 267.

[8] Arthur Broes, 'Chaucer's Disgruntled Cleric: The Nun's Priest's Tale', *Publications of the Modern Language Association*, 78 (1963), 156–62 (p. 158).

[9] The Middle English word *clerke* derived from both Old English *cleric* (also *clerec*, *clerc*) and Old French *clerc*. The word entered into Old English and Old French from the Latin and Greek words for 'priest' or 'clergyman' (Latin *clericus*, Greek *klerikos*). The two main uses of the word in Middle English were to refer to a clergyman or a scholar. Since most medieval scholars at Oxford and Cambridge were headed for the priesthood, Chaucer's clerk of Oxenford certainly could be. Not all university scholars were ordained. Though we are not told whether or not the Clerk was, we do know that he does not yet have a *benefice* requiring the performance of priestly duties and that neither has he accepted secular employment. The Middle English word, *prest*, came from Old English *preost* by way of Late Latin *presbyter* (derived from Greek *presbyteros*, 'elder'). The primary use of the word in Middle English was to refer to a clergyman in the second of the holy orders (above a deacon and below a bishop) having authority to administer the sacraments and pronounce absolution. From Old English times onward, however, the word could also be used generally to refer to a member of the clerical profession: *Middle English Dictionary* (Ann Arbor: University of Michigan Press, 1952–2001), s.v. *prest* n.3, 1c., a.

bookish clerk, most likely studying to become a man of the church, whether or not he has yet been ordained, he would find it natural enough to position himself near the religious group as the pilgrims travel towards their goal. (It would, however, not have taken him long to realize that the Merchant had more in common with the Friar, Monk, and Prioress than he.) The Canterbury pilgrims include another priest — 'third' or 'fourth,' depending on whether the Clerk should be counted as a priest — and he, of course, is the Parson, specifically called a *clerk*: 'he was also a learned man, a clerk' (l. 480). He, though, is far removed from the Prioress's portrait in the *General Prologue* and is explicitly said to be travelling in the company of 'a Plowman, was his brother' (l. 529). The description of the Parson doesn't come until after the Franklin, the group including the Haberdasher, Carpenter, Weaver, Dyer and Tapster, and then the Cook, the Shipman, the Doctor of Phisik, the Wife of Bath have all been described. He is not likely to be anywhere near the Prioress.

If we understand 'preestes thre' to refer to the Monk, Friar, and Clerk, it is still possible to get 29 pilgrims:

1 Knyght
2 Squier
3 Yemen
4, 5 Nonne and 'hir chapeleyne'
6 Monk
7 Frere
8 Marchant
9 Clerk
10 Sergeant of Lawe
11 Frankeleyn
12–16 Haberdasshere, Carpenter, A Webbe, a Dyere, a Tapycer
17 Cook
18 Shipman
19 Doctour of Phisik
20 Wif of Bathe
21 Persoun
22 Plowman
23–27 Reeve, Millere, Somnour, Pardoner, Maunciple
28 Chaucer
29 Hooste.

Chaucer appears to include himself in the count when he adds 'and myself' after introducing the last of the portraits:

Ther was also a REVE, and a MILLERE,
A SOMNOUR, and a PARDONER also,
A MAUNCIPLE, and myself ... (*General Prologue*, ll. 542–44).

Harry, the host, however, appears to be excluded since Chaucer continues, 'there were namo' (*General Prologue*, l. 544). Even so, by the time we get to line 751 of the General Prologue, Chaucer embarks on a portrait of Harry much like all the preceding pilgrim portraits:

A semely man OURE HOOSTE was withalle
For to been a marchal in an halle.
A large man he was with eyen stepe —
A fairer burgeys was ther noon in Chepe —
Boold of his speche, and wys, and wel ytaught,

The Nun's Priest's Identity and the Purpose of his Tale

> And of manhod hym lakkede right naught.
> Eek therto he was right a myrie man. (ll. 751–57)

No one can deny that he is very much present on the road and involved in the process of getting to Canterbury. If any pilgrim is to go back to the Tabard, it is he: Harry is the host of the inn, a fact which may put him into a more enduring purgatory than the rest.

There are several similarities that make the Clerk and the priest who tells the *Nun's Priest's Tale* seem interchangeable, almost the same pilgrim. Most obvious are the references to the poor quality of their horses but also there are the facts that both tell tales that place their ideals of womanhood in agrarian settings and both are erudite. In the *Prologue* to the *Nun's Priest's Tale*, the host, trying to get a tale from the priest that will be merrier than the monk's which precedes it, calls the priest's horse a 'jade' (l. 2812; that is, a nag) which is 'bothe foul and lene' (l. 2813). In the *General Prologue's* description of the Clerk, we read: 'As leene was his hors as is a rake' (l. 287). More important, the Clerk and the Nun's Priest seem to share the same conception of ideal womanhood.

In the tales told by the Clerk and the Nun's Priest worthy women are found on farms. Before the technicolor world of the barnyard is set in motion in the *Nun's Priest's Tale*, the opening description presents the memorable black-and-white world of the poor widow. The long passage that begins the tale displays the old widow's virtues, her thrift, her care of daughters and animals, the poverty of her home and diet, and her moderate style of living from which spring peace and health:

> A povre wydwe, somdel stape in age,
> Was whilom dwellyng in a narwe cotage,
> Biside a grove, stondynge in a dale.
> This wydwe, of which I telle yow my tale,
> Syn thilke day that she was last a wyf
> In pacience ladde a ful symple lyf,
> For litel was hir catel and hir rente.
> By housbondrie of swich as God hire sente
> She foond hirself and eek hir doghtren two.
> Thre large sowes hadde she, and namo,
> Three keen, and eek a sheep that highte Malle.
> Ful sooty was hire bour and eek hir halle,
> In which she eet ful many a sklendre meel.
> Of poynaunt sauce hir neded never a deel.
> No deyntee morsel passed thurgh hir throte;
> Hir diete was accordant to hir cote.
> Repleccioun ne made hir nevere sik;
> Attempree diete was al hir phisik,
> And exercise, and herte suffisaunce.
> The goute lette hire nothyng for to daunce,
> N'apoplexie shente nat hir heed.
> No wyn ne drank she, neither whit ne reed;
> Hir bord was served moost with whit and blak–
> Milk and broun breed, in which she foond no lak,
> Seynd bacoun, and somtyme an ey or tweye,
> For she was, as it were, a maner deye. (*Nun's Priest's Tale*, ll. 2821–45)

A similar woman in a comparable setting is found in Part Two of the *Clerk's Tale*. We are told that not far from the opulent palace of the Marquis,

Carol F. Heffernan

> There stood a throop, of site delitable
> In which that poore folk of that village
> Hadden hir beestes and hir herbergage
> And of hire labour tooke hir sustenance,
> After that the erthe yaf hem habundance. (ll. 197–203)

There Janicula, an old man, lived with his daughter, Griselda, just as the widow lives with her two daughters and animals. His daughter has some of the qualities of the Nun's Priest's widow: she doesn't drink wine, and she doesn't seem interested in genteel life or material pleasure (major concerns of the Nun's Priest's travelling companion, the Prioress):

> No likerous lust was thurgh hire herte yronne.
> Wel after of the welle than of the tonne
> She drank, and for she wolde vertu plese,
> She knew wel labour but noon ydel ese. (*Clerk's Tale*, ll. 204–17)

She works hard on the farm like the widow of the *Nun's Priest's Tale*:

> A fewe sheep, spynnynge, on feld she kepte;
> She wolde noght been ydel til she slepte.
> And whan she homward cam, she wolde brynge
> Wortes or othere herbes tymes ofte,
> The whiche she shredde and seeth for hir lyvynge.
> And made hir bed ful harde and nothynge softe. (*Clerk's Tale*, ll. 223–28)

While their ideals of womanhood may be drawn from the peasantry, the Clerk and Nun's Priest belong to an exclusive fraternity whose members lead lives that centre on the scholar's cell.

The Clerk has studied logic and philosophy at Oxford and thinks more than he speaks, a quality which the Host suspects might interfere with the storytelling competition:

> This day ne herde I of youre tonge a word.
> I trowe ye studie aboute som sophyme;
> But Salomon seith 'every thyng hath tyme.' (*Prologue of the Clerk's Tale*, ll. 4–6)

The host turns to him, nonetheless, for 'som murie thyng,' just as he will later turn to the Nun's Priest for merriness after the dreary *Monk's Tale*, but warns the Clerk to avoid needless erudition or complex rhetoric in the company of the ordinary folk who are the Canterbury pilgrims:

> Youre termes, youre colours, and youre figures,
> Keepe hem in stoor til so be ye endite
> Heigh style, as whan that men to kynges write.
> Speketh so pleyn at this tyme, we yow preye,
> That we may understonde what ye seye. (*Prologue of the Clerk's Tale*, ll. 16–20)

The erudition of the Nun's Priest, left undescribed in the *General Prologue*, has to be inferred from the tale he tells. His broad knowledge of medieval medicine is apparent in the dialogue about dreams the Priest gives Chauntecleer and Pertelote and in Pertelote's enumeration of the many curative herbs to be found right in the barnyard: *lawriol, centaure, ellebor, katapuce,* and *gaitrys beryis* (ll. 2963–65). References to Boece (l. 3242), Bradwardyn (l. 3442), Augustyn (l. 3441), the Physiologus (l. 3271), kyng Priam (l. 3358), Eneydos (l. 3359) suggest reading not just in philosophy but also in classical and medieval secular literature. The Clerk, it will be recalled, learned the tale he told in Padua from Italy's poet lauriate, Petrarch. To be sure, the Priest's reference to *Eneydos* and the mock heroic style of his beast fable itself indicate that he is familiar with romance literature of the day as well as classical epic or, at least, legends derived from epic. No wonder in the eleven lines shared among the voices of the Host, Nun's Priest, and the narrator, Chaucer, which precede the *Nun's Priest's Tale*, there are so many words suggesting joy and gladness:

> 'Com neer, thou preest, com hyder, thou sir John!
> Telle us swich thyng as may oure hertes <u>glade</u>.
> Be <u>blithe</u>, though thou ryde upon a jade.
> What thogh thyn hors be bothe foul and lene?
> If he wol serve thee, rekke nat a bene.
> Looke that thyn herte be <u>murie</u> everemo.'
> 'Yis, sir,' quod he, 'yis, Hoost, so moot I go.
> But I be <u>myrie</u>, ywis, I wol be blamed.'
> And right anon his tale he hath attamed,
> And thus he seyde unto us everichon,
> This sweete preest, this goodly man sir John. (Emphasis mine; *Prologue of the Nun's Priest's Tale*, ll. 2810–20)

The fact that there is no direct description of the Nun's Priest in the *General Prologue* makes it tempting to wonder if that might be because the Clerk is so shortly to be fully described. Perhaps the scholarly clerk with no ecclesiastical benefice who rides on his undernourished horse is the pilgrim whom we should imagine as travelling to Canterbury in service to the Prioress. Serving as the Prioress's protector could be as good a job as the poor clerk has been able to find. Even today scholars unsure of their futures often are resourceful in uncovering inexpensive ways to travel. The title of the tale — *The Nun's Priest's Tale* — also conspires to keep the identity of the priest vague.[10] Could the generic title be Chaucer's way of keeping a sort of bookmark on a tale that might be kept in reserve for the Clerk to tell if there were ever to be enough complete tales to give each pilgrim two stories for the return trip as well as two for the trip to Canterbury ('ech of yow ... shal telle tales tweye / To Caunterbury-ward ... / And homward he shal tellen othere two'; *General Prologue*, ll. 792–94)?[11] But why hasten to compose a spare tale for the Clerk rather than some other pilgrim? The pilgrim Chaucer already has two stories: the *Tale of Thopas*, his 'tale of myrthe', (*Sir Thopas*, l. 706) in rhyme; and *The Tale of Melibee*, his 'tretys lyte' (*Sir Thopas* endlink, l. 963), in prose. Chaucer's *Sir Thopas* is a parody of old-fashioned tail-rhyme romances, while the *Tale of Melibee* is a moral treatise. Together the *Clerk's Tale* and the *Nun's Priest's Tale* repeat the pattern of pairing an ideal tale with a satiric one found in the two tales Chaucer gave himself (although *Thopas* is left incomplete and its author-persona may not get the joke). The tale told by the clerk is generally regarded as an ideal tale told by an ideal scholar, while the *Nun's Priest's Tale* is universally admired as a high-spirited satire, perhaps the greatest of all the Canterbury Tales.[12] It is told

---

[10] The sense of 'prest' intended in the title, *The Nonnes Preestes Tale*, could be the general one referring to 'any officeholder in the church.' See *MED* n.3, 1c.,a. It should be noted, however, that CT NP B. 4637 — 'Sire Nonnes Preest ... yblessed be thy breche and euery stoon' — is used as an illustration of the noun *prest* used figuratively in a phrase to mean 'a priest serving as chaplain to a nunnery or group of nuns.'

[11] Afterwards Harry tells the Franklin that the plan was for each pilgrim to tell a tale or two. By the time it is the Parson's turn to tell a tale, Harry is content with every pilgrim having told one tale (*Parson's Prologue*, 'Every man, save thou, has told his tale', l. 25).

[12] In this light it may be worth observing that Robert Kilburn Root, *The Poetry of Chaucer* (Boston: Houghton, Mifflin, 1906), p. 208, and T. W. Craik, *The Comic Tales of Chaucer* (New York: Barnes and Noble 1964), p. 81n, saw the *Nun's Priest's Tale* as a revelation of Chaucer in *propria persona*. Alfred David also suggests something close to this when he observes that the Nun's Priest is a character who represents a moment of fusion with 'a particular persona of Chaucer the artist.' He goes on to add, 'One may even draw an analogy between the position of the Priest, whose background is obviously humble, a spiritual guide to the ladylike nuns of St. Leonard's and

by a 'sweete preest' (*Prologue of The Nun's Priest's Tale*, l. 2820). Surely the adjective *sweete* would describe the quiet, gentle Clerk of whom the Host had earlier commented:

> Ye ryde as coy and stille as dooth a mayde
> Were newe spoused, sittynge at the bord. (*Prologue of the Clerk's Tale*, 2–3)

As the collection of Canterbury Tales stands, there are two clear possibilities: either the Clerk told two tales as Chaucer himself did or the Clerk told only the tale of Griselda and some other anonymous priest told the *Nun's Priest's Tale*. If the latter is, indeed, the case, we can at the very least imagine the Clerk within earshot of the telling of the beast fable and understanding perfectly what the purpose of a kindred spirit was in telling such a tale.[13] In the argument which follows, I by no means wish to suggest that the relation of the Nun's Priest to his tale cancels any of the numerous readings of the tale which has been seen in isolation as a superb beast fable and viewed in the context of the *Canterbury Tales* as a tale that subverts themes that run throughout the work.[14]

The purpose of the priest's tale

It is easy to view the *Nun's Priest's Tale* as the 'sweete' priest's acerbic yet witty commentary on his travelling companion, the Prioress. Like Chaucer the Pilgrim who describes the Prioress in the *General Prologue*, the Priest is fully aware of the degree to which she values the graces and trappings of cultivated life. With the very first line of his tale he immediately begins to displace the Prioress's standards with his own by opening the *Nun's Priest's Tale* with the description of the life of the old widow whose spiritual and moral values he shares. Whereas the Prioress sought to evade what were to her the constraints of a nun's life, by decorating the nun's habit, for example, by pleating its wimple (*General Prologue*, l. 151), wearing a cloak 'Ful fetys' (*General Prologue*, l. 157) and choosing a rosary made of coral, green stones, and 'gold ful sheene' (*General Prologue*, l. 160), the poor widow 'In pacience ladde a ful symple lyf' (*Nun's Priest's Tale*, l. 2826). One can just imagine the Prioress's thoughts having heard that part of the *Clerk's Tale* which gives the account of how the Marquis arranges for clothing and jewels to transform a peasant girl into a courtly lady for her wedding day:

> ...this markys hath doon make
> Of gemmes, set in gold and in asure,
> Brooches and rynges, for Griseldis sake;
> And of hir clothyng took he the mesure. (*Clerk's Tale*, ll. 253–56)

Doubtless the Priest and probably the Clerk, too, have had the opportunity to observe the Prioress's reaction at close range.

The Priest uses the poor widow's world as a referential frame which contrasts with and stands outside of the turbulence contained in the barnyard, which itself frequently provides instances of obvious identity with the Prioress. Within the barnyard world, the courtly values

---

the position of Chaucer as a poet writing for the ladies of the English Court': *The Strumpet Muse* (Bloomington: Indiana University Press, 1976), p. 224.

[13] This individuating approach may seem to run against Jill Mann's analysis of the conventional ingredients of the pilgrim portraits in *Chaucer and Medieval Estates Satire* (Cambridge: Cambridge University Press, 1973), and H. Marshall Leicester's argument that the tales give voices to their tellers and not the other way round in *The Disenchanted Self* (Berkeley: University of California Press, 1990). My reading of these primary texts, nonetheless, moves that way.

[14] See, for example, Jill Mann, 'The Speculum Stultorum and the Nun's Priest's Tale', *The Chaucer Review*, 8

of the Prioress with their emphasis on wealth as well as her pretention find a satiric echo in Pertelote, the chicken who is the rooster's favorite concubine. Pertelote is 'Curteys ... discreet, and debonaire, / And compaignable, and bar hyrself so faire' (*Nun's Priest's Tale*, ll. 2871–72). The priest's description of her is intended to recall that of the Prioress in the *General Prologue* that depicts her as being 'ful plesaunt, and amyable of port', someone who

> ... peyned hire to countrefete cheere
> Of court, and to been estatlich of manere,
> And to ben holden digne of reverencee. (*General Prologue*, ll. 138–41)

Much of the power of the priest's mocking satire comes from just this fact of the identification of the nun with a chicken. Pertelote's rooster lover, Chauntecleer, keeps her henlike glory before the reader as he gloats:

> ... whan I se the beautee of youre face,
> Ye been so scarlet reed aboute youre yen,
> It maketh al my dred for to dyen. (*Nun's Priest's Tale*, ll. 3160–62)

Furthermore, Chauntecleer is used by the Priest to indicate that when the Prioress shows herself off as a woman capable of moral outrage in her telling of the sentimental tale about the young Christian boy who is killed by Jews and cast into a latrine to die that — capable of moral outrage — is exactly what she is not. (The old widow of the *Nun's Priest's Tale* frame, on the other hand, puts no moral stance on display yet is recognizable as a person of real conscience). The Priest has Chantecleer refer to a story similar to the *Prioress's Tale* and gives the rooster a phrase that exactly repeats the nun's histrionic exclamation about the murder of the little clergeon: 'Mordre wol out' (*Prioress's Tale*, l. 576). Chauntecleer's story, alluded to in the course of his discussion of dreams, concerns the murder of a man by robbers who throw his dead body into a dung heap. The lines of commentary about the murder which are given to Chauntecleer by the Priest mockingly imitate the Prioress's storytelling style:

> Mordre wol out, that se we day by day,
> Mordre is so wlatsom and abhomynable
> To God, that is so just and resonable,
> That he ne wol nat suffre it heled be,
> Though it abyde a yeer, or two, or thre.
> Modre wol out, this my conclusioun. (*Nun's Priest's Tale*, ll. 3052–57)[15]

Chauntecleer surrounded by Pertelote and her sister hens suggests the Priest in company with the Prioress and the nun 'chapelayne'. But even before the reader gets to the barnyard chickens, much in the opening portrait about the widow's life — which, though a framing device, is still part of the tale — plays off against what is known about the Prioress. As with the parody (and deflation) of the Prioress's courtly bearing achieved through its mirror image in Pertelote mentioned above, when the old widow's meals are said to be slight and without sauce or fancy food, the Priest intends us and his fellow pilgrims to remember the nun's attention to feeding with elegance:

(1974–5), 262–82 and Alan T. Gaylord, 'Sentence and Solas in Fragment VII of the Canterbury Tales: Harry Bailly as Horseback Editor', *Publications of the Modern Language Association*, 82 (1967), 226–35.

[15] There is a reminder of *The Clerk's Tale* as well in Chauntecleer's story of the murder, for the victim is lodged overnight in a place that recalls the humble home Griselda shared with Janicula of which the Clerk said, '. . . hye God somtyme senden kan/His grace into a litel oxes stalle' (*Clerk's Tale*, ll. 206–7). The victim, who is one of two pilgrims, is lodged in what is described as 'a stalle,/Fer in a yeerd, with oxen of the plough' (*Nun's Priest's Tale*, ll. 2996–97). His companion pilgrim has a dream in which the victim calls to him saying, 'Allas, for in an oxes stalle/This nyght I shal be mordred ther I lye!' (l. 3005). If the Clerk were telling the tale, the echo would

> She leet no morsel from hir lippes falle,
> Ne wette hir fyngres in hir sauce depe.
> Wel koude she carie a morsel and wel kepe
> That no drope ne fille upon hire breste. (*General Prologue*, ll. 128–31)

Again, the effect is to undercut what the Prioress means to be a grace. The humble 'broun breed' (*Nun's Priest's Tale*, l. 2844) of the widow's table which feeds her and her daughters is less good than the 'wastel-breed' (*General Prologue*, l. 147) with which the Prioress feeds her hounds. Deflation again. Because the Priest in his poverty, signaled by the nag he rides, identifies with the life of the admirable old woman, he thus appropriates the moral high ground from the very outset of his taletelling. And later — after the matter of Chauntecleer's troubling dream is taken up on the very narrow perch where he has trouble making love to Pertelote, and the hen's interpretation proves wrong and that of her husband, the rooster, right — at the very moment the predatory fox enters the beast fable to capture the cock, the Priest seizes upon the opportunity to make an anti-feminist statement:

> Wommennes conseils been ful ofte cold;
> Wommannes conseil broghte us first to wo,
> And made Adam fro Paradys to go,
> Ther as he was ful myrie and wel at ese. (*Nun's Priest's Tale*, ll. 3256–58)

There is a striking reversal in the beast fable of the relationship between the Prioress and the Priest: whereas the Priest is critical of and feels superior to the Prioress, Chauntecleer is passionate about Pertelote to the point of uxoriousness. When Chauntecleer's lust for Pertelote leads him to wittily and purposefully mistranslate the Latin '*Mulier est hominis confusio*' (l. 3164) as 'Womman is mannes joye and al his blis' (l. 3166), the mistranslation manages at once to signal the rooster's submission to his desire for the hen and the Priest's needling the Prioress for her poor language skills. Having unwisely ignored his own view of the dream as a prophetic one and having allowed his guard to drop as a result of Pertelote's insistence that the dream arose from mere indigestion, Chauntecleer is ensnared by the flattery of the fox. The priest, however, depicts his rooster as intelligent enough to learn from his mistakes — at least the one about the dangers of flattery. Once he has escaped from the mouth of the fox and flown to the safety of the branches of a tree, Chauntecleer resists the fox's entreaties to come down:

> 'Nay thanne', quod he, 'I shrewe us bothe two.
> And first I shrewe myself, both blood and bones,
> If thou bigyle me ofter than ones.
> Thou shalt namoore, thurgh thy flaterye,
> Do me to synge and wynke with myn ye;
> For he that wynketh, whan he sholde see,
> Al wilfully, God lat him nevere thee!' (*Nun's Priest's Tale*, ll. 3426–32)

As a beast fable the tale the Priest tells must have a moral: that appears to be not only that a man who 'wynketh, whan he sholde see' (l. 3431) risks death, but also that a man who learns from his mistakes can triumph — a merry story, indeed.

The Priest's moral is directed more at *man*kind than *human*kind, for there is no change of fortune for Pertelote who continues to be Chauntecleer's concubine, as she has been 'Syn thilke day that she was seven nyght oold' (*Nun's Priest's Tale*, l. 2873). Thus to the Host, the Priest of the *Epilogue* looks a winner, a Priest triumphant, rooster-like with "So greet a nekke,

be a sign of playful wit; on the other hand, if the Nun's Priest were some other clergyman, the reason for the association is ambiguous but no less interesting.

and swich a large breest!' (l. 3457), a veritable 'trede-foul' (l. 3451) like Chauntecleer. To sum up then, the purpose of *The Nun's Priest's Tale* is to offer indirect criticism of the Prioress by showing how like Pertelote she is and how *un*like the widow, which is to say, *un*like the Priest, since he feels spiritually akin (as would the Clerk as well) to the old widow. The related theme of the dangers of listening to the counsel of women, a common antifeminist thread in clerical writing and, therefore, fitting to the character of a clergyman, seems to suggest that the Prioress — as a woman and, most especially, for all her specific private weaknesses — is probably not a good convent head and should certainly be regarded as intellectually inferior to her Priest. The Prioress is so obviously flawed as a nun that she deserves what she gets as a target of satire whether from a Clerk who is as glad to teach as he is to learn or from a Priest worthy to be a spiritual guide.[16] This said, there is something unattractively bullying and smug about satirists even when their criticism is so indirect, so artful, so light as to leave their targets oblivious of the fact that they have been hit. The satirist must always have that quality which keeps Harry in awe of the Clerk and the Nun's Priest sure of what he is doing in his tale — 'his monolithic certainty'.[17]

This new reading of the problematical 'preestes three' in the *General Prologue* has attempted to give a greater sense of identity to the anonymous Nun's Priest by suggesting that Chaucer conflated him with another clergyman: the Clerk. This association helps shed more light on the Nun's Priest's relationship to the tale he tells. It is my hope that I have contributed something to unpicking a notorious problem.[18]

---

[16] This section of the essay suggests the Prioress as a context for understanding the outlook and satire of the *Nun's Priest's Tale*. Peter W. Travis's study, *Disseminal Chaucer* (Notre Dame, Indiana: University of Notre Dame Press, 2010) mentions the *Prioress's Tale* three times and brings it together with the *Nun's Priest's Tale* only when citing Helen Cooper's remark about language, 'If the Prioress's Prologue had declared the inadequacy of words to express spiritual meaning, the Nun's Priest's Tale demonstrates how rhetoric can be manipulated to endow the most trivial of barnyard events with epic significance': *The Structure of the Canterbury Tales* (Athens, Georgia: University of Georgia Press, 1984), p. 186.

[17] The term was coined by Alvin Kernan in *The Cankered Muse: Satire of the English Renaissance* (New Haven, Conn.: Yale University Press, 1959), p. 22.

[18] An earlier version of this essay was presented at the New Chaucer Society Congress held at the University of Glasgow, Scotland, July 2004.

The Yew Rune, Yogh and *Yew*

Bernard Mees

The problem of the thirteenth rune of the older and Anglo-Saxon futharks (ᛇ~ᛇ) has a long and divergent historiography.[1] A number of values such as *eu* or close or open *e* were accepted by earlier generations of runologists.[2] Indeed even in the medieval period there seems to have been little consensus as to its phonological purpose. Various values are assigned to this staff in the English manuscript tradition: *i, eo, h* and *k*; and similarly, its use in Old English inscriptions varies from an earlier employment as *i* to a later *h*. There is somewhat less ambivalence among the attested rune names, however. The *Codex Salisburgensis* and the *Isruna Tracts* designate this rune *ih*, and the *Runic Poem* names it *eoh* mirroring Old English vocalic development. Therefore, the original rune name has traditionally been constructed as meaning 'yew' (OE *ēo, ēow, īw*), as a similar name, *ýr*, is recorded for one of the Nordic runes that represented *r* (ʀ), as if when the old value *z* was surrendered, that of the lost thirteenth rune was assumed.[3]

---

[1] The following abbreviations are used in this paper: *IEW* = Julius Pokorny, *Indogermanisches etymologisches Wörterbuch*, 2 vols (Bern: Francke, 1959–69); *IK* = *Die Goldbrakteaten der Völkerwanderungszeit*, ed. by Karl Hauck and others, Münster Mittelalter-Schriften, 24 (Münster: Fink, 1985–), I.2–III.2 (*Ikonographischer Katalog*, 1–3); *KJ* = Wolfgang Krause and Herbert Jankuhn, *Die Runeninschriften im älteren Futhark*, Akademie der Wissenschaften in Göttingen, Phil.-Hist. Klasse, Abhandlungen, III. Reihe, 65, 2nd edn (Göttingen: Vandenhoeck & Ruprecht, 1966); *NIæR* = *Norges indskrifter med de ældre runer*, ed. by Sophus Bugge and Magnus Olsen, Norges indskrifter indtil reformationen, 1/Norske historiske Kildeskriftfondsskrifter, 22, 4 vols (Christiania: Brøgger, 1891–1924).

[2] Cf. Peter Andreas Munch, 'Om indskriften paa det i Sønder-Jylland 1734 fundne guldhorn', *Annaler for nordisk oldkyndighed og historie* (1847), pp. 389–91 [repr. in Peter Andreas Munch, *Samlede afhandlinger*, ed. by Gustav Storm, 4 vols (Christiania: Cammermeyer, 1873-76), I, 399]; Julius Zacher, *Das gothische Alphabet, Vulfilas, und das Runenalphabet: Eine sprachwissenschaftliche Untersuchung* (Leipzig: Brockhaus, 1855), p. 25; Ludvig F. A. Wimmer, 'Runeskriftens oprindelse og udvikling i norden', *Aarbøger for nordisk oldkyndighed og historie*, 1 (1874), 1–270 (p. 120) (though cf. Ludvig F. A. Wimmer, *Die Runenschrift*, trans. by Ferdinand Holthausen, rev. edn. (Berlin: Weidmann, 1887), pp. 134–35); Rudolph Henning, *Die deutsche Runendenkmäler* (Strasbourg: Trübner, 1889), p. 67; *NIæR*, pp. 117–48; Carl J. S Marstrander, 'Om runenene og runenavnes oprindelse', *Norsk tidskrift for sprogvidenskap*, 1 (1928), 85–188 (pp. 118–19); Arthur G. Brodeur, 'The Riddle of the Runes', *University of California Publications in English*, 3 (1932), 1–15 (pp. 10–13); Otto von Friesen, *De germanska, anglofrisiska och tyska runorna*, ed. by Otto von Friesen, Nordisk kultur, 6 (Stockholm: Bonnier, 1933), pp. 3–79 (p. 9).

[3] Raymond I. Page, 'The Old English Rune *eoh, íh*, "Yew Tree"', *Medium Ævum*, 37 (1968), 125–36 [repr. in *Runes and Runic Inscriptions: Collected Essays on Anglo-Saxon and Viking Runes*, ed. by David Parsons (Woodbridge: Boydell, 1995), pp. 133–44]. In two of the manuscripts, British Library, Cotton Galba A.ii and St John's College, Oxford, 17, the names of the thirteenth and fifteenth runes have been exchanged, and as in the Nordic tradition, it is the old fifteenth rune which has received the name 'yew' (or actually *eth*, corrected to *eoh*).

The Yew Rune, Yogh and Yew

Thus runologists have generally assumed a vocalic value for the thirteenth runes, a value clearly shown in some of the oldest inscriptions. Formerly represented in the grammars as *ė* (i.e. close *e*), Wolfgang Krause's transliteration *ï* has now found favour in most studies.[4] Yet doubt remains as to the rune's original value. Elmer Antonsen proposes to read /æ:/ (i.e. $\bar{e}_1$), Leo Connolly has reconstructed /i(:)/, Ottar Grønvik and Elmar Seebold prefer [ç], Tineke Looijenga has mooted an original value /i(:)j/ or /ji(:)/ and Heinrich Beck, reviving an older interpretation, now sees the rune as representing an /i(:)/ not fully lowered to /e(:)/.[5]

Antonsen's reading /æ:/ is largely predicated on structural concerns — i.e. the notion that there was an imbalance between the inventory of Proto-Germanic short (*/i, e, a, u/) and long (*/i:, æ:, ɔ:, u:/) vowel phonemes. Yet of all the contributions it is Connolly's which is the most intriguing and the most original.[6] Following Antonsen's principle that the yew rune must have represented a phoneme lost during the Proto-Germanic period, but still attempting to reconcile its employment in both the early inscriptions and in the rune names (the chief failing of Antonsen's theory), he has reconstructed a Proto-Germanic vowel created through the influence of a Proto-Germanic laryngeal. This laryngeal, he proposes, retracted neighbouring Proto-Germanic *i* to a high central vowel that he transcribes as *ɨ*. He arrived at this theory after a number of studies on the inconsistent fate of inherited IE *e*, *ei* and *i* in the descendant dialects.[7] Nonetheless he is unable to provide proof of the use of the yew rune to represent this *ɨ*.

[4] KJ, p. 5.
[5] Elmer H. Antonsen, *A Concise Grammar of the Older Runic Inscriptions*, Sprachstrukturen, Reihe A: Historische Sprachstrukturen, 3 (Tübingen: Niemeyer, 1975), pp. 3–6; Elmer H. Antonsen, *Runes and Germanic Linguistics*, Trends in Linguistics: Studies and Monographs, 140 (Berlin: Mouton de Gruyter, 2002), pp. 44–45; Leo A. Connolly, 'The Rune ᛇ and the Germanic Vowel System', *Amsterdamer Beiträge zur älteren Germanistik*, 14 (1979), pp. 1–32; Ottar Grønvik, *Runene på Tunesteinen: Alfabet — språkform — budskap* (Oslo: Universitetsforlaget, 1981), pp. 29–32; Elmar Seebold, 'Die Stellung der englischen Runen im Rahmen der Überlieferung des älteren Fuþark', in *Old English Runes and their Continental Background*, ed. by Alfred Bammesberger, Anglistische Forschungen, 217 (Heidelberg: Winter, 1991), pp. 439–569 (pp. 469–70); Tineke Looijenga, 'The Yew-Rune in the Pforzen Inscription', in *Pforzen und Bergakker*, ed. by Alfred Bammesberger, Historische Sprachforschung Ergänzungsheft, 41 (Göttingen: Vandenhoeck & Ruprecht, 1999), pp. 80–87 (pp. 81–82); Tineke Looijenga, *Texts and Contexts of the Oldest Runic Inscriptions*, The Northern World, 4 (Leiden: Brill, 2003), pp. 138–42; Heinrich Beck, 'Runen und Schriftlichkeit', in *Von Thorsberg nach Schleswig: Sprache und Schriftlichkeit eines Grenzgebietes im Wandel eines Jahrtausends. Internationales Kolloquium im Wikinger Museum Haithabu vom 29. September–3. Oktober 1994*, ed. by Klaus Düwel, Edith Marold and Christiane Zimmermann, Ergänzungsbände zum Reallexikon der germanischen Altertumskunde, 25 (Berlin: De Gruyter, 2001), pp. 1–23 (pp. 1–6); Heinrich Beck, 'Zum Problem der 13. Rune (ᛇ)', in *Runica, Germanica, Mediaevalia*, ed. by Wilhelm Heizmann and Astrid von Nahl, Ergänzungsbände zum Reallexikon der germanischen Altertumskunde, 37 (Berlin: De Gruyter, 2003), pp. 77–83; and cf. Wolfgang Krause, *Die Sprache der urnordischen Runeninschriften*, Germanische Bibliothek Reihe 3: Untersuchungen und Einzeldarstellungen (Heidelberg: Winter, 1971), pp. 25–26; Heinrich Beck, 'Sprachliche Argumente zum Problem des Runenaufkommens', *Zeitschrift für deutsches Altertum und deutsche Literatur*, 101 (1972), 1–15; Richard Schrodt, 'Die Eibenrune und Idg. *ei* in Germanischen', *Zeitschrift für deutsches Altertum und deutsche Literatur*, 104 (1975), 171–79; Bernard Mees, 'Early Rhineland Germanic', *North-Western European Language Evolution (NOWELE)*, 49 (2006), 13–49 (p. 35).
[6] Connolly, 'The Rune ᛇ and the Germanic Vowel System'.
[7] Leo A. Connolly, 'Indo-European *i* > Germanic *e*: An Explanation by the Laryngeal Theory', *Beiträge zur Geschichte der deutschen Sprache und Literatur (Tübingen)*, 99 (1977), 173–205, 333–58; Leo A. Connolly, '$\bar{e}_2$ and the Laryngeal Theory', *Beiträge zur Geschichte der deutschen Sprache und Literatur (Tübingen)*, 101 (1979), 1–29; Leo A. Connolly, 'Altnordisch *e* < indogermanisch *i*', *Zeitschrift für vergleichende Sprachforschung*, 97 (1894), 267–80; Leo A. Connolly, 'On Identifying Laryngeal Reflexes in Germanic', *American Journal of Germanic Linguistics and Literatures*, 11 (1999), 205–22.

Connolly's linkage of the yew rune to the development of *e*, *ei* and *i* is reminiscent of the theory that first led to the transcription *ē*. This transcription derives from the positing that the thirteenth rune represented a Germanic non-low front vowel, intermediate between *e* and *i*. Indeed when long, this vowel is often proposed to have derived from an intermediate value (i.e. *ē*) suggested to have been produced by the monophthongisation of *ei* before it developed to *ī*,[8] bearing in mind that such a development occurred in both pre-classical Latin and Hellenistic Greek.[9] Yet the few inscriptions in the older futhark that employ the yew rune lexically show a value /i(:)/, and when long not necessarily one derived from *ei*.[10] The thirteenth rune only appears in inscriptions where it seems to be orthographically redundant. Thus some philologists have claimed that it was redundant from the time of the inception of the futhark, a redundancy that occurs in alphabetic scripts found throughout the Mediterranean (as witnessed by their abecedaria).[11] Yet the thirteenth rune does not clearly formally derive from any single Mediterranean letter. Indeed it has been claimed by some to have been especially created for the Germanic script, as if it represented a sound unknown in the tradition from which it was borrowed. Antonsen's theory seems conclusive: the yew rune probably represented a phone later lost from Germanic.[12]

---

[8] Friedrich Ranke *apud* Wolfgang Jungandreas, 'Die germanische Runenreihe und ihre Bedeutung', *Zeitschrift für deutsche Philologie*, 40 (1935), 105–21 (p. 106).

[9] The old theory is perhaps best summarised in an article contemporary to that of Connolly by Karl Schneider, 'Zum gemeingermanischen runischen Schriftsystem (Älter, Runennamen, Struktur der 24er-Reihe, kimbrische Schöpfung)', in *Integrale Linguistik: Festschrift für Helmut Gipper*, ed. by Edeltrud Bülow and Peter Schmitter (Amsterdam: Benjamins, 1979), pp. 541–71. Antonsen and others seem to (mis)understand this theory as proposing that the yew rune represents the diphthong itself. Antonsen reaffirms his view in Schneider's *Festschrift*, but others, such as Alfred Bammesberger, are still inclined to link the thirteenth rune with IE *ei*: Elmer H. Antonsen, 'Zum Ursprung und Älter des germanischen Fuþarks', in *Festschrift für Karl Schneider zum 70. Geburtstag am 18. April 1982*, ed. by Kurt R. Jankowsky and Ernst S. Dick (Amsterdam: Benjamins, 1982), 3–15 (pp. 10–12); Alfred Bammesberger, 'The Development of the Runic Script and its Relationship to Germanic Phonological History', in *Language Change and Language Structure: Older Germanic Languages in a Comparative Perspective*, ed. by Torvil Swan, Endre Mørck, Olaf Jansen Westvik, Trends in Linguistics: Studies and Monographs, 73 (Berlin: De Gruyter, 1994), pp. 1–25 (pp. 6–8). Another similar approach is that of Helmut Birkhan who posits the influence of a neighbouring East Celtic dialect (Celtic usually monophthongises IE *ei* to *ē*): Helmut R. J. Birkhan, *Germanen und Kelten bis zum Ausgang der Römerzeit: Der Aussagewert von Wörtern und Sachen für die frühesten keltisch-germanischen Kulturbeziehungen*, Österreichische Akademie der Wissenschaften, Phil.-Hist. Klasse. Sitzungsberichte, 272 (Vienna: Böhlau, 1970), pp. 178–80.

[10] In addition, as Krause points out, the name of the ice rune is also usually derived from a form with IE *ei*- (see *IEW* 301). According to Connolly, however, the only sure Continental attestation of the thirteenth rune with a value *i* in Krause's corpus, on the Freilaubersheim fibula, may represent *ī* < *eH₁i*. Wolfgang Krause, 'Untersuchungen zu den Runennamen II', *Nachrichten der Akadamie der Wissenschaften in Göttingen, Phil.-Hist. Klasse*, 2 (1948) 93–108; KJ, p. 5; Connolly, 'The Rune ᛇ and the Germanic Vowel System', p. 28.

[11] e.g. Михаил Иванович Стеблин-Каменский (Mikhail Ivanovich Steblin-Kamenskiĭ), 'Какую систему гласных выражал первоначально рунический алфавит?', Скандинавский Сборник, 4 (1959), 153–58; 'Noen fonologiske betrakninger over de eldre runer', *Arkiv för nordisk filologi*, 77 (1962), 1–6 (pp. 5–6).

[12] The only other option would seem to be to assume some magico-religious reason for the creation of this staff. Despite the appearance of pairings in the rune-row similar to those sometimes used in alphabetic magic, such solutions are usually overly speculative. The most voluminous example of this type of analysis is the gematric theory of Heinz Klingenberg based around the number thirteen, one that most runologists have treated with circumspection: Heinz Klingenberg, *Runenschrift — Schriftdenken — Runenschriften*, Germanische Bibliothek, Reihe: Untersuchungen und Einzeldarstellungen, 3 (Heidelberg: Winter, 1973). Similarly, others have pointed to the magical and religious significance of the yew tree and its connection with the ON Yggrdrasil and Ullr; see Karl Schneider, *Die germanischen Runennamen: Versuch einer Gesamtdeutung; ein Beitrag zur idg./germ. Kultur- und Religionsgeschichte* (Meisenheim a G.: Hain, 1956), p. 285; Harry Andersen, 'Three Controversial Runes in the Older Futhark', *North-Western European Language Evolution (NOWELE)*, 4 (1984), 97–110 and 5 (1985),

The Yew Rune, Yogh and Yew

Rather than beginning with theoretical concerns, however, a more grounded approach would surely be to start with a survey of how the rune is actually used in early epigraphy before bringing in other considerations. The earliest attestation of the thirteenth rune is in the Kylver stone rune-row (KJ 1), for example, and it appears in all of the elder rune-row inscriptions save the short partial rows of Aquincum (KJ 7), Beuchte (KJ 8) and the Gudme II bracteate (*IK* 392). It also has the same orientation as has Latin S (i.e. ʃ) in each of these inscriptions. This includes the example on the Vadstena bracteate (*IK* 337, 1) where as an anticlockwise (i.e. sinistroverse) inscription, this makes the character retrograde to the rest of the text. Similarly, the character is generally direct (ʃ) in the body of inscriptions collected by Krause: the only other retrograde example is one of the two yew runes on the Krogsta stone where this staff is (apparently mistakenly) employed for the graphically similar **t** (↑; KJ 100). This is also the case in most of the English inscriptions. Yet in the four examples on English coins and the two English rune-rows, the yew rune is always inscribed as a retrograde (ʅ), a practice also to be noted on a non-provenanced Danish bracteate (*IK* 197).[13] A doubtful example of a retrograde form has also emerged on a find on a strap-end from Long Buckby, Northamptonshire, that dates from the late eighth century; although the top of the rune is missing, Ray Page plausibly read ']i h ‖ t' — i.e. a partial, perhaps of the common anthroponymic element *briht*.[14] On the other hand, the manuscripts containing runes usually feature the direct form, although an apparent formal confusion with Latin Z is evident in the Codex Cotton Otho B.x.[15]

The thirteenth rune also hardly varies its shape throughout the centuries of its employment.[16] In the Lindkær/Over Hornbæk III bracteate rune-row (*IK* 110) it has been reduced to the shape of an **l**-rune (i.e. ⌐), a reduction which also appears to have occurred on an Anglian coin[17] and possibly on the Broholm bracteate (*IK* 225). These variants, however, seem to be mistakes on the behalf of the craftsmen so concerned. The yew rune is thus very stable in form, if not in orientation or in phonological value.

Of the rune-row inscriptions, only that from Charnay (KJ 6) gives us any clue as to the phonological value of this rune, in the graphically isolated sequence ʃia. Seebold reads [aiç] here, yet this is unlikely as this assumes that both the **a** and ʃ are retrograde to this sinistroverse

---

3–22. Cf. Ralph W. V. Elliot, 'Runes, Yews and Magic', *Speculum*, 32 (1957), 250–61; Robert Bevan-Jones, *The Ancient Yew: A History of 'Taxus Baccata'* (Macclesfield: Windgather, 2002). It should be noted that in the very inscription that appears to invoke the power of the yew, however, this rune does not appear, although the ice rune does: Tineke Looijenga, 'Yew Wood and Runic Inscriptions in the Frisian *Terp*-Area', in *Old English Runes and their Continental Background*, ed. by Alfred Bammesberger, Anglistische Forschungen, 217 (Hedelberg: Winter, 1991), pp. 335–42. Nor does it appear in what is often taken to be the only runic testament to Ullr, the inscription on the Thorsberg chape.

[13] For the coins see Mark Blackburn, 'A Survey of Anglo-Saxon and Frisian Coins with Runic Inscriptions', in *Old English Runes and their Continental Background*, ed. by Alfred Bammesberger, Anglistische Forschungen, 217 (Heidelberg: Winter, 1991), pp. 137–89 (pp. 155–56, 159); Raymond I. Page, *An Introduction to English Runes*, 2nd edn (Woodbridge: Boydell, 1999), pp. 123, 125–26; for the rune-rows see Page, *An Introduction to English Runes*, pp. 79–80.

[14] Raymond I. Page, 'New Anglo-Saxon Rune Finds', *Nytt om runer*, 15 (2000), 10–11 (p. 11).

[15] This is a quite different picture to that expounded by Bengt Odenstedt, who claims the distribution of retrograde versus direct is about even: *On the Origin and Early History of the Runic Script: Typology and Graphic Variation in the Older Futhark*, Acta Academiae Regiae Gustavi Adolphi, 59 (Uppsala: Almqvist & Wiksell, 1990), pp. 75–77. Cf. the reviews of Odenstedt by Düwel and Williams: Klaus Düwel's in *Göttingische gelehrte Anzeigen*, 224 (1992), 234–41 and Henrik Williams, 'Which Came First, Π or Π?', *Arkiv för nordisk filologi*, 107 (1992), 192–205.

[16] Seebold, 'Die Stellung der englischen Runen', p. 470 may have found a late variant similar to the **n** or **g** runes in the unclear inscriptions on the Lundeborg (*IK* 295) and Gudme I bracteates (*IK* 391).

[17] Blackburn, 'A Survey of Anglo-Saxon and Frisian Coins', p. 155; Page, *An Introduction to English Runes*, p. 123.

reading (note too that the main Charnay inscription is clearly dextroverse as is standard in Continental inscriptions).[18] I have suggested that the sequence (which is found along with another isolated sequence **kr**) may be an abbreviation for the common early Christian *nomen sacrum* Iaô (and **kr** likewise Christus) much as Ute Schwab sought to interpret many of the shorter sequences in German inscriptions as typically Christian forms.[19] Considering that it is graphically separated from the main inscription, however, ʃ**ia** may not represent a lexeme at all.[20]

With the form on the Charnay fibula may be grouped a number of other inscriptions in the older futhark. The By stone's final sequence **rmþ**ʃ (KJ 71), the Denmark X bracteate legend ʃ**lwl** (*IK* 39), the Kitnæs III-C bracteate's **l**ʃ**t** (*IK* 94.1), and the anticlockwise Nebenstedt II bracteate inscription **llet × oʀ·r**ʃ **i̱**ʃ**·aþʀmtl** and the similar Darum IV bracteate legend **lae:t ⁕oʀʀ**ʃ**ll**ʃ**aþʀet** (*IK* 129.1–2) are all of disputable value for the present purpose. Krause (KJ 55, nn. 1–2) has remarked on two similarly problematic Norwegian inscriptions from Hammeren and Oppauran that read **alf**ʃ (*NIæR* I.373–82: sinistroverse; perhaps an anthroponym *Alfi*) and **ea**ʃ**u** (*NIæR* II.732–40). To this category also belongs the Krogsta stone, side A of which bears the uninterpreted **mwsꞁeij**, along with a second attestation which, as has already been mentioned, shows that the thirteenth rune seems to have been confused with the **t** rune in **s**ʃ**ainaʀ** [stainaz].

More evidence is forthcoming from the Nebenstedt I bracteate which bears the inscription **gl**ʃ**augiʀu** ʃ**uṛṇrl** (*IK* 128). Krause (KJ 133) has related the first element to ON *gljá* 'glitter', and thus reconstructs a value /i/. Seebold prefers to see a cognate form of OIr. *glicc* 'clever, skilful' here and so is able to accommodate a value [iç].[21] The third element is ambiguous for although a strong *wīhu* 'I consecrate' (cf. Goth *weihan* 'sanctify, make holy') is a possible form, the Kragehul spear shaft (KJ 27) spells this verb as **wiju** and the Vimose buckle (KJ 24) has **wija**, suggesting an Early Nordic **wīhju* with the loss of medial *-h-*; compare the Nydam axe haft's **wi̱hgu̱**.[22] Seebold also brings to attention the scrambled Broholm (*IK* 225) form that he reconstructs as **wlho** and which he suggests is probably [wi:ço] with a deformed yew rune.[23] Moreover, a Danish bracteate of unknown provenance features a spelling **wiꞁu**

---

[18] Seebold, 'Die Stellung der englischen Runen im Rahmen', p. 498.

[19] Ute Schwab, 'Runen der Merowingerzeit als Quelle für das Weiterleben der spätantiken christlichen und nichtchristlichen Schriftmagie?', in *Runische Schriftkultur in kontinental-skandinavischer und -angelsächsischer Wechselbeziehung: Internationales Symposium in der Werner-Reimars-Stiftung vom 24.–27. Juni 1992 in Bad Homburg*, ed. by Klaus Düwel, Ergänzungsbände zum Reallexikon der germanischen Altertumskunde, 10 (Berlin: De Gruyter, 1996), pp. 376–433; Mindy MacLeod and Bernard Mees, *Runic Amulets and Magic Objects* (Woodbridge: Boydell, 2006), p. 42.

[20] Cf. Robert Nedoma, who eschews any attempt to interpret the sequence: 'Schrift und Sprache in den ostgermanischen Runendenkmälern', *North-Western European Language Evolution (NOWELE)*, 58/59 (2010), 1–70 (p. 39).

[21] Seebold, 'Die Stellung der englischen Runen im Rahmen', p. 487. Antonsen reads **glæaugizu æurgz**, and links the first element to OE *glær*, ON *glæsa*, Lat. *glēsum* 'amber'. He is unable to offer an interpretation for the third element, nor has he for the Kragehul spearshaft's **wiju** (whereas he interprets the Vimose buckle's **wija** as belonging to the sequence **auwija**, i.e. *auja* with West Germanic development). Antonsen's value *æ* has obviously hampered his attempt to offer an interpretation. Antonsen, *A Concise Grammar of the Older Runic Inscriptions*, no. 63; Elmer H. Antonsen, *Runes and Germanic Linguistics*, Trends in Linguistics: Studies and Monographs, 140 (Berlin: Mouton de Gruyter, 2002), pp. 44–45.

[22] Marie Stoklund, 'Runer 1993', *Arkæologiske udgravninger i Danmark* (1993), 259–74 (pp. 269–70). Cf. Adolf Noreen, *Altisländische und altnorwegische Grammatik (Laut- und Flexionslehre) unter Berücksichtigung des Urnordischen*, Sammlung kurzer Grammatiken germanischer Dialekte 4: Altnordische Grammatik, 1, 4th edn (Halle a. S.: Niemeyer, 1923), p. 167; Grønvik, *Runene på Tunesteinen*, p. 195, n. 28.

[23] Seebold, 'Die Stellung der englischen Runen im Rahmen', p. 470.

The Yew Rune, Yogh and Yew

which could indicate an employment as [ç] (KJ 133, *IK* 197).²⁴ The use of the thirteenth rune elsewhere on the bracteate, however (in **jjjwᛚa** and possibly in **dwudeᛚwwna**), suggests that, despite the appearance of the **j**-rune putatively employed here as a logograph, ᛚ is being used as an alternative to **i** to represent the associated semivowel.²⁵ Thus, despite the plausibility of Seebold's interpretation, his reading of ᛚ here as [ç] is far from indisputable.

Grønvik proposes that the troublesome last character in the legend **awaleubwiniᛋ** on the Nordendorf I fibula be read [ç] in order to discover an enclitic pre-OHG *-h* 'and' (i.e. 'Awa and Leubwini'), citing the Gothic form *-h* (*-uh*) < IE *-kʷe*.²⁶ A plausible interpretation, nonetheless it can hardly represent proof of the value of the thirteenth rune, although it is clearly preferable to interpreting the last rune as an ideograph as does Krause.²⁷ More recently an unclear graph in the inscription on the Pforzen buckle has been promoted by Klaus Düwel as comprising an apparent ligature of **a** + ᛋ, representing the diphthong *ai*.²⁸ The first line of the inscription does seem to read **aigilandiaᛋlrun**, i.e. *Aigil andi Ailrūn*. Given the peculiar nature of the ligaturing and the lack of expected *-a* in the putative second anthroponym, however, this inscription might be open to other interpretations both lexical and phonological.²⁹

A value *ē₂* has been assumed for the Rubring stone's **kᛚndo** (perhaps for an early High German *kēn dō(ē)*).³⁰ Yet this interpretation was clearly made on *a priori* grounds. Indeed despite its inclusion in Stefan Opitz's catalogue, given its irregular and (Lower) Austrian provenance it is probably of modern authorship — i.e. a Nazi-era forgery.³¹ More categorical is the sequence **daþᛋna** on the Freilaubersheim fibula (KJ 144) which is generally held to represent the anthroponym *Daþina*.³² Clearly there is no hint of a consonantal value here. By this date (c. 575), however, English examples of the thirteenth rune have appeared.

---

[24] Seebold, 'Die Stellung der englischen Runen im Rahmen', pp. 474–77; Elmar Seebold, 'Völker und Sprache in Dänemark zur Zeit der germanischen Wanderungen', in *Nordwestgermanisch*, ed. by Edith Marold and Christiane Zimmermann, Ergänzungsbände zum Reallexikon der germanischen Altertumskunde, 13 (Berlin: De Gruyter, 1995), pp. 155–86 (pp. 169, 173, 182).

[25] Seebold, 'Die Stellung der englischen Runen im Rahmen', pp. 474–77; Seebold, 'Völker und Sprache in Dänemark', pp. 169, 173, 182 reads **jjjwᛚadwudeᛚwwnaekwwd wiᛚuhu??** which he interprets as 'GUTES JAHR (x3) weiht X, durch dieses Pferd weihe, weihe, weihe ich'.

[26] Ottar Grønvik, 'Die Runeninschrift der Nordendorfer Bügelfibel I', in *Runor och ABC: Elva föreläsningar från ett symposium i Stockholm våren 1995*, ed. by Staffan Nyström, Runica et Mediævalia, 4 (Stockholm: Stockholms Medeltidsmuseum, 1987), pp. 111–29.

[27] KJ 151; cf. Robert Nedoma, *Personennamen in südgermanischen Runeninschriften: Studien zur altgermanischen Namenkunde I,1,1*, Indogermanische Bibliothek, Reihe: Untersuchungen, 3 (Heidelberg: Winter, 2004), pp. 361–62.

[28] Klaus Düwel, 'Die Runenschnalle von Pforzen (Allgäu) — Aspekte der Deutung, 3, Lesung und Deutung', in *Pforzen und Bergakker*, ed. by Alfred Bammesberger, Historische Sprachforschung Ergänzungsheft, 41 (Göttingen: Vandenhoeck & Ruprecht, 1999), pp. 36–54 (pp. 38–39).

[29] Ute Schwab, 'Die Runenschnalle von Pforzen (Allgäu) — Aspekte der Deutung, 4, Diskussion', in *Pforzen und Bergakker*, pp. 55–79 (p. 57); Elmar Seebold, 'Bemerkungen zur Runenschrift von Pforzen', in *Pforzen und Bergakker*, pp. 88–90 (p. 88); Nedoma, *Personennamen in südgermanischen Runeninschriften*, pp. 167–71.

[30] Otto Haas, 'Ein problematischer Fund', *Archaeologia Austriaca*, 24 (1958), 71–73; Walter Steinhauser, 'Die Runenschrift von Rubring an der Enns und der Eisriese Iring', *Archaeologia Austriaca*, 44 (1968), 1–20.

[31] Stefan Opitz, *Südgermanische Runeninschriften im älteren Futhark aus der Merowingerzeit*, 2nd edn (Kirchzarten: Burg, 1981), no. 37; see further Robert Nedoma, 'Zur Inschrift auf dem Stein von Rubring', in *Runica, Germanica, Mediaevalia*, ed. by Wilhelm Heizmann and Astrid von Nahl, Ergänzungsbände zum Reallexikon der germanischen Altertumskunde, 37 (Berlin: De Gruyter, 2003), pp. 481–95.

[32] Nedoma, *Personennamen in südgermanischen Runeninschriften*, pp. 279–80.

Yet there are English inscriptions that support the value *h*, although of these some probably represent [x] rather than [ç]. The Great Urswick stone bears the anthroponym **toroʃtredæ**, *Torhtred(æ)*[33] and although *h* is usually counted a palatal before final *t* in Old English, this development that had begun in West Saxon by the ninth century is only evident when *h* before *t* begins to have a palatalising effect on *eo* and *io*,[34] and the svarabhakti **o** in this inscription hardly warrants a value [ç] for ʃ here. Somewhat more probably palatal, however, is the example in **almeʃttig** for *almehtig* on the Ruthwell cross.[35] There are also three examples in coin legends, one from the eighth and two from the ninth century, that similarly show the yew rune with a value *h*: **tilberlt**, *Tilberht* (also **tilberlt**), **dEBelt** (a contraction of *Dægberht*) and **wiltred**, *Wihtred*.[36] These though as can be seen by the occasional penetration of Roman letters are all quite late; yet again clear evidence for a palatal value in the element *-berht* is lacking (we might expect *-**byrlt** or *-**birlt**). And a further extension of this rune to represent *k* is indicated in another late coin legend where Latin *rēx* is spelt as **rEls**,[37] an innovation perhaps influenced by the Old English development *-*hs* > -*ks* (cf. PG *sehs > OE *siex, syx, six*).[38]

The earliest Anglo-Frisian example of the yew rune is on the Caistor-by-Norwich gaming piece which bears the inscription **raʃhan** that is usually interpreted now as /raihan/.[39] And such a reading would seem to support Düwel's interpretation of the Pforzen inscription's **aʃlrun**. Seebold sees the Caistor employment, however, as a natural extension of the usage [iç] to represent /i/ before /h/: after all, the Ing rune appears to be used as [iŋ] (instead of the usual [iŋg]) before a seemingly redundant **g** on the Opedal stone (KJ 76).[40] Yet such an interpretation assumes that Proto-Germanic *ai here is still unmonophthongised (we might expect, rather, [ra:xan], cf. OE *rāha, rā*), and the palatalisation of *h* is usually held to postdate the relevant monophthongisation in proto-English.[41] Another English example of this rune is in the Thames silver mount legend **sberædhtʃbcailerhadæbs** which appears to be an

---

[33] Page, *An Introduction to English Runes*, pp. 150–51.

[34] Karl Brunner, *Altenglische Grammatik: Nach der angelsächsischen Grammatik von Eduard Sievers*, Sammlung kurzer Grammatiken germanischer Dialekte, A: Hauptreihe, 3, 3rd edn (Tübingen: Niemeyer, 1965), §122, §206, 6; Richard M. Hogg, *A Grammar of Old English, Volume 1: Phonology* (Oxford: Blackwell, 1992), pp. 167–70.

[35] Page, *An Introduction to English Runes*, pp. 147–48; Waxenberger, 'The Yew-Rune', pp. 393–96.

[36] Blackburn, 'A Survey of Anglo-Saxon and Frisian Coins with Runic Inscriptions', pp. 155–56; Page, *An Introduction to English Runes*, pp. 123, 125.

[37] Blackburn, 'A Survey of Anglo-Saxon and Frisian Coins with Runic Inscriptions', p. 159; Page, *An Introduction to English Runes*, p. 126.

[38] Page, *Runes and Runic Inscriptions*, p. 144, prefers to read a malformed RE**ss**, as appears in the other Beonna legends: surely, however, given the value *k* for the thirteenth rune in some manuscripts the otherwise inexplicable form RE**ss** is actually a corruption of **rEʃs**.

[39] Page, *An Introduction to English Runes*, pp. 19, 179–80.

[40] Seebold, 'Die Stellung der englischen Runen im Rahmen', p. 469. Cf. Grønvik, *Runene på Tunesteinen*, pp. 196–97, n. 28, who proffers the development *i* (_ç) > *i* (_*ç) or (_$) > *i*, citing this inscription and the similarly early examples from Nebenstedt (in **uʃu** and **gliʃa-**).

[41] Ingrid Sanness Johnsen, 'Den runologiske plassering av innskriften fra Caistor-by-Norwich', *Arkiv för nordisk filologi*, 89 (1974), 30–43 (pp. 39–41); Richard M. Hogg, 'Old English Palatalization', *Transactions of the Philological Society* (1979), pp. 89–113 (pp. 90–91); Bengt Odenstedt, 'On the Transliteration of the ʃ-Rune in Early English and Frisian Inscriptions', in *Festskrift til Ottar Grønvik på 75-årsdagen den 21. oktober 1991*, ed. by John Ole Askedal, Harald Bjorvand and Eyvind Fjeld Halvorsen (Oslo: Universitetsforlaget, 1991), pp. 53–65 (p. 58); Gaby Waxenberger, 'The Yew-Rune and the Runes ᚾ, ᚷ, ᛡ and ᛁ in the Old English Corpus (Epigraphical Material)', in *Runes and their Secrets: Studies in Runology*, ed. by Marie Stoklund and others (Copenhagen: Museum Tusculanum, 2006), pp. 385–414 (pp. 390–91).

attempt to produce a palindrome.⁴² The central portion is alphabetic (**a, b, c**), it is then flanked by the yew and ice runes, and flanked again by what may be a name encrypted in pairs: **sb/er/æd/ht** = s[æd]b[er][ht], *Sædberht*.⁴³ The Northamptonshire find probably also evidences a vocalic value for the yew rune as it precedes an **h** and then a **t** rotated 90 degrees clockwise. Similarly, the two Anglo-Saxon rune-row inscriptions, on the Thames scramasax and the partial row on the Brandon pin (both from the eighth–ninth centuries) provide no help phonologically, although both examples are retrograde (ᛇ).⁴⁴ The value *i*, however, is more obviously betrayed in the Loveden Hill urn inscription's **sᛇþæbad**, representing the anthroponym *Sīþæbad*, and the Dover stone legend **+jᛇslheard** which can only represent the anthroponym *Gīs(i)lheard*.⁴⁵ Similarly, the Thornhill II stone bears the legend **eateᛇnne**, i.e. *Ēadþegn(e)*, where the thirteenth rune represents [j̊] if not yet [j] which, as the use of **j** for this allophone in the late Dover stone inscription suggests, probably derives from an identification with *i* by way of *j*.⁴⁶ More examples with a clear value of *i* separate from a following *h* include the **hælᛇj** and the **hᛇræ** of the Gandersheim (Brunswick) casket inscription whose authenticity is doubted by Page⁴⁷ and the title **ioseP ᛇ** for the expected genitive *Josep(h)i* (where, as Klaus Düwel points out to me, the rune exhibits horizontal rather than oblique branches) that appears twice on the cover of the *Hegesippus Codex*, a Latin translation of Josephus' *Bellum Iudaicum*.

It thus seems that the earliest value of the yew rune known to us is *i*. It is also clear that in English sources this rune later came to represent *h*. This may have been part of a process of development from a high front vowel > palatal semivowel > palatalised voiced spirant > voiceless palatal spirant > voiceless velar spirant > voiceless velar stop (i.e. [i] > [j] > [j̊] > [ç] > [x] > [k]), which may correspond to the suggested development of the name **īha-* > OE *īh* [i:ç] > *ēoh* [eox]. Yet it may equally have been suggested by the manuscript tradition as the alternate values (*i* or *h*) of the *Codex Salisburgensis* suggest. The late (ninth–tenth-century) date offered for the Dover stone inscription, which retains a value *i*, also points to the latter interpretation. It is similarly possible that the consonantal values stem from the time when the runes *calc* (ᛣ) and *gar* (ᚸ) were introduced to (somewhat inconsistently) distinguish allophones of OE /k/ and /g/, the yew rune signifying a similar distinction from *h*;⁴⁸ and indeed the northern English provenance (Thornhill, Great Urswick, Ruthwell and the Wihtred and Dægberht stycas) of the instances of the use of the thirteenth rune with a velar value seen alongside the presence of *calc* and *gar* in the northern lapidary inscriptions might seem supportive of this suggestion were it not for the analysis of the coins of the East Anglian moneyers Tilberht and Werferth offered by Mark Blackburn.⁴⁹ Alternatively, as the rune name for **h** began with [h], the otherwise redundant ᛇ~ᛁ may, under the influence of its name, have been thought better to represent [ç] and [x] (irrespective of palatalisation), the

---

⁴² Page, *An Introduction to English Runes*, p. 182.
⁴³ Cf. Raymond I. Page, 'Anglo-Saxon Runes and Magic', *Journal of the British Archaeological Association*, 3rd series, 27 (1964), 14–31 (p. 29) [repr. Page, *Runes and Runic Inscriptions*, p. 121]; MacLeod and Mees, *Runic Amulets and Magic Objects*, pp. 82–83.
⁴⁴ Waxenberger, 'The Yew-Rune', pp. 396–97.
⁴⁵ Page, *An Introduction to English Runes*, pp. 47, 115, 137, 180–81; Waxenberger, 'The Yew-Rune', p. 391–92.
⁴⁶ Waxenberger, 'The Yew-Rune', pp. 394–96.
⁴⁷ Page, *An Introduction to English Runes*, p. 14; cf. Waxenberger, 'The Yew-Rune', p. 392.
⁴⁸ Cf. David N. Parsons, *Recasting the Runes: The Reform of the Anglo-Saxon Futhorc*, Runrön, 14 (Uppsala: Institutionen för nordiska språk, Uppsala universitet, 1999), p. 84.
⁴⁹ Blackburn, 'A Survey of Anglo-Saxon and Frisian Coins with Runic Inscriptions', pp. 155–56; cf. Raymond I. Page, 'Language and Dating in OE Inscriptions', *Anglia*, 77 (1959), 385–406, (pp. 388, 398–99) [repr. Page, *Runes and Runic Inscriptions*, pp. 31, 38].

medial allophones of /h/.⁵⁰ Nevertheless, when representing *i* it often appears near an **h**-rune or where one might be expected, possibly indicating that the spirant in its name influenced its employment from an early period.

A second consideration traditionally brought to bear in discussions of the purpose of the yew rune relates to its origin. Jens Jensen, for example, assuming a vocalic value for the thirteenth rune, has noticed that each *ætt* of the futhark contains two vowels.⁵¹ His theory that the futhark is grouped by a tradition of the classical grammarians (e.g. Donatus, *Ars gram*. 1, 1) as the Irish Ogams are usually held to be is flawed by an attempt to use modern phonological categorisations, however, not those of antiquity (such as the *semivocales* and *mutae*).⁵² The runes are clearly based on the Mediterranean alphabetic tradition and proponents of a Roman origin for the futhark have tended to link the yew rune with the similarly shaped Roman letter Z.⁵³ Yet as /z/ was clearly served by another character (ᛉ, putatively descended from Roman Y), a Roman thesis either points to a novel creation or perhaps a replacement for Greek Υ (i.e. [y]), even if Greek words which feature upsilon are typically written with I in Roman inscriptions — e.g. NIMPHIS 'to the nymphs' (*CIL* XII 1092, XIII 8522 etc.). Richard Morris has proposed a link instead with the rare epichoric Greek variant of iota that has an identical form to the yew rune,⁵⁴ which may have a reflection in Etruscan.⁵⁵ From a North Etruscan perspective, however, the thirteenth rune seems closest in shape to a character from the Camunic tradition which is extremely rare and appears in inscriptions where its phonological value, ancestry and arguably even graphemic status are unclear.⁵⁶ Moreover, similar forms appear in two Rhaetic inscriptions, both of which have usually been interpreted in the past as defective forms of North Etruscan lambda (ᒋ). Nonetheless, they appear to represent labial values: i.e. Rhaetic ʃ**AŚUNU** seems to represent the Italic hieronym

---

⁵⁰ Page, 'The Old English Rune *eoh*, *íh*, "Yew Tree" ', p. 129 [repr. Page, *Runes and Runic Inscriptions*, p. 138].

⁵¹ Jens J. Jensen, 'The Problem of the Runes in the Light of Some Other Alphabets', *Norsk tidskrift for sprogvidenskap*, 23 (1969), 128–46.

⁵² For the ogams see Wolfgang Keller's review of Helmut Arnzt, *Das Ogom* (Leipzig 1935) in *Beiblatt zur Anglia*, 47 (1936), 33–35; Wolfgang Keller, 'Die Entstehung des Ogom', *Beiträge zur Geschichte der deutschen Sprache und Literatur*, 62 (1938), 121–32 (pp. 125–26); Rudolf Thurneysen, 'Zum Ogom', *Beiträge zur Geschichte der deutschen Sprache und Literatur*, 61 (1937), 188–208 (pp. 203–4).

⁵³ Wimmer, *Die Runenschrift*, p. 134; Sigurd Agrell, 'Der Urprung der Runenschrift und die Magie', *Arkiv för nordisk filologi*, 43 (1927), 97–107 (pp. 105–6); Fritz Askeberg, *Norden och kontinenten i gammal tid: Studier i forngermansk kulturhistoria* (Uppsala: Almqvist & Wiksells, 1944), p. 83; Odenstedt, *On the Origin and Early History of the Runic Script*, p. 164; Henrik Williams, 'The Origin of the Runes', *Amsterdamer Beiträge zur älteren Germanistik*, 45 (1996), 211–18.

⁵⁴ Richard L. Morris, *Runic and Mediterranean Epigraphy*, North-Western European Language Evolution Supplement, 4 (Odense: Odense University Press, 1988). For the iota variant itself see Margherita Guarducci, *Epigrafia greca*, 4 vols (Rome: Istituto poligrafico dello Stato, Libreria dello Stato, 1967–78), I 102, 181, 183, 194.

⁵⁵ Guilio Buonamici, *Epigrafia etrusca* (Florence: Rinascimento del libro, 1932), p. 122.

⁵⁶ Thomas L. Markey, 'A Tale of Two Helmets: The Negau A and B Inscriptions', *Journal of Indo-European Studies*, 29 (2001), 69–172 (p. 92). All the inscriptions seem to be a potter's marks, i.e. anthroponymic abbreviations: cf. ʃ**-S-U** (*Museo Archeologico Nationale delle Valle Camonica: Guida dai materiali al territorio*, ed. by Filli Rossi (Milan: ET, 1989), p. 16) and **U**ᒋ, Museo Archeologico Nationale della Valle Camonica, inv. no. ST 79011 (as autopsied by Thomas L. Markey, to whom we are grateful for the reference).

*Vesuna*⁵⁷ and ⌐**AUSPE**⁵⁸ is probably an anthroponym comparable in the first instance to Rhaetic **ΦAUSUT**,⁵⁹ and then Etruscan *Haspa* and the commoner *Hasti, Hastia, Hausti, Fasti, Fastia* 'Fausta'. The development of this character may represent a response to the 'pernicious homography' noted by Markey whereby the frequent development of North Etruscan alpha to an 'open' form (i.e. ⌐, much as has obviously occurred with runic **a**) provoked either the loss, functional replacement or a distinguishing variation in the inherited form of digamma (also ⌐), the ancestor of Roman F (hence, presumably, the upturned branches of runic **f**, ⌐).⁶⁰ In fact the proclivity for Etruscoid characters to show a variation of labial and velar fricative values is well known.⁶¹ Hence an identification with this North Etruscan ∫~⌐ may indicate that the later consonantal value was closer to the original sound represented by the yew rune than the vocalic. Yet this value is clearly shared by the **h**-rune, a fact that once again implies that the yew rune was phonologically superfluous from the time of the inception of the futhark.

A similar redundancy has also been proposed for the Ing rune (◊, ⌐, ⌐), a character whose presence among the Old Germanic letters seems similarly idiosyncratic. After all, the Mediterranean scripts did not employ a separate character (*figura*) for the sound usually associated with this staff — hence Antonsen's demand that the rune be connected with Greek agma,⁶² the name given to gamma by ancient grammarians when it served to indicate velar nasals.⁶³ Yet the Ing rune seems to be unnecessary in the futhark. Although often thought to be employed for [ŋ] or [ŋg], it is frequently omitted when expected: in fact, except for in the Årstad inscription's **uŋwinaz** (which was read by Krause as a late form of a genitive *Jungawinaiz) and in the unclear Leţcani find's **raŋo** (where the rune has also been read as a **z** or a mirror rune), in elder inscriptions the Ing rune seems merely to be used as shorthand for ⟨iŋg⟩, the first syllable of its Proto-Germanic name.⁶⁴ Gerd Høst, after an inspection of the Årstad stone *in situ*, however, has declared that Krause's reading is incorrect, and as Antonsen had divined, the apparent **ŋ** is in fact a **k** (Krause's **uŋ** better to be read as **ek**).⁶⁵ As there

---

⁵⁷ Stefan Schumacher, *Die rätischen Inschriften. Geschichte und heutiger Stand der Forschung*, Innsbrucker Beiträge zur Kulturwissenschaft, Sonderheft, 79 (Innsbruck: Verlag des Instituts für Sprachwissenschaft der Universität Innsbruck, 1992), no. SZ-15; Markey, 'An *interpretatio Italica* among the Casalini (Sanzeno) votives and another Helbig hoax', in *L'Umbro e le altri lingue dell'Italia mediana antica: Atti del I Convegno Internazionale sugli Antichi Umbri, Gubbio, 20–22 settembre 2001*, ed. by Augusto Ancillotti and Alberto Calderini (Perugia: Jama, 2009), 97–136 (pp. 102–8).

⁵⁸ Stefan Schumacher, 'Neufunde "rätischer" Inschriften', *Studi etruschi*, 59 (1994), 307–20 (no. HI-5).

⁵⁹ Schumacher, *Die rätischen Inschriften*, no. NO-7.

⁶⁰ Markey, 'A Tale of Two Helmets', pp. 99ff.

⁶¹ Bernard Mees, 'The North Etruscan Thesis of the Origin of the Runes', *Arkiv för nordisk filologi*, 115 (2000), 33–82 (pp. 64–65); Markey, 'A Tale of Two Helmets', p. 95; Thomas L. Markey, 'Early Celticity in Slovenia and at Rhaetic Magrè (Schio)', *Linguistica*, 46 (2006), 145–72.

⁶² Antonsen, *Runes and Germanic Linguistics*, pp. 102–3.

⁶³ Edgar H. Sturtevant, *The Pronunciation of Greek and Latin*, William Dwight Whitney Linguistic Series, 2nd edn (Philadelphia: Linguistics Society of America / University of Pennsylvania, 1940), pp. 35–39; W. Sidney Allen, *Vox Graeca: A Guide to the Pronunciation of Classical Greek*, 3rd edn (Cambridge: Cambridge University Press, 1987), pp. 35–39.

⁶⁴ KJ 58; Wolfgang Krause, 'Die gotische Runeninschrift von Letcani', *Zeitschrift für vergleichende Sprachforschung*, 83 (1969), 53–61; Mindy MacLeod, *Bind-Runes: An Investigation of Ligatures in Runic Epigraphy*, Runrön, 15 (Uppsala: Institutionen för nordiska språk, Uppsala universitet, 2002), pp. 44–46. This excepts the **iriŋg**[of the doubtful Rubring inscription; see also Bernard Mees, 'Runo-Gothica: The Runes and the Origin of Wulfila's Script', *Die Sprache*, 43 (2002), 55–79 (p. 74) for a re-reading of the apparent **ŋ** of the Letcani inscription as a mirror-rune **þ**.

⁶⁵ Gerd Høst, 'Die Årstad-Inschrift — eine Neuwertung', in *Runor och ABC: Elva föreläsningar från ett symposium i Stockholm våren 1995*, ed. by Staffan Nyström, Runica et Mediævalia, 4 (Stockholm: Stockholms

is no other example in a lexical employment in Krause's corpus where ŋ clearly does not also represent a vocalic value, it seems that, with the exception of the English inscriptions, this staff always bears a syllabic value, and thus the notion that the 'lantern' variant of the form (↑, ⌧) is a bind-rune of **i** and **ŋ** (| and ◊) must be false.[66] Gerhard Alexander, following William Moulton's reconstruction of the Proto-Germanic obstruents, maintains that the Ing rune was required to distinguish the plosive allophone of PG */g/ that appeared after */n/ from the usual fricative realisation, implying that it was not originally redundant, but became confused with [ŋ] — a theory consistent with its reconstructed rune name *Ingwaz.[67] Yet runic inscriptions usually omit nasals before homo-organic obstruents. In modern Germanic dialects, the /ŋ/ phoneme only develops from */ng/ (not */nk/ or */nh/), and the timeframe for the development of */ng/ > /ŋ/ is unclear in Germanic. The apparently trustworthy evidence of the sixteenth-century English orthoepists for retention of [ŋg] pronunciations might be called into question given the appearance of fourteenth-century spellings such as *lenth* and *strenth*.[68] And despite the confident assertions of some handbooks, neither is the evidence of the manuscript languages categorical. Middle High German alternations such as *dinc* : *dinges* might merely reveal a reinterpretation of [ŋ] (if not [ŋg]) as [ŋk]. Similarly, Old Norse verbal forms such as *ganga, gakk, gengu, gekk* surely represent a historical development (as the geminate *kk* continues the **nk* of an earlier time), and once again may show an *[ŋ] (if not [ŋg]) devoicing to an *[ŋk]. Much of this behaviour is consistent with the generativist theory that reinterprets modern /ŋ/ as an abstract morphophonemic /ng/ cluster (with synchronic *n* → *ŋ* and *g, ɣ* → *k*, Ø rules) which explains similar behaviour in modern languages today, such as in some dialects of Dutch and German (and compare the non-standard English pronunciations [ɛniθiŋk] and [ɛniθən], *anything*).[69] Moreover, not only is the status of traditional /ŋ/ quite unlike that of other Germanic phonemes (both in its positional distribution and in its variation

---

Medeltidsmuseum, 1987), pp. 155–61; Antonsen, *A Concise Grammar of the Older Runic Inscriptions*, pp. 12, 34; cf. Elmer H. Antonsen, 'What Kind of Science is Runology?', *Det Konglige Norske Videnskapers Selskabs Forhandlinger* (1995), 125–39 (pp. 127–29), Antonsen, *Runes and Germanic Linguistics*, pp. 4–5.

[66] The 'lantern' form clearly cannot be a bind-rune in the Grumpan rune-row, and the inscription on the Årstad stone was the only example in a lexical employment where the staffless form was interpreted by Krause as only [ŋg]. As this rune presumably derives from a reflex of archaic Greek qoppa (ϙ), and as Etruscan inscriptions preserve forms both with and without a *hasta* (and, as in runic, favour the former), this cannot be the case; cf. Kai-Erik Westergaard, *Skrifttegn og symboler: Noen studier over tegnformer i det eldre rune-alfabet*, Osloer Beiträge zur Germanistik, 6 (Oslo: Germanistisches Institut der Universität Oslo, 1981), pp. 136–88; Michael P. Barnes, 'The New Runic Finds from Illerup and the Question of the Twenty-Second Rune', *Saga og sed* (1984), 59–76; Bengt Odenstedt, 'Om typologi och grafisk variation i den äldre futharken', *Arkiv för nordisk filologi*, 100 (1985), 1–15; Ottar Grønvik, 'Über den Lautwert der Ing-Rune und die Auslassung von Vokal in den älteren Runeninschriften', *Indogermanische Forschungen*, 90 (1985), 168–95.

[67] Gerhard Alexander, 'Die Herkunft der Ing-Rune', *Zeitschrift für deutsches Altertum und deutsche Literatur*, 104 (1975), 1–11; William G. Moulton, 'The Stops and Spirants of Early Germanic', *Language*, 30 (1954), 1–46 (pp. 31–32, 42); William G. Moulton, 'The Proto-Germanic Non-syllabics (Consonants)', in *Toward a Grammar of Proto-Germanic*, ed. by Frans van Coetsem and Herbert L. Kufner (Tübingen: Niemeyer, 1972), pp. 141–73 (p. 173). In fact this is the only place in which PG */g/ was clearly a plosive as geminate Proto-Germanic mediae were at the very least rare; Louis L. Hammerich, 'Die germanische und die hochdeutsche Lautverschiebung', *Beiträge zur Geschichte der deutschen Sprache und Literatur*, 77 (1955), 1–30, 165–203 (p. 175), and a recent Lepontic find witnesses North Etruscan qoppa representing Celtic /gʷ/; Francisco Rubat Borel, 'Lingue e scritture delle Alpi occidentali prima della romanizzazione: stato della questione e nuove ricerche', *Bulletin d'études préhistoriques et archéologiques alpines*, 16 (2005), 9–50 (pp. 15–19).

[68] Eric J. Dobson, *English Pronunciation 1500–1700*, 2 vols, 2nd edn (Oxford: Clarendon, 1968), II, 971–73.

[69] Noam Chomsky and Morris Halle, *The Sound Pattern of English*, Studies in Language (New York: Harper & Row, 1968), p. 85; Theo Vennemann, 'The German Velar Nasal: A Case for Abstract Phonology', *Phonetica*, 22 (1970), 65–82; Pierre Swiggers, 'On the Underlying "Velar Nasal" in Dutch', *Leuvense Bijdragen*, 74 (1985), 185–92.

with [ŋg]), in some modern dialects (e.g. the West Midlands and Northern English dialects, where *sing* is [siŋg], not [siŋ] and in some southern Norwegian dialects where *lange* is [laŋgə], not [laŋə]) it is absent (as a discrete structural unit) altogether.[70] Hence as the Ing rune only represents the nasal before */g/ in the older inscriptions, runic ŋ may well have been required for a PG */ŋ/.[71] In fact its absence when expected, e.g. in Reistad's **iuþingaʀ/idringaʀ** (KJ 74) might stem from a dialectal variation in the development of */ng/ such as still exists today. Clearly, the use of the ŋ-rune had broadened by the Old English period (e.g. the Ruthwell Cross's **uŋket**). Yet as the velar nasal was recognised by the classical grammarians (it had a *nomen*, agma, and *potestas*, but no separate *figura*), the extension of the use of the rune also to allophonic [ŋ] in Old English inscriptions (considering that late inscriptions such as that of the Ruthwell cross show a connection with the manuscript tradition) may have been due to the influence of classical grammatical learning, much as seems to be the case with a number of the values given to the Ogam signs in Irish manuscripts.[72] But can a similar innovation be detected in the case of the thirteenth rune?

The rune names of the futhark are mainly acrophonic and so their names can be used to assess the phonological values of the corresponding staves. It is also clear that the rune names change when the values of the staves change. This is most obviously the case with the rune name **ansuz* that in Old English became *os*, just as the associated fourth rune changed in value from *a* to *o*. The putative change in value of the thirteenth rune in the English tradition from *i* to *h* (or [ç]), however, did not necessitate a similar change in the rune name. This may indicate that the name *īh* suggested a new value for the yew rune.

The reconstruction of the name *yew* for the thirteenth rune seems to be corroborated by the Nordic name (mentioned above) and a Gothic name *uuaer* (< **hwair* 'cauldron') from the *Codex Salisburgensis* that similarly refers to a newly designated sound (in this case *hw*). In Gothic the acrophonic principle seems to have provoked a change in the inherited letter name — from **eihws* 'yew' to **hwair* (*uuaer*). Why this change occurred precisely is not clear, but the equation of *uuaer* with **eihws* and thus the thirteenth rune is supported by the correspondence of every other Gothic letter name to one from the older futhark (except that of ⟨q⟩ which is modelled, as in the English tradition, upon that of ⟨p⟩).[73]

The Proto-Germanic reconstruction of the runic letter name, however, is not so clear. Many different forms have been proffered, most runologists accepting an ambivalent **ī(h)waz*. Alfred Bammesberger has reconstructed two separate lexemes, **īwa-* and **īha-*, but evidence from outside Germanic suggests a different explanation.[74] Clearly the Indo-European root is

---

[70] Grønvik, *Runene på Tunesteinen*, pp. 27–29; Helge Sandøy, *Norsk dialektkunnskap* (Oslo: Novus, 1985), p. 75; Peter Ladefoged and Ian Maddieson, *The Sounds of the World's Languages* (Oxford: Blackwell, 1996), pp. 2–3; Heinz J. Giegerich, *English Phonology: An Introduction*, Cambridge Textbooks in Linguistics (Cambridge: Cambridge University Press, 1996), p. 36.

[71] Cf. Alfred Bammesberger, 'Frisian and Anglo-Saxon Runes: From the Linguistic Angle', *Amsterdamer Beiträge zur älteren Germanistik*, 45 (1996), 15–23 (p. 21, n. 8); Frederick W. Schwink, 'The Velar Nasal in the Adaptation of the Runic Alphabet', *American Journal of Germanic Linguistics and Literatures*, 12 (2000), 235–49.

[72] Damien McManus, *A Guide to Ogam*, Maynooth Monographs, 4 (Maynooth: An Saggart, 1991), pp. 34–41.

[73] Mees, 'Runo-Gothica: The Runes and the Origin of Wulfila's Script', pp. 61–63; Elmar Seebold, 'Fuþark, Beith-Luis-Nion, He Lamedh, Abğad und Alphabet: Über die Systematik der Zeichenaufzählung bei Buchstaben-Schriften', in *Sprachen und Schriften des antiken Mittelmeerraums: Festschrift für Jürgen Untermann zum 65. Geburtstag*, ed. by Frank Heidermanns, Helmut Rix and Elmar Seebold, Innsbrucker Beiträge zur Sprachwissenschaft, 78 (Innsbruck: Institut für Sprachwissenschaft der Universität Innsbruck, 1993), pp. 411–44 (pp. 419–20).

[74] Alfred Bammesberger, 'The Development of the Runic Script and its Relationship to Germanic Phonological

ei- and the Old English names *ēoh* and *īh* suggest a voiceless velar enlargement. Yet this seems to appear only in Germanic; with the extension *-w-*, the term already means 'yew' (or at least 'red plant') in other Indo-European languages: cf. OE *īh*, *ēoh*, *īw*, *ēow*, *ēo*, OHG *īha*, *īwa*, *īga*, OS (pl.) *īchas*, ON *ýr*; Gaulish *ivo-*, Old Irish *eó*, *í*, Middle Welsh *ywen*, Old Cornish *hiuin*, Breton *ivin* (< **iwo-*); Old Prussian *iuwis* 'yew', Lithuanian *ievà* 'black alder', Latvian *ieva* 'bird-cherry', Old Czech *jíva*, Russian *iva*, Serbo-Croatian *ïva* 'willow' (< **īwa*); Latin *īva* 'bunch of grapes, vine', Greek οἴη, ὄη, ὄα 'mountain ash' (< **oiwa*); and Armenian *aygi* 'grapevine' (< **oiwiyā*). In fact Sanskrit *eito* 'coloured' and Hittite *GIŠe(y)a(n)-* 'sacred evergreen' (< the Sumerogram for 'tree' + **eyo-*) suggest that *-wo-* produces the meaning 'yew, red plant' from the root **ei-* 'red, mottled, yellow'.[75] These cognate forms indicate a late Indo-European formation **ei-wo-* (with *o*-grade ablaut in Armenian and Greek, zero grade in Celtic) or as Connolly proposes perhaps a laryngealised reconstruction **H(e)Hi-wo-*.[76] As there are in fact three attested Germanic forms, **īwa-*, **īga-* and **īha-*, it has been suggested (Walde and Pokorny 1927–32:I. 165) that *-g-* and *-h-* derived from a strengthening of original *-w-* similar to that seen in *Jugend* (vs. Latin *juventus*). The two velar extensions (the Old High German lenis velar is supported by an Old English toponymic element **īg*),[77] however, suggest a lenition (of *-h- > -g-*) typical of that produced by Verner's law.

An Indo-European **H(e)Hi-* might be used to justify both the old theory that the thirteenth rune represented some sort of /e(:)/ as well as Connolly's laryngealist value /i(:)/ (but not Antonsen's structuralist /æ:/). Yet the reconstruction of this name is not at all unproblematic. Did the rune name only ever show the velar extension? We have no sure employment of the rune as shorthand for its name which might confirm its name as we have for the Ing rune, and the comparative Gothic and Nordic evidence is unclear. In fact the Gothic names might not even be authentic, although they do seem to show specifically Gothic characteristics.[78] Only the Old English evidence is categorical: the English name is *ēoh* or *īh*, whereas the usual Anglo-Saxon name for the yew was *ēo*, *ēow* or *īw*.

History', in *Language Change and Language Structure: Older Germanic Languages in a Comparative Perspective*, ed. by Torvil Swan, Endre Mørck, Olaf Jansen Westvik, Trends in Linguistics: Studies and Monographs, 73 (Berlin: De Gruyter, 1994), pp. 1–25 (p. 8).

[75] Cf. Franz Specht, *Der Ursprung der indogermanischen Deklination* (Göttingen: Vandenhoeck & Ruprecht, 1944 [1947]), p. 63; *IEW*; Page, 'Anglo-Saxon Runes and Magic', p. 127 [repr. Page, *Runes and Runic Inscriptions*, pp. 135–36]; Paul Friedrich, *Proto-Indo-European Trees: The Arboreal System of a Prehistoric People* (Chicago: University of Chicago Press, 1970), pp. 121–25; Т. В. Гамкрелидзе (T'amaz Gamqreliże) and Вяч. Вс. Иванов (Viacheslav Vsevolodovich Ivanov), Индоевропейский язык и Индоевропейцы: реконструкция и историко-типологический анализ праязыка и протокультуры, 2 vols (Tbilisi: Издательство Тбилисского университета, 1984), II, 628–30 (Thomas V. Gamkrelidze and Vjačeslav V. Ivanov, *Indo-European and the Indo-Europeans: A Reconstruction and Historical Analysis of a Proto-Language and a Proto-Culture*, trans. by Johanna Nichols, Trends in Linguistics: Studies and Monographs, 80, 2 vols (Berlin: De Gruyter, 1995), I, 540–41).

[76] Connolly, 'The Rune ᛇ and the Germanic Vowel System', p. 15, n. 28.

[77] Albert Hugh Smith, *English Place-Name Elements*, English Place-Name Society, 25–26, 2 vols (Cambridge: Cambridge University Press, 1956), I, 305.

[78] Cf. Theodor von Grienberger, 'Die germanischen Runennamen, 1. Die gotischen Buchstabennamen', *Beiträge zur Geschichte der deutschen Sprache und Literatur*, 21 (1896), 185–224; James W. Marchand, 'Les Gots ont-ils vraiment connu l'écriture runique?', in *Mélanges de linguistique et de philologie, Fernand Mossé in memoriam* (Paris: Didier, 1959), pp. 277–91; Wolfgang Krause, *Handbuch des Gotischen*, Handbücher für das Studium der Germanistik, 3rd edn (Munich: Beck, 1968), pp. 63–66; Norbert Wagner, 'Zu den Gotica der Salzburg-Wiener Alcuin-Handschrift', *Historische Sprachforschung*, 107 (1994), 262–83; Mees, 'The North Etruscan Thesis of the Origin of the Runes', pp. 56–63.

The Yew Rune, Yogh and Yew

As we have already seen, the runic letter name probably influenced the phonological value given to ſ~1 in Old English manuscripts. The original name of the rune cannot be reconstructed without some ambiguity, but given the evidence of at least two Continental inscriptions with a value of *i*, the name **īhaz* is eminently plausible. Indeed, as the lexeme *īh* only seems to have survived into Old English to represent the name of this rune, the fact that this rune is not signified by the usual Old English term for 'yew' points to both the importance and antiquity of this name.

Yet the name *īh* is but one of a number of rune names beginning with *i*. The other two are that of the ice rune (|), clearly (ultimately) a reflex of archaic Greek iota (also the ancestor of Roman I) and the Ing rune (◇, ⇡, ⊕), ultimately derived (it is usually argued) from archaic Greek qoppa (ϙ; cf. Roman Q). If the thirteenth rune bore an acrophonic name then its original value would have been similar in sound to *i*. But if it, like the Ing rune, did not have an acrophonic name, it would surely have originally had the extension which survives in the Old English tradition. The survival of the medial velar value in the name recorded in English manuscripts may have been ensured by a cognisance of the consonantal value allowed for this rune, even though it seems only to appear at a later date than the vocalic. The fact that the thirteenth rune never appears in initial position in clearly lexical inscriptions is also suggestive of the fricative interpretation of Grønvik and Seebold. Yet although [ç] sometimes appears in opposition to [x] in modern German, few theorists would accept the existence of a PG */ç/ phoneme separate to */h/. In fact the evidence for a comparatively late palatalisation of *h* in English even puts the Proto-Germanic *[ç] assumed by Seebold in doubt. Thus this value, like most of the vocalic values promoted for ſ~1, is merely an allophonic variant of a phoneme more typically represented by a separate staff (i.e. ᚺ, ᚻ) and is, moreover, a doubtful one at that. After all, the employment of a separate character for an allophone of /h/ is unparalleled among the Mediterranean scripts. Rather, we would expect the thirteenth rune to have represented a phoneme.

Connolly's theory has the strength of reconciling the value suggested by the rune name with a phoneme later lost to Germanic. This */ɨ(:)/ he derives from the influence of a laryngeal, represented as *X* after its vowel-colouring effect had become phonemic (in fact he uses *X* to signify any laryngeal whose description is uncertain). This Germanic laryngeal he suggests was the result of the merger of the proposed Indo-European non-, *a*- and most of the *o*-colouring laryngeals, the vocalic effects of which had already become phonemic before the Proto-Germanic period (thus IE *eH_2i- > PG *aXi-). He detected the putative presence of this laryngeal while attempting to explain the vagaries of descent of inherited IE *e, *ei and *i among the different Germanic dialects. Indeed similar arguments have been proffered to explain other features such as the irregular velarisation of IE *-*w*- in a group of Germanic terms first assembled by Sophus Bugge and the *Verschärfung* of semivowels in North and East Germanic first identified by Adolf Holtzmann.[79] In fact the influence of at least some laryngeals in early Proto-Germanic, at least where Holtzmann's law is concerned, seems to have been accepted by a majority of theorists.[80] Connolly's value for the thirteenth rune derives

---

[79] Sophus Bugge, 'Zur altgermanischen Sprachgeschichte. Germanisch *ug* aus *uw*', *Beiträge zur Geschichte der deutschen Sprache und Literatur*, 13 (1888), 504–15; Adolf Holtzmann, *Altdeutsche Grammatik: Umfassend die gotische, altnordische, altsächsische und althochdeutsche Sprache*, I (Leipzig: Brockhaus, 1870–75), pp. 108–9.

[80] Cf. Henry Lee Smith, 'The *Verschärfung* in Germanic', *Language*, 17 (1941), 93–98; William M. Austin, 'A Corollary to the Germanic *Verschärfung*', *Language*, 22 (1946), 109–11; 'Germanic Reflexes of Indo-European -*Hy*- and -*Hw*-', *Language*, 34 (1958), 103–11; Edgar C. Polomé, 'A West Germanic Reflex of

from an Indo-European element containing a laryngeal we might reconstruct as *$H_1(e)H_1i$-, one that probably served as the root of the Indo-European lexeme *yew*.[81] All of this, however, assumes that the thirteenth rune is to be derived from some Mediterranean ⟨i⟩ (or Z substituting for Y). Yet what if it was in origin an ⟨h⟩?

As noted before, the vocalic sound which is the earliest surely attested value for this staff supports Connolly's reconstruction of the thirteenth rune as representing a Proto-Germanic *$i̯$ created by the influence of an intervocalic Proto-Germanic laryngeal (the colourless laryngeal surviving into Proto-Germanic only in intervocalic positions).[82] Connolly could not prove the existence of this value, however, through an analysis of the inscriptions. This is quite possibly because the use of the thirteenth rune had already changed by the time of its first lexical attestation (i.e. the fourth/fifth century). Connolly also postulates that this Proto-Germanic laryngeal had been lost some time prior to the first attestation of the yew rune. Indeed he proposes that the laryngeal probably disappeared soon after the fixing of Germanic stress on the initial syllable, a development suggested by some investigators not to have been completed until as late as the second century A.D.[83] Moreover, Connolly has also sought to demonstrate that a retained laryngeal affected the outcome of Verner's law in some classes of Germanic strong verbs.[84] Many laryngealist solutions merely equate the uncertain with the effect of these rather difficult to isolate phones. Yet granted the indeterminacy of attested values and the evidence of the development of the rune name, the thirteenth rune is not implausibly to be associated with the Proto-Germanic laryngeal proposed as the cause of the developments first delineated by Bugge and Holtzmann that was lost early in the Proto-Germanic period.

The comparatively late appearance of the yew rune in a lexical employment suggests that the sound that it originally represented had already been lost by the time of the provenance of

---

the Verschärfung', *Language*, 25 (1949), 182–89; 'Laryngaaltheorie en Germaanse Verscherping', *Handelingen der Zuid-Nederlandse Maatschappij voor Taal- en Letterkunde en Geschiedenis*, 4 (1950), 61–75; 'Theorie "laryngeale" et germanique', in *Mélanges de linguistique et de philologie, Fernand Mossé in memoriam* (Paris: Didier, 1959), pp. 387–402; 'Are there Traces of Laryngeals in Germanic?', in *Die Laryngealtheorie und die Rekonstruktion des indogermanischen Laut- und Formensystems*, ed. by Alfred Bammesberger, Indogermanische Bibliothek, Reihe: Untersuchungen, 3 (Heidelberg: Winter, 1988), I, 383–414; Winfred P. Lehmann, *Proto-Indo-European Phonology* (Austin: Univerity of Texas Press, 1955), pp. 36–52; *Germanic Evidence: Evidence for Laryngeals*, ed. by Werner Winter, Janua linguarum; Series maior, 11 (The Hague: Mouton, 1965), pp. 212–23; Rosemarie Lühr, 'Germanische Resonantengemination durch Laryngal', *Münchener Studien zur Sprachwissenschaft*, 35 (1976), 73–92; Jay Jasanoff, 'Observations on the Germanic Verschärfung', *Münchener Studien zur Sprachwissenschaft*, 37 (1978), 77–90; Neville Edgar Collinge, *The Laws of Indo-European*, Amsterdam Studies in the Theory and History of Linguistic Science, Series 4: Current Issues in Linguistic Theory, 35 (Amsterdam: Benjamins, 1985), pp. 93–101; Seiichi Suzuki, 'The Germanic Verschärfung: A Syllabic Perspective', *Journal of Indo-European Studies*, 19 (1991), 163–90; Garry W. Davis and Gregory K. Iverson, 'The Verschärfung as Feature Spread', in *Germanic Linguistics: Syntactic and Diachronic*, ed. by Rosina Lippi-Green and Joseph C. Salmons, Amsterdam Studies in the Theory and History of Linguistic Science, Series 4: Current Issues in Linguistic Theory, 137 (Amsterdam: Benjamins, 1996), pp. 103–20; Laura C. Smith, 'What's All the Fuss with Sixteen Words? A New Approach to Holtzmann's Law', *Göttinger Beiträge zur Sprachwissenschaft*, 1 (1998), 75–100.

[81] The precise value and position of the laryngeals in Indo-European *yew*, however, are difficult to determine. Connolly posits two, one initially, one intervocalically, i.e. *H_eHiwo-, and considers that at least one was H_3. Heiner Eichner, 'Die urindogermanische Wurzel *H_2reu "hell machen" ', *Die Sprache*, 24 (1978), 144–62 (p. 151), instead suggests up to three, one after the diphthong, one in the extension, and possibly a third initially, claiming H_1 or H_3 as the likely candidates for the first two laryngeals, i.e. *$(H_{1/3})eiH_{1/3}$-we-H_2-.

[82] Connolly, 'ē₂ and the Laryngeal Theory', p. 27.

[83] e.g. Robert Woodhouse, 'Verner's and Thurneysen's laws in Gothic as Evidence for Obstruent Development in Early Germanic', *Beiträge zur Geschichte der deutschen Sprache und Literatur*, 120 (1998), 194–222.

[84] Connolly, ' "Grammatischer Wechsel" and the Laryngeal Theory'.

most of the early inscriptions and that its attested values may all be secondary. Our only clear evidence for its original value is its name, a name that seems to have suggested its attested values, and the possibility (if not likelihood) that the yew rune continues either an archaic Greek iota, Roman Z substituting for Y or a North Etruscan reflex of digamma in the Germanic script. When it betrays a consonantal value, it is a velar, as is the usual description of a laryngeal (thus the transcriptions *H* and *X*), and a similar value is often thought to have resulted upon the hardening of a laryngeal in Germanic.[85] As the Indo-European laryngeals in initial position are usually considered to be the first to have been lost, and as laryngeals probably only survived into Germanic in word-medial positions, a rune denoting a laryngeal is not likely to have had an acrophonic name. According to Edward Sapir (1938 = 1990–94:V.126–31), a laryngeal is often absorbed when in a cluster with a sonorant consonant. Consequently, he used a typological comparison with similar developments in some American Indian languages to explain the development of Gk. *he-* < IE **we-* as an assimilation of voicelessness from a proximate laryngeal — i.e. IE **Hwe-* > **u̯e-* > *he-*. And as has long been suspected, a similar assimilation may have occurred in Holtzmann's *Verschärfung* when *-Hw-* and *-wH-* developed to *-ggw-* in North and East Germanic.[86] Moreover, the development of IE **-w-* to *-g-* or *-k-* first noted by Bugge may also have been influenced by the close presence of a laryngeal. A similar velarisation of the extension *-w-* to *-h-* has occurred in some forms of the Germanic term for 'yew', and in fact in some dialects it seems under Verner's law to have further developed to *-g-*. Indeed the reconstruction of the Gothic name with a totally unexpected medial *-hw-* appears to confirm the presence of a laryngeal preceding the semivocalic extension in the Proto-Germanic form of the rune name. The effect of laryngeals on semivowels in Germanic might well vary between dialects (and even within them) as the Gothic rune name *sugil* (cf. OE *sygel*) versus Wulfilian *sauil* (< IE *sH_2uel-*, *seH_2ul-*) has been suggested to show by Winfred Lehmann.[87] And so when this sound was lost, if it had a corresponding rune, this staff would probably at first have been associated with *h*.[88] Thus the phonological redundancy of the thirteenth rune would soon have become apparent, only its name remaining (as the pairs of names were probably learned as a mnemonic),[89] and a new value, *i*, might well have become associated with this rune, a value derived from its name.

[85] And this laryngeal would most probably be H_3, perhaps a pharyngealised voiceless velar fricative, possibly with some labial quality. Indeed, in Connolly's reconstruction H_1 and H_2 seem to have already been lost or had merged with H_3 by this time, and so his *X* would probably have had a description similar to H_3.

[86] See Henry Lee Smith, 'The *Verschärfung* in Germanic'; Austin, 'A Corollary to the Germanic *Verschärfung*'; Austin, 'Germanic Reflexes of Indo-European *-Hy-* and *-Hw-*'; Polomé, 'A West Germanic Reflex of the *Verschärfung*'; Polomé, 'Laryngaaltheorie en Germaanse Verscherping'; Polomé, 'Theorie "laryngeale" et germanique'; and Lehmann, *Proto-Indo-European Phonology*, pp. 36–52; Lehmann, 'Germanic Evidence', pp. 212–23.

[87] Lehmann, *Proto-Indo-European Phonology*, p. 49; cf. Eric P. Hamp, 'Indo-European **au* before Consonant in British and Indo-European "Sun" ', *Bulletin of the Board of Celtic Studies*, 26 (1975), 97–102; Mees, 'Runo-Gothica: The Runes and the Origin of Wulfila's Script', p. 60.

[88] Cf. Armenian, where inherited initial H_2 and H_3 produce *h-*, and Hittite, where the reflex of H_2 (and occasionally H_3) is represented by *h*, a character that usually describes a voiceless velar fricative, but in Akkadian represented values that continued various Proto-Semitic velar fricatives, laryngeals and pharyngeals: *An Introduction to the Comparative Grammar of the Semitic Languages: Phonology and Morphology*, ed. by Sabatino Moscati, Porta linguarum orientalium; Neue Serie, 6 (Wiesbaden: Harrassowitz, 1964), p. 39; Robert S. P. Beekes, 'The Nature of the Proto-Indo-European Laryngeals', in *The New Sound of Indo-European: Essays in Phonological Reconstruction*, ed. by Theo Vennemann, Trends in Linguistics: Studies and Monographs, 41 (Berlin: Mouton de Gruyter, 1989), pp. 23–33.

[89] Williams, 'The Origin of the Runes', p. 217; Mees, 'The North Etruscan Thesis of the Origin of the Runes', p. 73.

The English manuscript tradition quite clearly indicates that two values were associated with the thirteenth rune and the evidence of the inscriptions seems to mirror this ambivalence. Evidently some inscribers remembered the association with *h* as recorded in the velarity of the medial consonant of the rune name; others derived a value *i* from the acrophonic principle of most of the other names. After the last Proto-Germanic laryngeal was lost, it is possible that its approximate value may have been retained in its runic letter name which in the English tradition always contains the velar as opposed to semivocalic extension that is exclusive to the Germanic terms for 'yew'.

Erik Brate was the first to posit that the medial value of the associated rune name may have been the original value of the thirteenth staff.[90] Eduard Sievers tentatively modified Brate's value *ç* to *hw*, clearly after considering the Gothic evidence. This solution was subsequently sponsored by Bruce Dickins and C. L. Wrenn.[91] Other investigations attempting to find a unique vocalic value for the yew rune have proved unsatisfactory, employing controversial descriptions of the vocalic system, or promoting values which are surely only allophonic realisations of one of the Proto-Germanic vowel phonemes usually accepted by theorists. A laryngeal value for this rune, however, reconciles the evidence of the rune name, the evidence suggested by a North Etruscan prototype for the runic script, and relies on an identity with a Proto-Germanic phoneme that was lost by the time of the dialectal period.

The major problem with such an identity, however, is that there is no clear evidence that the laryngeals reconstructed for Indo-European lasted long enough in Germanic to have required separate representation in the futhark. Not even a hint of a laryngeal has been detected so far in the earliest evidence from classical sources, the Negau (Ženjak) B inscription (the form **TEIVA** perhaps being especially relevant to a consideration of an early Germanic *eiwaz); or indeed the early runic inscriptions themselves. Moreover, as runic **t** and **b**, derived (ultimately) from archaic Greek tau and beta, still represent *t* and *b*, and the inherited archaic Greek heta has retained its value as the Germanic staff **h**, the Germanic adoption of these letters must post-date the first effecting of Grimm's law; and clearly, laryngeals have no effect on the operation of the Common Germanic sound shift (cf. esp. Greek κεφαλή, Lat. *caput*, ON *hǫfuð*, OE *heafod*, Goth. *haubiþ*, OS *hobid*, OHG *houbit* < IE **kepH-* 'head'). The variation between voiced and voiceless forms in the extension of the rune name where *-*w*- was velarised, if not evidence for such velarisation occurring at different times in different dialects, may well derive from the different accentuation in the forms of the term that would have applied before the loss of nominal ablaut in Germanic: i.e. **H₁éi-(H)wo-/H₁(e)i-(H)wó-* > **īga-/īha-*. As Bammesberger has suggested, there remains the possibility of the influence of a semantically separate vṛddhi formation (putatively meaning 'yew wood') in early Germanic as a lengthened-grade form of *yew* might well have existed in Proto-Germanic.[92] Yet not only are such formations rare in Germanic, vṛddhi constructions are not attested for this lexeme in other Indo-European dialects. Indeed, we might even expect formations influenced

---

[90] Erik Brate, 'Runologiska spörsmål', *Konglige Vitterhets Historie och Antikvitets Akademiens månadsblad*, 5 (1886), 1–25 (pp. 1–9); Erik Brate, 'Runradens ordningsföljd', *Arkiv för nordisk filologi*, 36 (1920), 193–207 (p. 199).

[91] Eduard Sievers, 'Runen und Runeninschriften', in *Grundriß der germanischen Philologie. I*, ed. by Hermann Paul (Strasbourg: Trübner, 1891), pp. 238–50 (table after p. 250); Bruce Dickins, 'A System of Transliteration for Old English Runic Inscriptions', *Leeds Studies in English*, 1 (1932), 15–19; Charles Leslie Wrenn, 'Magic in an Anglo-Saxon Cemetery', in *English and Medieval Studies presented to J. R. R. Tolkein on the Occasion of his Seventieth Birthday*, ed. by Norman Davis and Charles Leslie Wrenn (London: Allen & Unwin, 1962), pp. 306–21.

[92] Bammesberger, 'The Development of the Runic Script and its Relationship to Germanic Phonological History', p. 8.

The Yew Rune, Yogh and Yew

by an *ēigwa- to show some variation between high and middle vowels in the root given the connection between *ēi and the problematic ē₂ promoted by some authors.[93] The laryngealist explanation of velarisation in some Germanic forms, given no evidence for a medial laryngeal in their Indo-European cognates, remains unconvincing. Moreover the *Verschärfung* and the velarisations of *-w- to -g- and -k- first collected by Bugge might equally be explained as the result of an expressive process similar to the gemination of West Germanic.[94]

A close *e* value was that which originally led to the transcription *ė*. Yet given the attestations as *i*, surely Krause's *ï* remains more practical wherever the thirteenth rune is attested as a vowel. And surely a transcription *ç* is quite inadequate for this rune when it represents a consonant as its palatal status is far from clear. Similarly, the less phonologically judgemental transcription preferred latterly by Page unfortunately bears the connotation of Connolly's (IPA) value /ɨ(:)/ and there seems little point in adding to the already idiosyncratic inventory of Germanic phonological transcriptions by employing the well-established IPA symbol ɨ to refer to something quite different as would Page.[95] Yet Dickins's transcription 'ȝ' seems in part to represent a relationship of runic *ēoh* to Middle English *yogh*. Indeed the variable Middle English use of ⟨ȝ⟩ (for the palatal semivowel and both voiced, and finally and before *t*, also voiceless fricatives) appears somewhat to parallel that of the earlier runic sign. Moreover, the relationship between the two names proposed by Anna Paues, i.e. *ēoh* > **yoh* > *yogh* in parallel to the developments of the names of ME *thorn* and *wynn* from those of runic þ and w,[96] is quite possible when we consider that a similar vocalic development had occurred in some toponyms by the Middle English period,[97] and that the final -*h* might well have been re-interpreted as a devoiced final -*g*. Her contention that the shape of the yew rune can be seen reflected in ⟨ȝ⟩ is also strengthened by a preponderance of reversed (ᛇ) instances of the rune in the later English tradition as is represented by the two rune-row inscriptions and the coin legends, and the confusion of the thirteenth rune with ⟨z⟩ in the manuscript futhorc of the Codex Cotton Otho B.x. In fact given that ⟨þ⟩ clearly derives from runic þ, and ⟨p⟩ equally from runic w, it seems rather unlikely that ⟨ȝ⟩ merely represents a variant of scribal ⟨g⟩ as was argued by Henry Bradley — *yogh* instead appears to represent a conflation of miniscule ⟨g⟩ and runic ᛇ.[98] So despite the inevitable confusion with the IPA value [ʒ] or Middle English *gh*, we might prefer to maintain the Old English transcription of Dickins whenever the rune

---

[93] Grønvik, *Runene på Tunesteinen*, p. 203; Joseph B. Voyles, *Early Germanic Grammar: Pre-, Proto- and Post-Germanic Languages* (San Diego: Academic Press, 1992), pp. 72–74. Cf. Mees, 'Early Rhineland Germanic', pp. 34–36.

[94] Jerzy Kuryłowicz, 'The Germanic *Verschärfung*', *Language*, 43 (1967), 445–51; Robert S. P. Beekes, 'Germanic "Verschärfung" and no Laryngeals', *Orbis*, 21 (1972), 326–36; Elmar Seebold, 'Die Übergang von idg. -w- zu germ. -k- und -g-', *Indogermanische Forschungen*, 87 (1982), 172–94; Thomas L. Markey, 'The Laryngeal Theory and Aspects of Germanic Phonology', in *Die Laryngealtheorie und die Rekonstruktion des indogermanischen Laut- und Formensystems*, ed. by Alfred Bammesberger, Indogermanische Bibliothek, Reihe: Untersuchungen, 3 (Heidelberg: Winter, 1988), pp. 322–23 (pp. 322–23); Polomé, 'Are there Traces of Laryngeals in Germanic?', pp. 69–70; Joseph B. Voyles, 'Laryngeals in Germanic', *American Journal of Germanic Linguistics and Literature*, 1 (1989), 17–53; Voyles, *Early Germanic Grammar*, pp. 27–28; and Bernard Mees, 'The Stentoften Dedication and Sacral Kingship', *Zeitschrift für deutsches Altertum und deutsche Literatur*, 140 (2011), 281–305.

[95] Raymond I. Page, 'On the Transliteration of English Runes', *Medieval Archaeology*, 28 (1984), 22–45 (pp. 31–32) [repr. Page, *Runes and Runic Inscriptions*, pp. 256–57]; Page, *An Introduction to English Runes*, p. 40.

[96] Anna C. Paues, 'The name of the letter ȝ', *Modern Language Review*, 6 (1911), 441–54.

[97] Jürgen Giffhorn, *Phonologische Untersuchungen zu den altenglischen Kurzdiphthongen* (Munich: Fink, 1974), pp. 117–19.

[98] Henry Bradley, 'Discussion of Paues', *Modern Language Review*, 7 (1912), 520–21.

can be shown to represent a consonant and Krause's **ï** elsewhere, rather than Page's somewhat unfortunate 'ï'.[99]

In runic, a second inherited sign for *h* would appear to have been redundant. It seems likely that it would have been readily re-employed for another consonantal value if one was required to represent early Germanic. Yet there is no evidence of a palatal allophone of PG */h/ at such an early stage, let alone a */ç/ phoneme. Moreover, as Markey has pointed out, the North Etruscan alphabet used to record Venetic developed an additional iota which could well be the prototype of runic **ï**:[100] this punctuated iota (·**i**·) developed a graphemic independence from the usual Venetic iota as it had come to form the second part of the Venetic perigram for /f/; i.e. an earlier **vh** had been replaced by a spelling **v**·**i**· after **h** had become redundant phonologically in Venetic.[101] It may well, then, have come to be associated with the Rhaetic ʃ~ʅ as both were, in effect, secondary forms of digamma. The remarkable variation in inherited kappa in the North Etruscan alphabet used in the Val Camonica includes forms reminiscent of the Venetic **ii** perigram (many even reduced in size) and it is obvious that this doubling of iota (used to indicate palatal glides in Venetic) can explain the formation of runic **j**.[102] Indeed the few inscriptions where these Camunic 'kappas' appear also make much more sense phonologically if a semivocalic value is assumed for this runic **j**-like letter: compare Piancogno's **IIIIANOAŚ**,[103] i.e. **I{I}JANOAŚ** rather than **KKANOAŚ**, and perhaps Pla d'Ort's **ZEI×SIJAU** (**ZEI×SIIIAU**) rather than **ZEI×SIKAU**.[104] The letter transcribed as **Í**, the 'Claudian *i*' known from other epichoric Italian traditions, also appears in a Camunic inscription where it clearly indicates a glide, i.e. in **EŚUÍI**, 'to Esus' (?),[105] and some of the abecedaria from Foppe di Nadro suggest that **Í** may have gradually usurped the position of ksi in the Camunic ordering.[106] The appearance of both **Í** and **II** in Camunic, the North Etruscan tradition long considered to be closest to runic, suggests two new variants of iota were added to the prototype upon which the runes may have been based, one replacing a redundant sibilantic character, the other usurping the grapheme which had already come to serve in some Rhaetic centres as a disambiguating replacement for digamma in light of the development of an 'open' form of alpha. A comparatively late Camunic graph identical in form to the yew rune has of course been isolated and although it is both of unclear phonological value and origin, it may well be that it has replaced the earlier Camunic 'Claudian *i*' (i.e. **Í**), perhaps under Venetic influence. Both variant *i*-graphs (which under a North Etruscan thesis may have produced runic **j** and **ï**) ultimately seem to be modelled on orthographical developments in Venetic. Yet they still appear to have entered the prototype upon which the runes are based (given a North Etruscan derivation) as if it were that of the Val Camonica rather than a more easterly tradition.

[99] Cf. Looijenga, *Texts and Contexts of the Oldest Runic Inscriptions*, pp. 139–41.
[100] Markey, 'A Tale of Two Helmets', pp. 91–92.
[101] Michel Lejeune, *Manuel de la langue vénète*, Indogermanische Bibliothek, I. Reihe: Lehr- und Handbücher (Heidelberg: Winter, 1974), p. 23.
[102] Mees, 'The North Etruscan Thesis of the Origin of the Runes', pp. 63–64.
[103] Maria Grazia Tibiletti Bruno, 'Nuove iscrizioni camune', *Quaderni camuni*, 49–50 (1990), 29–169 (no. PC 35*a*, 47).
[104] Tibiletti Bruno, 'Nuove iscrizioni camune', no. Pl. 2*b*,64.
[105] Tibiletti Bruno, 'Nuove iscrizioni camune', no. CC 68; Alessandro Morandi, 'Epigrafia camuna. Osservazioni su alcuni aspetti della documentazione', *Revue belge de philologie et d'histoire*, 79 (1998), 99–124 (p. 104); Alessandro Morandi, *Celti d'Italia, tomo II: Epigrafia e lingua dei Celti d'Italia* (Rome: Spazio Tre, 2004), no. 270.
[106] Tibiletti Bruno, 'Nuove iscrizioni camune', nos FN 4*d*,60; 5*e*,61; and 6*f*,62.

Yet few runologists support a North Etruscan origin for the runes today, so like a laryngeal explanation for the thirteenth rune, a derivation of the yew rune from an archaic *i/h* grapheme might seem rather speculative and hence unlikely. After all, the later English and Gothic velar values associated with the letter name *yew* may only have arisen after the redundancy of what had become a second rune for *i* was recognised, the medial values suggested by the rune name being adopted independently. Nonetheless there is something of a tradition of confluence between descendants of iota and heta and the values *i* and *h* in many Mediterranean orthographies: recall the orthographical heta~iota variation in Venetic (i.e. **vh~v·i·** for *f*), Messapic displays a similar bivalency for heta (i.e. Anlaut *h-*~Inlaut *-y-*)[107] and there is even a formal confusion between some forms of ⟨h⟩ and ⟨i⟩ both in epigraphical Latin (i.e. of half-H and Claudian *i*) and archaic Greek (heta/eta-cum-spiritus asper and iota). Indeed not only is half-H a particularly notable feature of Rhenish epigraphy, the appearance of a variation between -EI-, -I- and -E- attested in Germano-Roman material from the Rhineland is also reminiscent of what might be happening with the yew rune as this variation is usually concomitant with a following -H-.[108] Given the frequency of suffixal *-īg-* in Germanic, **īgaz/*īhaz* would also seem a likely name for a rune connected with this sequence.[109] Nevertheless the comparatively late emergence of velar values in Germanic use for the thirteenth rune suggest that the bivalency in runic was not inherited. In fact it may well have been that much as ŋ had come to represent /ing/, ï at one stage became a semi-ideographic way of writing /i:g/ (or rather /ï:g/).[110]

Yet despite the rejection here of a laryngealist approach to the problem of the origin of the rune itself, of all the explanations for the development of velarity in the three attested Northwest Germanic terms for 'yew', only the ones based in the laryngeal theory seem to offer much promise. Seebold's explanation for the terms assembled by Bugge can only explain the underlying *-w-* > *-g-* (and a further devoicing of *-g-* > *-h-* seems unparallelled; indeed surely the opposite development would be more likely in a language where fricatives were subject to positional voicing).[111] Similarly, Voyles's reliance on an IE **-g-* infix cannot apply to **īhaz* and Franz Specht's reliance on an alternation of **-w-* and **-k-* at the Indo-European level has no broadly accepted parallels.[112] Criticising Wren, Page even went so far as to dispute the reconstruction **īhwaz* completely, but offered no explanation for the crucial emergence of voiceless velarity.[113] It has long been recognised that Germanic alternations of *-w-*, *-g-* and *-h-* can be linked to the inconsistent development of inherited labiovelars, however,[114] a linkage which accords well with the connection often assumed between the thirteenth rune and Gothic ⟨ƕ⟩.

---

[107] Hans Krahe, *Die Sprache der Illyrier I: Die Quellen* (Wiesbaden: Harrassowitz, 1955), p. 14.

[108] Mees, 'Early Rhineland Germanic'.

[109] Hans Krahe and Wolfgang Meid, *Germanische Sprachwissenschaft, III: Wortbildungslehre*, Sammlung Göschen, 234, 7th edn (Berlin: De Gruyter, 1969), pp. 192–93.

[110] And in late Gothic the name **eihws* appears to have been surrendered in favour of a more suitably acrophonic **hwair* > *uuaer*. Indeed given developments such as **teiws* > *tyz*, *þiuþ* > *thyth* and **aihws* > *eyz* among the other *Codex Salisburgensis* names, **eihws* might well otherwise have produced a homonym to the name for Gothic ⟨e⟩; see Mees, 'Runo-Gothica: The Runes and the Origin of Wulfila's Script', pp. 60–62.

[111] Seebold, 'Die Übergang von idg. -w- zu germ. -k- und -g-'.

[112] Voyles, 'Laryngeals in Germanic', p. 41; Specht, *Der Ursprung der indogermanischen Deklination*, pp. 63–65.

[113] Wren, 'Magic in an Anglo-Saxon Cemetery', p. 309; Page, 'The Old English Rune *eoh*, *íh*, "Yew Tree"', p. 126 [repr. Page, *Runes and Runic Inscriptions*, p. 134].

[114] Cf. Thomas L. Markey, 'Delabialisation in Germanic', *Folia Linguistica Historica*, 1 (1980), 285–94.

Karl Brunner lists examples of this alternation such as West Saxon *bræw*, Anglian *brēg*, Gothic (dat.) *brahva* 'brew' (< IE **bhreu-*) and Old English *hweogol, hweowol, hwēol, hweohhol* 'wheel' (< IE **kʷekʷl-*) where delabialisation has occurred before what in Indo-European were accented back vowels (including PG **ō* < IE **ā*).[115] Nevertheless, the development in *yew* is also parallelled at least in part by occasional forms where velarity develops from a labial glide in strikingly similar variants such as OE *nīge* and *nīwe* 'new' (cf. OFris. *ny*, OS *nigi*, runic Norse *niuha*, PG **niujaz* < IE **newios*), OE *hīgan, hīgu* and *hīwan* 'family' (< IE **k̂eiwo-*) and OE *Tīg* for the usual *Tīw* (PG **Tīwaz* < IE **Deiwos*).[116] Yet it is also clear that glides (G) sometimes develop to obstruents (C — although still maintaining an articulatory feature developed from the glide) in some instances where syllable contacts of an unstable nature have arisen upon the loss of a laryngeal (H). Thus in cases of Holtzmann's *Verschärfung*, the loss of a laryngeal in structures such as VG$HV would have produced the unwieldy syllabification *VG$V; and so instead of merely resyllabifying, the glide has been geminated across the syllable boundary ($) and 'sharpened', producing VC$C^{G}V (e.g. IE **bheu\$H_2-eye* > PG **big\$g^w-ī* > ON *byggvi*).[117] Of course the sharpening of glides to obstruents is suggested in this model to be due to an assimilation from a proximate laryngeal. Yet whatever the merits of the putative laryngeal assimilation (and even the laryngealists admit that similar developments occur in modern Faroese long after the loss of the Indo-European laryngeals),[118] the syllable contact approach does seem to provide the key to the development of the medial variability of Germanic *yew*. Clearly, under this approach a Proto-Germanic **ei\$waz* might well develop to **ei\$h^waz*, the sharpening of the semivowel serving to lower the sonority of the onset of the second syllable (perhaps even under the influence of the loss of a putative laryngeal). And a Proto-Germanic **eih^waz* might well produce the later variants **īh^waz* (in Gothic, cf. *brahva*), **īhaz* (cf. OE *hweohhol*) and a Vernerised **īgaz* (cf. Angl. *brēg*, OE *hweogol*).[119]

Yet the best evidence for an additional phoneme in Proto-Germanic that is reminiscent of attested values of the yew rune is the second- and third-century EI spellings attested in Germano-Roman theonyms recorded on votive epigraphs from the Rhineland. After all, the earliest evidence for the value of the thirteenth rune unmistakably points to a high front vowel — its attestations as a fricative are all appreciably later. The attested values were probably influenced by the yew-rune's letter name, and although the term for 'yew' is itself somewhat problematic, it is far from clear that the medial value in its letter name is the original value of this rune. The resort to the laryngeal theory to explain the problem of the Germanic front vowels has produced results no more conclusive than have similar explanations for other unexpected variations in the phonological development of Germanic. And neither have investigations of putative model alphabets proved categorical in this regard. In contrast, the votive epigraphs from the Rhineland which are contemporary with the earliest runic inscriptions exhibit evidence for a variability in the representation of Germanic front vowels similar to that which has long been seen as the likely origin of the yew rune. The use of the digraph EI to signal a variation in timbre from those vowels typically represented by I and

---

[115] Brunner, *Altenglische Grammatik*, §213, n. 1; cf. §234, n. 3, §250, n. 2.
[116] Mees, 'The Stentoften Dedication and Sacral Kingship'.
[117] Suzuki, 'The Germanic *Verschärfung*: A Syllabic Perspective'; Davis and Iverson, 'The *Verschärfung* as Feature Spread'; and Mees, 'The Stentoften Dedication and Sacral Kingship'.
[118] Markey, 'The Laryngeal Theory and Aspects of Germanic Phonology', pp. 322–23.
[119] Smith, *English Place-Name Elements*, II, 50.

The Yew Rune, Yogh and Yew

E is the result of the monophthongisation of inherited *ei* in Greek and Latin. Nonetheless a monophthongisation cannot be the cause of all of the similar Rhenish spellings — Rhenish -EIH- clearly continues *-$\bar{\imath}$g- rather than *-eig-.[120] Instead, this variation must stem from a varying description analogous to the Greek and Latin values, yet derived from some other development — presumably an *a*-umlaut that was restricted to secondarily stressed *$\bar{\imath}$.[121] And if such variations do result from a third early Germanic high front vowel phoneme intermediate between /e:/ and /i:/ (perhaps also to be linked with the development of the controversial *$\bar{e}_2$),[122] then surely this is the original value of the thirteenth rune.

Indeed it is not difficult to see how a digraphic spelling might have been thought better replaced by a (slightly confused) reuse of one of the two Greek letters at the end of the Roman alphabet (i.e. Y or Z) by an early Germanic writer. The Germano-Roman EI spellings only occur medially, however, and they are only employed in a regular manner when they appear in the later parts of polysyllabic Germano-Roman forms. In fact there is no evidence from anywhere in early runic epigraphy that an additional vowel phoneme of this kind needs to be reconstructed for Early Nordic. Hence the reasonable suspicion remains that just as the medial -*w*- in the inherited Proto-Germanic form *eiwaz* underwent sharpening in some Germanic dialects to *$\bar{\imath}$h(w)az and *$\bar{\imath}$g(w)az, a similar development is attested by the phonological values associated with the yew rune in later texts.

Much as it is only in the Old English tradition that the Ing rune has assumed an unambiguously agma-like role, it may well be that the Anglo-Saxon use of the yew rune represents some sort of standardisation of the function of this troublesome character. The name *eiwaz* 'yew' contains a syllable juncture of the type that can lead to sharpening in Germanic and such a value is reminiscent of those represented by the Middle English letter yogh. If the yew rune's original function was to indicate (relatively unsystematic) articulatory strengthenings of semivowels, then it would not be too surprising to witness its later attested phonological indeterminacy. In fact its association with [x] and [ç] suggests that it may originally have represented a lip-rounded laryngeal or glottal fricative (as 'sharpening' is most commonly associated with labiovelar environments) not too dissimilar to Connolly's -*X*- (or rather -*Xw*-), its use being confined to /i(:)/ in dialects which had lost this phonological segment. Given its name and the attested later values, it would seem not unwarranted to assume that the yew rune's original function was to indicate a (perhaps only preliminarily) sharpened glide of the type first studied by Holtzmann and Bugge.

---

[120] Mees, 'Early Rhineland Germanic', pp. 15–18, 30.

[121] Mees, 'Early Rhineland Germanic', pp. 32–36.

[122] Cf. Frans van Coetsem, *Das System der starken Verba und die Periodisierung im älteren Germanischen*, Mededelingen der Koninklijke Niederlandse Akademie van Wetenschappen, Afdeling Letterkunde, Nieuwe reeks, 19.1 (Amsterdam: Noord-Hollandse Uitgevers Maatschaapij, 1956), pp. 22–46; '$\bar{e}^2$-Perikelen', *Mededelingen van de Vereniging voor Naamkunde te Leuven en de Commissie voor Naamkunde te Amsterdam (Naamkunde)*, 38 (1962), 1–16; 'Proto-Germanic Morphophonemics', in *Toward a Grammar of Proto-Germanic*, ed. by Frans van Coetsem and Herbert L. Kufner (Tübingen: Niemeyer, 1972), pp. 175–209; *The Vocalism of the Germanic Parent Language: Systemic Evolution and Sociohistorical Context*, Indogermanische Bibliothek, I. Reihe: Lehr- und Handbücher. Untersuchungen zur vergleichende Grammatik der germanischen Sprachen, 4 (Heidelberg: Winter, 1994), pp. 94–119; Mees, 'Early Rhineland Germanic', pp. 35–37.

Sententia in Narrative Form: Ælfric's Narrative Method in the Hagiographical Homily on St Martin

Hiroshi Ogawa

I

It is generally agreed that Ælfric is the greatest prose writer in the vernacular in Anglo-Saxon England and his massive body of composition testifies to a distinctive creative method, which may be defined, in relation to the antecedent works he draws upon, as fundamentally 'a process of selection, adaptation and independent argument'.[1] He usually abbreviates his source materials, but his exact method of adaptation is varied, depending on different items of relevance on individual occasions, such as the nature of the source text, the audience and/or reader he had in mind, and the genre of the work he was engaged in producing. This last aspect, with particular reference to the distinction between the homily and the hagiography, was the subject of my recent article on the *Passio Apostolorum Petri et Pauli* (*ÆCHom* I, 26).[2] There I showed how Ælfric is successful, both thematically and stylistically, in adapting a Latin *Passio* to his purpose of writing a preaching homily, by making (among other things) thematic use of narrative and homiletic modes of discourse, having, for example, the two martyr saints speak in the homilist's own voice addressing the Anglo-Saxon audience when the occasion arises in the course of the hagiographical narrative.[3] While self-contained as a study of the Peter and Paul homily, the article poses a new problem to consider: how differently does Ælfric respond to the same subject and source material when writing for a homily and when writing for a hagiography? In this essay I propose to discuss this question with reference to the two lives of St Martin of Tour that Ælfric wrote, one for the *Catholic Homilies* (Second Series xxxiv; *Dictionary of Old English* short title *ÆCHom* II, 39) and the other for the *Lives of Saints* (xxxi; *DOE* short title *ÆLS* 31), drawing on essentially the same range of Latin

---

[1] *The Blackwell Encyclopaedia of Anglo-Saxon England*, ed. by Michael Lapidge, John Blair, Simon Keynes and Donald Scragg (Oxford: Blackwell, 1999), s.v. *Ælfric of Eynsham*.

[2] Hiroshi Ogawa, 'Hagiography in Homily – Theme and Style in Ælfric's Two-Part Homily on SS Peter and Paul', *Review of English Studies*, 61 (2010), 167–87.

[3] 'Hagiography in Homily', pp. 182–85. 'A saint as preacher' (as Godden in the study below calls it) seems to be a feature of earlier saints' lives in the *Catholic Homilies*; see, for example, *Assumptio Sancti Johannis Apostoli* (*ÆCHom* I, 4), lines 95–128. But it has disappeared in later ones, including the one on Martin, as we shall see. See M. R. Godden, 'Experiments in Genre: The Saints' Lives in Ælfric's *Catholic Homilies*', in *Holy Men and Holy Women: Old English Prose Saints' Lives and Their Contexts*, ed. by Paul E. Szarmach (Albany, NY: State University of New York, 1996), pp. 261–87 (pp. 278–82).

sources.[4] The two lives and their shared Latin sources make an ideal trilogy for comparative study. By reading the homily on St Martin in light of the source texts on one hand and, on the other, its hagiographical counterpart written later for a different purpose, we can best see how Ælfric revises the Latin *Vita* and the associated materials to create his own homily in a way which gives it a distinctive form and significance as a preaching text about the saint's life.

The life in the *Catholic Homilies* has often been referred to as Ælfric's 'shorter life' compared with the work in the *Lives of Saints* collection, which follows its source texts more closely and is much longer (1495 rhythmical prose lines in the standard edition) — 'as long as any three average Ælfrician homilies'.[5] One focus of discussion from this point of view has been omissions of contents that have made the work shorter. 'The entire homily,' says G. H. Gerould, 'is a plain tale in rapid, unadorned prose of the saint's life and death, as brief as was consistent with clarity yet by no means ill fashioned'.[6] However, of real importance, from my point of view, are the new emphases Ælfric introduces into the hagiography as he adapts it and the exact ways in which he makes the omissions and other relevant adaptations to reinforce those emphases. To discuss all this demands full analysis of his narrative method and general use of language in adapting the hagiographical materials into a work appropriate for a collection of homilies.

Before proceeding to the analysis, we may be wise to recall what M. R. Godden has described as Ælfric's 'change of heart about the genre',[7] which is evident in later saints' lives in the *Catholic Homilies*. One might assume that the homiletic mode of discourse, seen in the Peter and Paul homily and other earlier saints' lives in the *Catholic Homilies* (see above, n. 3), would be a continuing basis for Ælfric's hagiographical homilies, informing later ones in the series as well. In fact, however, the later saints' lives, from the life of Cuthbert (*ÆCHom* II, 10) onwards, show Ælfric departing from his earlier pattern in favour of a new form, as Godden goes on to explain:

> The earlier, nonalliterative saints' lives often begin with some kind of homiletic address from preacher to audience, but the lives of Cuthbert, Benedict, and Martin launch straight into narrative without a hint of the audience's presence. They are also very much longer than most of the homilies. The sense or pretense of a preaching text is clearly fading; Ælfric seems to have largely abandoned the attempt to adapt hagiography to a preaching

---

[4] They are: Sulpicius Severus's *Vita Sancti Martini* for the main part, supplemented by the same author's *Dialogi* and Alcuin's summary of Sulpicius (*Vita Sancti Martini Turonensis*), the *Epistula Tertia* by Sulpicius for the death of the saint, and *Historia Francorum* by Gregory of Tours for the post-mortem part. For details of the precise extent of Ælfric's indebtedness to each of these, see *Ælfric's Catholic Homilies: Introduction, Commentary and Glossary*, ed. by M. R. Godden, Early English Text Society, s. s., 18 (Oxford: Oxford University Press, 2000), pp. 623–33. Citation from Ælfric's two lives is made below from *Ælfric's Catholic Homilies. The Second Series*, ed. by M. R. Godden, Early English Text Society, s. s., 5 (London: Oxford University Press, 1979); and *Ælfric's Lives of Saints*, ed. by W. W. Skeat, Early English Text Society, o. s., 76, 82, 94, and 114 (London: Oxford University Press, 1881–1900; repr. in two volumes, 1966); and citation from Sulpicius's works is from *Sulpicii Severi Libri Qui Supersunt*, ed. by C. Halm (Vienna: Gerold, 1866), with page and line. For *Historia Francorum*, see n. 41.

[5] D. R. Letson, 'The Form of the Old English Homily', *American Benedictine Review*, 30 (1979), 399–431 (p. 422).

[6] Gordon Hall Gerould, 'Ælfric's Lives of St. Martin of Tours', *JEGP*, 24 (1925), 206–10 (p. 207). More recently, Jonathan Wilcox has noted the radically different lengths of the two versions, seeing them as a consequence of the distinct contexts in which they were used ('The Audience of Ælfric's *Lives of Saints* and the Face of Cotton Caligula A. xiv, fols. 93–130', in *Beatus Vir: Studies in Early English and Norse Manuscripts in Memory of Phillip Pulsiano*, ed. by A. N. Doane and Kirsten Wolf (Tempe: Arizona Center for Medieval and Renaissance Studies, 2006), pp. 229–63 (pp. 243–44).

[7] Godden, 'Experiments in Genre', p. 280.

genre even before he had completed the *Catholic Homilies* and begun to treat the saint's life as a distinct kind of discourse.[8]

The life of Martin, as one of these later works of the genre, testifies to the change. The life has no opening address to the audience or reminder of the feast for the saint as the occasion on which it is delivered but 'launches straight into narrative'.[9] Nor does it feature the protagonist saint taking on the role of a preacher speaking in Ælfric's own voice where appropriate (as it would have been in, for example, lines 161–77, discussed below in IV). Ælfric does not even provide comments by expanding on the saint's words and deeds, though he could well have chosen to do so in several passages (see lines 24–26 and 41–43, both discussed in II). In the one commentary where Ælfric does insert a doctrinal issue (lines 82–85), he raises a point which he does not make very well (see below, n. 27). Clearly, Ælfric has now reached a new solution for his problem about the genre.

How then does Ælfric register his sense of a preaching homily into which he attempts to reshape the hagiographical materials of his Latin sources in the Martin homily? My contention in the following sections is that Ælfric relies on specialized uses of homiletic diction and a narrative method designed to enhance the sanctity and virtues of the protagonist saint, thereby incorporating into the narrative what is in effect a commentary on his sayings and deeds. These points will emerge as we analyse the homily and Ælfric's emphases within it in comparison with the original form of the saint's *vita* and also the different emphases in his later, longer life of the saint.

II

Ælfric's life of St Martin in the *Catholic Homilies*, titled *Depositio Sancti Martini Episcopi*, is a 'birth-to-beatification homily' (as opposed to the Episodic type),[10] describing the blessed life of the title saint from his birth in a heathen family to his death in glory (and a post-mortem incident). For this homily, as for his later telling in the *Lives of Saints*, Ælfric draws mainly upon the *Vita* of the saint by Sulpicius Severus, supplemented by four associated materials (see above, n. 4). As mentioned above, abridgement by omission is Ælfric's basic approach to the copious source materials, a feature long known and best summarized by Godden:

> Ælfric's technique [...] was to abridge by summarising most of the incident and omitting much of the contextual detail; in particular the background of ecclesiastical history (the exile of Hilarius by Arians, their oppression of Martin, his conflict with other bishops and clergy, the gradual evangelisation of areas surrounding Tours) mostly disappears, though some aspects, such as the qualities of the monastic life which Martin sustained while bishop of Tours, are given fuller treatment. What Ælfric produces is an account of Martin's virtues and miracles rather than a sequential history.[11]

Godden's summary embraces two types of omission: omission of an incident itself and omission of some detail in an incident. The examples of the former Godden mentions are from earlier chapters of the *Vita* (cap. 6-cap. 10), while an example from later chapters is the omission of cap. 20 of the *Vita* with its account of Martin's dealings with Emperor Maximus.

---

[8] Godden, 'Experiments in Genre', p. 281.
[9] But Ælfric does give both a hint of the audience's presence and a reminder of the feast day in the closing portion of the homily; see V.
[10] For these terms, see Letson, 'The Form', pp. 420–21.
[11] Godden, *Commentary*, pp. 622–23.

Sententia *in Narrative Form*

This latter omission appears to have given Ælfric an impetus. He now goes on to omit most of the remaining chapters of the *Vita* (though not cap. 24), and where he does not entirely omit, he draws on Alcuin's condensed account rather than on the original account of the miracles Sulpicius gives in the *Dialogues*.[12] It seems as if Ælfric now felt he had had enough miracles to tell and should hasten to the final climax of the narrative, to which he turns with a few words of excuse: 'Ne mage we awritan ealle his wundra on ðisum scortan cwyde. mid cuðum gereorde. ac we wyllað secgan hu se soðfæsta gewat' (lines 266–69).[13]

While omissions of entire events reveal where Ælfric puts emphasis and where he does not in his account of the saint as *godes andetere* 'confessor of God' (line 1) and *godes cempa* 'soldier of God' (line 7), even more important are omissions of the other kind — omissions of contextual detail from incidents he does relate. Thus, Ælfric usually omits to mention place-names and personal names in accounts of miracles and other incidents. He also often pares the narrative to Martin and his immediate adversary, making other people in Sulpicius's account invisible. Omissions of this kind not only help to abridge the source text, but, more importantly, to represent Martin as a type rather than as an individualized saint. This aspect of Ælfric's narrative technique acquires greater significance, particularly when omission of contextual detail is combined with a certain set of diction which tends to be formulaic and even symbolic.

But before we discuss that point, we should note another of Ælfric's techniques which is related to the point Godden makes in the summary quoted above about the homily not being a sequential history. Ælfric does not do anything, apart from adding two incidents (lines 146–52 and 152–54) that ultimately come from the *Dialogues*,[14] to disrupt the order of events given in the *Vita*, but he tends to 'detemporize' them. This is partly because he follows the *Vita*, for the latter 'follows the chronology of the subject's life until success is attained, and then summarizes thematically further achievements'.[15] But even where the *Vita* gives a chronological account in the earlier part, Ælfric often minimizes the temporal element in his narrative, pushing chronology into the background. For example, he downgrades a temporal phrase denoting time when in the *Vita*, either omitting it entirely or replacing it with the

---

[12] See Frederick M. Biggs, 'Ælfric as Historian: His Use of Alcuin's *Laudationes* and Sulpicius's *Dialogues* in His Two Lives of Martin', in *Holy Men and Holy Women*, ed. by Szarmach, pp. 289–315 (p. 297). Ælfric had occasionally derived his account from Alcuin rather than Sulpicius in the preceding parts; see Godden, *Commentary*, pp. 628–31.

[13] 'We cannot write down all his miracles in this short discourse, with familiar language, but we will say how the righteous man departed.' Translation of the homily here and in the other footnotes is cited from *The Homilies of the Anglo-Saxon Church. The First Part, Containing the Sermones Catholici, or Homilies of Ælfric*, ed. by Benjamin Thorpe, 2 vols. (London: Ælfric Society, 1844–46; repr. New York: Johnson Reprint, 1971), ii, pp. 498–519.

[14] Godden (*Commentary*, p. 628) writes that they 'probably come [...] from Alcuin, who summarizes them together'. Letson also points out that 'Alcuin adds two related miracles, the raising of the widow's son and the healing of the dumb girl' after the first two miracles Martin performed. From the evidence we have now, however, he seems to give a confused picture in saying that these miracles 'are found at a late point in Sulpicius' and that Ælfric 'seems to misplace both of these miracles, locating them after Martin's consecration' ('The Form', p. 423 and n. 48). As a matter of fact, the miracles originate ultimately from Sulpicius's *Dialogues* II.4 and III.2 respectively. There the first miracle at any rate is narrated as occurring after Martin's election as Bishop of Tours, though Alcuin appears to give both as pre-election events. Nor does Letson seem to make it clear why Ælfric, by placing them where he does, 'breaks the thematic arrangement' (n. 48). For a full discussion, see Biggs, 'Ælfric as Historian', pp. 296–97.

[15] Biggs, 'Ælfric as Historian', p. 295. On the same page Biggs cites from Clare Stancliffe to give more specific details: 'as Clare Stancliffe writes, "chapters 2–10 do contain a chronological account of Martin's career up to his election as bishop and the foundation of Marmoutier; the following fourteen devoted to his miraculous deeds as bishop are strictly arranged according to subject-matter" '.

inexpressive *ða* 'then' or its equivalent, as in lines 105 *Sum ungesceadwis man hine sylfne aheng* (*Vita* 118.14 *Nec multo post, dum [...], indicatur unum ex familia seruulum [...]*), 110 *Þæt turonisce folc hine ða geceas him to leodbiscope* (*Vita* 118.25 *Sub idem fere tempus ad episcopatum [...] petebatur*), and, in a cataloguing passage from the later part, 198 *Tetradius hatte sum hæðen þegen [...]; Martinus eac com to anes mannes huse* (*Vita* 126.10 *Eodem tempore Taetradii [...]. Per idem tempus in eodem oppido ingressus [...]*).[16] The force of focusing on the events themselves in this way is shown clearly by the contrast it makes to Ælfric's treatment in the *Lives of Saints* version, where he renders the *Vita*'s wording in each of the three sentences faithfully as: *ÆLS* 31.239 *Eft æfter sumum fyrste [...]*, 254 *On þære ylcan tide [...]*; and 506 *Ða wæs sum heah-þegen [...]. On ðære ylcan tide on þam ylcan fæstene [...]*,[17] respectively.

Ælfric's 'detemporization' makes its narrative significance felt more clearly in stretches of sentences which involve a *ða* (*ða*) 'when' clause, rendering a *cum*-clause in the *Vita*. The latter has four instances of the temporal clause in its earliest part prior to Martin's baptism, invariably placing it before its main clause. Ælfric, while following the *Vita* in all four except one (Martin at age fifteen) in the *Lives of Saints* version, is varied and flexible in the homily. He takes over one of the four as it is in the *Vita* (112.2 *cum esset annorum decem, [...] ad ecclesiam confugit*, which he renders as 'ða ða he tyn wyntre on ylde wæs. ða arn he to cyrcan',[18] line 8), but omits the reference to Martin at age twelve (*Vita* 112.4) and puts the reference to age fifteen after the main clause (line 17, rendering *Vita* 112.11). Then, most importantly, he concludes the pauper episode by explaining how Martin was impressed by Christ's appearance in his dream, saying with the last of the temporal clauses: 'Martinus ða fægnode þære fægeran gesihðe. and wearð þa gefullod forhraðe on criste ða ða he on ylde eahtatyne geara wæs'[19] (lines 42–44). He places Martin's age at that time at the end as if it were an afterthought, rendering the temporal frame less important than in the *Vita*'s original account (113.26 *cum esset annorum duodeuiginti, ad baptismum conuolauit*).[20] The *Vita* has a sentence before this implying the passage of time prior to the baptism; so does the *Lives of Saints* version, following the *Vita* closely again. By contrast, in the homily version Ælfric connects the vision and the baptism by the single word *forhraðe* 'immediately'. The passage of time is rendered invisible, making the pauper episode thematically more important and dramatizing the baptism as its denouement.

---

[16] line 105: 'Some irrational man hanged himself', (Latin) 'Not long after these events, while Martin [...], he was told that one of the slaves of the family [...]'; line 110: 'The people of Tours then chose him for their diocesan bishop', (Latin) 'Nearly about the same time, Martin was called upon to undertake the episcopate [...]'; line 198: 'There was a heathen named Tetradius [...]. Martin also came to a man's house', (Latin) 'At the same time the servant of one Tetradius [...]. About the same time, having entered [...] in the same town'. In the last of these passages, Ælfric might have drawn on Alcuin's condensed version; see Godden, *Commentary*, p. 630, note to lines 196–211. Translation of Sulpicius's works in the footnotes is all taken from Alexander Robert, 'The Works of Sulpicius Severus', in *A Select Library of Nicene and Post-Nicene Fathers of the Christian Church*, Second Series, Volume XI, ed. by Philip Schaff and Henry Wace (Oxford: Parker, 1894), pp. 1–122.

[17] 'Again after some time [...]'; 'At that same time [...]'; 'There was a certain great noble [...]. At the same time in the same fortified town'. Translation of the *Lives of Saints* version is Skeat's in his Early English Text Society edition, ii, pp. 218–313.

[18] (Latin) 'when he was of the age of ten years, he betook himself [...] to the Church'; 'when he was only ten years of age, he ran to church.'

[19] 'Martin then rejoiced at the fair vision, and was then speedily baptized in Christ, when he was eighteen years of age.'

[20] 'being now of the age of eighteen years, he hastened to receive baptism.' (Roberts's translation reads 'twenty years'.)

What is of hagiographical importance for Ælfric is the progress of events from giving the cloak through the vision to the baptism. His emphasis is not on the time at which they occur.

The importance of baptism in a saint's life is self-evident. But Ælfric seems to give it special emphasis as one of the three moments that punctuate Martin's life, the others being his retirement from military service (treated as consequent upon his baptism) and his election as Bishop of Tours. This last event is defined, both in the *Vita* and Ælfric's homily, as the highest point of Martin's attainment after which chronology is no longer relevant, and Ælfric obviously derived this from the *Vita*, as we have seen above. However, the form of emphasis on the baptism seems to be original with Ælfric, an emphasis which he gives, somewhat paradoxically, by referring to Martin being not yet baptized immediately *after* explaining his early virtues, on two occasions — first, in relating that Martin was as good as a Christian from his youth: 'He wæs swiðe geswæs eallum swincendum. and on mislicum yrmðum mannum geheolp. wædligum and wanscryddum. and næs ðeah ða gyt gefullod'[21] (lines 24–26), and then in Christ's words in the vision: 'Martinus me bewæfde efne mid ðyssere wæde. þeah ðe he ungefullod gyt farende sy'[22] (lines 41–42). The *Vita* does refer to Martin being a catechumen at both points,[23] but in a detached sentence *before* describing the virtues in the former (112.15–27) and in the intercalated position in the latter (113.19); the narratives in Ælfric's later telling show the same treatments (*ÆLS* 31.51, 82). The constant placement of the phrase with the addition of *þeah* 'nevertheless; though' at the end is Ælfric's own form of emphasis that he specially deploys for the homily. This distinctive manner of reference makes 'baptized/unbaptized' the underlying theme in the earliest part of the saint's life as Ælfric restructures it. He expresses the theme in narrative form, and significantly chooses not to add any comment to explain it. For the two references come from exactly where biblical quotations are made in the *Vita*, of Matt 6. 34 (somewhat obliquely) and Matt 25. 40 respectively, and Ælfric could have taken up the quotations and preached about the moral lesson of the event he had just told. But he merely places the phrase *næs ðeah ða gyt gefullod* at the very end in the first reference, as his own theme in place of the biblical teaching — an equivalence which Ælfric himself partly shows with his later telling: he quotes the verse from Matthew (more directly than the *Vita*, with 'swa swa þæt god-spel sægð . Ne þenc þu be mergene',[24] *ÆLS* 31.57) but mentions Martin not being baptized six lines earlier in a disconnected way. By the same token, Ælfric adds the word *fæger* 'fair' to the *Vita*'s *quo uiso* 'after this was seen' as his equivalent to the biblical quotation he omits in the vision scene. Simple though it is, the word with its rich associations of blessedness has a thematic force,[25] which is sufficiently powerful to make the equivalence convincing and to warrant its use again later when Ælfric refers to the angels coming to assist Martin in performing his first miracle (line 103; see below).

III

If abridgement is Ælfric's basic approach to his source texts, he shows other ways to make it effective and meaningful in achieving his larger end of rewriting a hagiography as a homily.

---

[21] 'He was very kind to all afflicted, and helped men under divers miseries, the poor and ill-clothed, and, nevertheless, was not yet baptized.'

[22] 'Martin clothed me with this garment, though he be yet going unbaptized.'

[23] Ælfric does not reflect the distinction between being baptized and being a catechumen made in the *Vita*. For a detailed discussion, see Godden, *Commentary*, p. 624, note to lines 1–18.

[24] 'even as the gospel saith: "Take no thought for the morrow." '

[25] For a recent study of this word, see Antonette diPaolo Healey, 'Questions of Fairness: Fair, Not Fair, and Foul', in *Unlocking the Wordhord: Anglo-Saxon Studies in Memory of Edward B. Irving, Jr.*, ed. by Mark C. Amodio

We have seen something of this larger pattern already. But it can be seen more clearly in long stretches of sentences such as the following passage on Martin in conflict with Emperor Julian, where Ælfric is perhaps at his best in combining omission and other techniques:

> *ÆCHom* II, 39.45 Æfter ðisum gelamp on ðære leode gewinn. þæt Iulianus se casere gecwæð to gefeohte. and dælde his cempum cynelice sylene. þæt hi on ðam gewinne werlice ongunnon; Þa nolde martinus geniman his gife. ne on ðam gefeohte his handa afylan. ac cwæð þæt he wolde criste ðeowian. on gastlicum gecampe æfter his cristendome; Ða cwæð se wælhreowa þæt he wære afyrht for ðan toweardan gefeohte. na for criste eawfæst; Þa andwyrde martinus unforht ðam casere; Ic wille ðurhgan orsorh ðone here mid rodetacne gewæpnod. na mid readum scylde. oððe mid hefegum helme. oþþe heardre byrnan; Ða het se hæðena cyning healdan martinum þæt he wurde aworpen ungewæpnod ðam here; Þa nolde se hælend his ðegen forlætan. ac gesibbode þæt folc sona þæs on merien. þæt hi to ðæs caseres cynegyrde gebugon.[26]

Ælfric first omits to relate that the warfare took place in Gaul, an omission which enables him to rewrite it as a civil war ('on ðære leode gewinn'), not as an invasion by a foreign nation as in the *Vita*'s 'inruentibus intra Gallias barbaris' (114.7) and its close rendering in the *Live of Saints* version (*ÆLS* 31.94–95). Changing the setting in this way, Ælfric pares down the incident to a one-to-one confrontation between Martin and Julian, with no other relevant party visible around them. The conflict is further sharpened by being placed within a homiletic framework that derives its force from opposing sets of epithets used for the two — Martin, who would not *afylan* 'defile' his hands in the war but rather be engaged in a *gastlicum gecampe* 'ghostly warfare', *orsorh* 'fearless' in the face of Julian *se wælhreowa* 'the cruel' and *se hæðena cyning* 'the heathen king'. All these epithets, setting them in absolute antithesis in terms of Christian and pagan, good and evil,[27] are Ælfric's own, introduced without any prompt from the *Vita*; in fact, they represent his hallmark which is more widely used in this homily, as we shall

---

and Katherine O'Brien O'Keeffe (Toronto: University of Toronto Press, 2003), pp. 252–73.

[26] 'After this it happened, in the civil war, that the emperor Julian gave order for a battle, and distributed a royal donation to his soldiers, and they conducted themselves manfully in that conflict. But Martin would not take his gift, nor defile his hand in the battle, but said that he would serve Christ in ghostly warfare after his christianity. Then the tyrant said that he was afraid because of the battle at hand, not pious for Christ. Martin then boldly answered the emperor, "I will fearlessly go through the host, armed with the sign of the rood, not with red shield or with heavy helm, or hard corselet." Then the heathen king commanded Martin to be held, that he might be cast unarmed amid the army. But Jesus would not forsake his servant, but reconciled the folk forthwith on the morrow, so that they submitted to the emperor's sceptre.'

[27] Ælfric extends this dualism to Martin and his father in referring to the latter's damnation, using the words *geðeah* 'throve' and *forweard* 'perished' for the two respectively: 'Be ðam we magon tocnawan þæt gehwilce geðeoð to heofenan rice. þeah ðe heora frynd losian. þa ða se mæra wer swa micclum geðeah. and his fæder forweard on fulum hæðenscipe' [By this we may know that any may thrive to the kingdom of heaven, though their friends perish, when this great man so greatly throve, and his father perished in foul heathenship] (lines 82–85; 'frynd' should be translated 'relatives', not 'friends'). This is the one comment of his own Ælfric adds in the homily. Ælfric would seem to mean that one should not wonder why many people are able to go to heaven when their kinsmen are damned, given that Martin was a great saint yet his father was so evil that Martin could not save him from damnation. In other words, Ælfric might be representing Martin's father as an exemplar — the worst of fathers, as evil perhaps as Emperor Julian *se wælhreowa*, whom even a saint like Martin could not help. For the evilness of Martin's father, see lines 14–16. But the point of making the comment seems not very clear, as Godden points out (*Commentary*, p. 626, note to lines 74–85). For a discussion of saints' lives as a genre that does not admit 'any (even momentary) ambiguity' between a protagonist Christian and his or her pagan relative, see Thomas D. Hill, '*Imago Dei*: Genre, Symbolism, and Anglo-Saxon Hagiography', in *Holy Men and Holy Women*, ed. by Szarmach, pp. 35–50 (p. 40).

see.²⁸ This thematic use of diction reaches its climax in this passage when Martin answers the Emperor's slander, saying that he is unafraid of going through the host, *mid rodetacne gewæpnod. na mid readum scylde. oððe mid hefegum helme. oþþe heardre byrnan* 'armed with the sign of the cross, not with red shield or with heavy helmet or hard corselet'. Godden notes that '[t]he red shield, heavy helm and hard mail-shirt [...] correspond simply to Latin *clipeus* 'shield' and *galea* 'helmet''.²⁹ Since all this heavy equipment is rejected as powerless by Martin, one may perhaps discern 'a mock-heroic line' in this expansion that Ælfric makes, as J. Wogan-Browne suggests.³⁰ On the other hand, Wogan-Browne fails to note a point which Ælfric seems to make in the *mid*-phrases just quoted, *mid rodetacne gewæpnod* in particular. By using the phrase in literal contrast to *ungewæpnod* in the sentence immediately following, Ælfric makes the Emperor call *ungewæpnod* 'unarmed' what Martin himself calls *gewæpnod* 'armed', epitomizing the direct division between the Christian and pagan, the good and evil, views.³¹ In this way, he expresses, in narrative form, the moral of the story unobtrusively but as clearly as by explaining it in commentary; he states the *sententia* with the explicitness appropriate to a preaching homily. Comparing Ælfric's two lives of Martin, Wogan-Browne further says that 'the earlier life [...] allows Martin's background and military career to bulk much larger'.³² But this does not seem to be wholly convincing, for the saint's military career is to all appearances minimized in the Martin homily. Thus, Ælfric does not stop to say that Martin continued to hold military office for two years after he was baptized, though he says so in his later telling (*ÆLS* 31.92–93, following the *Vita* 114.4–6).³³ Even in an earlier passage about giving a cloak to a pauper, Martin is said to have nothing to give the pauper but his cloak ('Ða næfde martinus nan ðing to syllenne þam nacedan ðearfan [...] buton his gewædum', lines 29–31), rather than his cloak and his armour, as in the later version ('naht butan his gewædum . and his gewæpnunge', *ÆLS* 31.67). Ælfric clearly minimizes Martin's military career even at this point, in sharp contrast to those who accompanied him, whom he plainly calls soldiers ('cempan', line 35). His method is essentially the same at the crucial point under discussion. Martin the *miles Christi* standing against the heathen Emperor Julian is the main focus of this entire passage, as the *gewæpnod*-vocabulary and other epithets demonstrate.

The homiletic mode of discourse in the passage on Martin and Julian, sustained by this use of affective vocabulary, is carried on to the end, giving a fitting conclusion to the confrontation as Ælfric tells it. Now we read in the *Vita*, and the *Lives of Saints* version following it closely, that before Julian's order to send Martin to the ordeal was carried out, the heathen nation surrendered the next morning. Sulpicius then adds a concluding authorial commentary to the effect that this could not have happened except by God's intervention to save the saint, which

---

[28] For example, the word *orsorh*(*lice*) occurs further in lines 70 and 301, and *wælhreow* in lines 20 and 59 (referring in both to Emperor Julian) and 301 (referring to the devil). Godden also notes this formulaic use of some epithets in this homily; see below n. 68.

[29] Godden, *Commentary*, p. 625, note to lines 45–58.

[30] Jocelyn Wogan-Browne, 'The Hero in Christian Reception: Ælfric and Heroic Poetry', in *La funzione dell'eroe germanico: storicità, metafora, paradigma*, ed. by Teresa Pàroli (Rome: Il Calamo, 1995); repr. in *Old English Literature*, ed. by R. M. Liuzza (New Haven and London: Yale University Press, 2002), pp. 215–35 (p. 224).

[31] It may also be interesting to note that the confrontation reads like a passage from a story of a martyr and a persecutor, an impression which the word *aworpen* '(to be) cast away' in the Emperor's command reinforces. Ælfric and anonymous writers often use the word or its equivalent in describing martyred saints tortured in a variety of forms by persecutors who are *wælhreow*.

[32] Wogan-Browne, 'The Hero in Christian Reception', p. 224.

[33] On this point, see Paul E. Szarmach, 'Ælfric Revises: The Lives of Martin and the Idea of the Author', in *Unlocking the Wordhord*, ed. by Amodio and O'Keeffe, pp. 38–61 (pp. 47–48).

starts by asking the reader: *quis dubitet* [...] 'who would doubt [...]?' (114.24–115.2). The *Lives of Saints* version again follows this treatment (*ÆLS* 31.121–30). Ælfric in the Martin homily transforms all this into a single sentence (the last sentence of the quotation) in which he asserts what happened as a truth: 'Þa nolde se hælend his ðegen forlætan. ac gesibbode þæt folc sona þæs on merien. þæt hi to ðæs caseres cynegyrde bugon'. As the initial *þa* certifies, the sentence is part of the narrative, continuing the action line of the incident being told. But it is a narrative with which Ælfric replaces Sulpicius's commentary; it is a commentary turned into narrative. It is a statement which, not unlike any of the Gospel narratives, is expressed as a truth, not by an impersonal narrator but by the homilist Ælfric, who is the omniscient author here.

The omniscient Ælfric also makes himself felt earlier in the pauper episode, where he says: 'On þære ylcan nihte æteowode crist hine sylfne martine on swefne'[34] (lines 38–39), representing Christ's appearance to Martin as a truth, rather than 'On þære ylcan nihte he geseah on swefne þone hælend' (*ÆLS* 31.75–76, where the emphasis is on Martin's dream, as it is in the *Vita* 113.15 *cum se sopori dedisset, uidit Christum* [...]).[35] This homiletic mode takes a slightly different form in the account of Martin's first miracle of restoring life to a man who died before baptism. The man then begins to report how he was recalled from a dark place by the saint's intercession. After its first sentence, however, his reported speech abruptly reverts into the author's account, reopened with the narrative formula *Ða comon þær*:[36]

> *ÆCHom* II, 39.99 and he wearð ða geedcucod æfter lytlum fyrste. and sona gefullod. gesundful leofode to manegum gearum. and gewisslice sæde þæt he wære gelæd to leohtleasre stowe. and swærlice geswenct. on sweartum witum; Ða comon þær fleogende twegen fægre englas. and hine gelæddon ongean to life for martines bene. swa swa he bæd æt gode.[37]

The words 'for martines bene. swa swa he bæd æt gode' at the end certify that the *Ða comon* sentence in which they occur is not part of the restored man's report but a statement made by Ælfric. It would be easy to see anacoluthon here and say that Ælfric could have avoided this grammatical irregularity; both the *Vita* (118.5–10) and Ælfric's later telling (*ÆLS* 31.227–36) make it clear that the entire passage is the man's report, the former by recurrent infinitives (*excepisse* [...] *fuisse* [...] *esse* [...] *reduci*) depending on the verb phrase *referre erat solitus* 'he was wont to report' and the latter by the narrator-author's confirmation of the report that it did so happen then ('and hit wearð þa swa', *ÆLS* 31.236). Here again, however, we should probably see a deliberate change on Ælfric's part in favour of the homiletic mode. Ælfric chooses to recount the coming of the angels and what ensued not as a reported story but as a truth, as appropriate to a homily. It is probably in light of this mode that Ælfric here again exploits opposing sets of affective epithets describing the place where the man was brought and the angels who helped him — words for 'lightless, dark, black' ('to leohtleasre stowe. and swærlice geswenct. on sweartum witum', featuring heavy alliteration on the *s*-words) are used to describe the former and a word for 'fair, bright' ('fægre') to describe the latter. This opposition between 'dark' and 'bright' parallels the opposition between Christian and pagan

---

[34] 'On the same night Christ appeared to Martin in a dream'.
[35] 'In the same night he saw in a dream Jesus'; (Latin) 'when Martin had resigned himself to sleep, he had a vision of Christ [...]'.
[36] Ælfric uses this formula later in line 187, again announcing the arrival of angels to assist Martin.
[37] 'And he was then after a little space requickened, and forthwith baptized, lived prosperous for many years, and, moreover, said, that he had been led to a lightless place, and heavily afflicted with dire torments. Then there came flying two fair angels, and led him again to life, at the supplication of Martin, as he had prayed of God.'

in the passage on Martin and Emperor Julian, while the word 'fægre' for the angels may also echo 'þære fægeran gesihðe' of Christ in the pauper episode. Like these two previous passages, the passage on Martin's first miracle shows Ælfric narrating as an omniscient homilist and enforcing his view with the dualism of opposing epithets for 'good' and 'evil' as a method of expressing *sententia* in narrative form.

IV

As can be seen from the previously quoted passages, Ælfric's techniques of omitting contextual detail and casting the *sententia* of hagiographical events in the narrative make his prose 'striking in its starkness'.[38] The starkness has stylistic and thematic dimensions. Stylistically, it is a product of a narrative prose focusing upon the progress of the action mostly told with verbs in the preterite tense. The succession of these assertive verb forms has a thematic consequence. It helps to heroicize the protagonist saint as a man of absolute sanctity, at all times unswerving in being a *godes cempa* and unhesitating in acting as such. This is part of the picture we saw earlier of Martin standing *orsorh* against Emperor Julian (lines 45–58). But the heroicization is seen more distinctly in later passages where Martin as a bishop confronts his adversaries. Perhaps the best example is a passage drawing upon the *Vita*, cap. 13. Martin has overthrown an idol-fane and then attempts to destroy a pine-tree standing close by, to the great anger of the people who have worshipped it (lines 161–63). Ælfric continues:

> ÆCHom II, 39.163 Ða noldon ða hæðenan þam halgan geðafian. þæt he swa halig treow æfre hynan sceolde; Cwæð þeah heora an þæt he hit underfenge feallende to foldan. and hi hit forcurfon. gif he on god truwode þurh trumne geleafan; Þa geðafode martinus. þæt mid gebylde. and wearð gebunden under ðam beame geset ðider ðe he bigde mid healicum bogum. and næs him nan wen þæt he ahwar wende buton to ðam halgan. swa swa he ahyld wæs; Hwæt ða ða hæðenan aheowon þæt treow mid ormætre blisse. þæt hit brastliende sah to ðam halgan were. hetelice swiðe; Þa worhte he ongean ðam hreosendum treowe þæs hælendes rodetacn. and hit ðærrihte ætstod. wende ða ongean. and hreas underbæc. and fornean offeoll ða ðe hit ær forcurfon; Þa awurpon ða hæðenan sona heora gedwyld. and to heora scyppende sæmtinges gebugon mid micclum geleafan ðurh martines lare.[39]

As usual, Ælfric leaves out what are, to him, irrelevant details in the *Vita* — the accompanying monks worrying about Martin and the distant crowd watching and wondering — leaving Martin and those actively engaged in resisting him in direct confrontation with each other. What is new in and characteristic of this passage is the sensational language with which Ælfric describes the enraged heathens intent on revenge and the danger of the falling tree in the successive two clauses ('Hwæt ða ða hæðenan [...] mid ormætre blisse [...] hit brastliende sah [...] hetelice swiðe') and in the second clause after these ('hit ðærrihte ætstod [...] hreas

---

[38] This is a phrase Godden uses for the homily on St Cuthbert ('Experiments in Genre', p. 277). Godden shows that the later hagiographical homilies in the *Catholic Homilies*, those on Cuthbert and Martin among them, share important features of style that separate them from the earlier ones in the series; see 'Experiments in Genre', pp. 276–82.

[39] 'Then the heathens would not allow the saint that he should ever destroy so holy a tree; though one of them said, that he should receive it as it fell to earth, and they would cut it down, if he trusted in God with firm belief. Martin then consented to that with boldness, and was set bound under the tree, where it bent with its high boughs, and they had no expectation that it would turn anywhere, save to the holy man, as it was inclined. Whereupon the heathen hewed the tree with boundless delight, so that it sank crackling towards the holy man, very violently. Then made he towards the falling tree the sign of the Saviour's rood, and it straightways stood still, turned then again,

underbæc'). Ælfric's aim is obviously to set the roaring dangers as a foil to the saint, who is shown, in between those dangers in the intervening clause, as heroically determined and steadfast ('Þa worhte he [...] rodetacn'). This sharp contrast between the violent and the calm, the moving and the steadfast, is intensified by an alteration Ælfric introduces as a consequence of excluding the watching crowd from the scene: the pine-tree, turned backwards by virtue of Martin's prayer, almost falls upon the violent heathens themselves, not on the crowd who are standing safely away, as in the *Vita* (123.14–15) and its close rendering in the *Lives of Saints* (*ÆLS* 31.417–18). The alteration, by making the intended harm come upon the intenders themselves, makes their role as a foil more poignant. The saint then never again comes to the fore. It is the enraged heathens who now transform, from *mid ormætre blisse* 'with excessive delight (to harm Martin)' to *mid micclum geleafan* '(turning to Martin's God) with great devotion'. This transformation is paralleled by a larger progress of action that frames the entire passage. Destruction of the idol, begun at Martin's initiative ('Se halga towearp [...]', line 161), is brought to completion by the heathen worshippers, who are now willing to cast away their false belief ('awurpon [...] heora gedwyld', the last line but one in the quotation), thereby completing the conversion and embracing the saint's example. The two -*wearp*/-*wurpon* words at the opening and ending form an envelope pattern, highlighting the two parallel changes that are central to the event.

This narrative framework and the narrative tension it produces are reinforced by the use of 'downgraded' speech in the passage. In the *Vita*, one among the heathen worshippers protests to Martin in direct speech, urging him to prove his claims about his God (122.23–26). This is 'downgraded' to indirect speech in Ælfric's passage, as seen above ('Cwæð þeah heora an þæt [...]', the second line). More importantly, in the *Vita* Martin is assigned, before being set under the ordeal, an indirect speech in which he instructs the people on the folly of worshipping the tree (122.20–22). The author of *De Falsis Diis* and other related passages, Ælfric could have developed this bit of teaching into a mini-homily of his own, much as he does in similar contexts in earlier hagiographical homilies in the *Catholic Homilies*, including the one on the passion of Peter and Paul (see I). Here he does not, however. On the contrary, he omits Martin's speech entirely, leaving only a faint hint of it in the phrase *ðurh martines lare* 'through Martin's teaching' at the very end of the passage. The correspondence to Martin's original speech in the *Vita* makes it possible to interpret this *ðurh*-phrase as a narrative equivalent of a commentary, not unlike the narrative statements delivered from the omniscient author's point of view in the two earlier passages we have discussed (*ÆCHom* II, 39.45–58; 99–105).[40] But it is more significant to note that there is no *lar* given by the saint in the passage being discussed as Ælfric has restructured it. Martin is, at least in this passage, a man who teaches

---

and fell backwards, and nearly fell on those that had before cut it down. The heathens then forthwith renounced their error, and immediately turned to their Creator, with great faith, through Martin's instruction.'

[40] The prepositional phrase of this kind is a recurrent feature of this homily and often seems to stress God's power that a miraculous event testifies to; see, for example, 'he ða frecednysse þæs færlican attres mid gebedum afligde. þurh fultum drihtnes' [he with prayers drove away the peril of the sudden venom, through the Lord's aid] (lines 88–90); 'and hine unwurðne of deaðe aræde. þurh his ðingrædene wið þone soðan god' [and raised him unworthy from death, through his intercession with the true God] (lines 108–09); 'englas [...] cuðlice to spræcon for his clænan life' [Angels [...] familiarly spake with him, because of his pure life] (lines 220–21); 'ac he wearð gehæled [...] þurh þæs hælendes gife' [but he was healed [...] through the grace of Jesus] (lines 244–45); and 'an wod man [...] wearð gewittig ðurh þæs weres geearnungum' [an insane man [...] became sane through the man's merits] (lines 256-58; see below). Godden mentions the first and fourth of these examples, noting that the *þurh*-phrase there is not from either the *Dialogues* or Alcuin's condensed account (*Commentary*, p. 632, note to lines 239–68).

not with words but through action; the disappearance of Martin's speech emphasizes the saint as a man of action.

The significance of the 'downgraded' speech may be seen more clearly in contrast with those few contexts where Ælfric does use direct speech. In those parts of the *Vita* and associated texts on which Ælfric draws for his homily, there are fourteen instances of direct speech involving different speakers.[41] Of these, Ælfric retains eight; the rest, assigned mostly to Martin's adversaries in the Latin texts, are rendered into indirect speech, including a single case of the '*het* 'commanded' + infinitive' construction for Martin. Of Ælfric's eight examples of direct speech, one each is for Christ (in Martin's vision; see II) and Martin's disciples (in their response to the saint who has just imparted foreknowledge of his own destiny to them; see V). In the other examples, the saint himself is the speaker: lines 52 (announcing his final determination to Emperor Julian), 77 (in a reply to the devil, making the latter vanish; the latter's original direct speech (*Vita* 116.10) is 'downgraded' to indirect speech), 234 (in another reply to the devil, causing him to vanish again and with the same change in mode of speech from the *Vita* (134.9); see below), 277 (in teaching his disciples about the greedy fowls which he likens to the devils; see V), 292 (in a prayer to God), and 301 (in the final speech of victory over the devil on the deathbed). The contexts present all these as climactic moments in each event in which the speech occurs. So does the alternation of direct and indirect speech for the saint in his confrontation with the Emperor; his first speech (put in direct speech in the *Vita*) as well as the Emperor's reply is rendered in indirect speech before his direct speech at the last moment, as seen above. By comparison, in his later telling Ælfric takes over all the direct speeches from the source texts except one (which he renders using the '*het* + infinitive', as in the homily), regardless of the speaker. All this testifies to the force for which Ælfric employs direct speech in the Martin homily, as a form to be exploited only at significant points in the hagiographical narrative.[42] In light of this evidence, the omission of Martin's speech referred to at the end of the previous paragraph confirms where Ælfric's emphasis falls in the narrative of the event: not on 'the saint as preacher' but on Martin as a man of heroic action.

To return to the saint's heroicization, idealization and glorification as its slightly varied form may be seen at work in a few passages Ælfric rewrites rather radically, including the two discussed by Frederick M. Biggs.[43] In one, lines 216–20, Ælfric describes Martin as falling down on the steps at the holy altar ('on ðam healicum gradum æt þam halgum weofode'), either understanding Alcuin's *per gradus* 'on the steps' in a specialized sense or rewriting *de cenaculo* 'from the upper storey' in the *Vita*. In either event, Ælfric thereby makes the incident more appropriate to a saint and more deserving of the angel's subsequent visit and healing. In the other passage, lines 256–60, an insane man is healed by sitting where the saint had rested earlier, by the latter's virtues ('geearnungum'), not by virtue of his bedstraw ('stramine'), as in the source. Ælfric replaced the particularizing *stramine* with the inexpressive *geearnungum*, either because he found the word 'superfluous' in Alcuin's condensed account (if that is his

---

[41] *Vita* 113.19, 114.13, 114.18, 116.10, 116.12, 122.23, 127.6, 134.9, 134.15; *Epistula III* 147.24, 148.8, 148.16, 149.17; and *Historia Francorum* 32.10. Reference to this last work is to *Gregory of Tours, Historia Francorum*, ed. by B. Krusch and W. Levison (Hannover: Hahn, 1937–51), Fascicule I, by page and line.

[42] On Ælfric's manipulative use of direct and indirect speech, see Ruth Waterhouse, 'Ælfric's Use of Discourse in Some Saints' Lives', *Anglo-Saxon England*, 5 (1976), 83–103. On his usage in the later life of Martin, see Judith Gaites, 'Ælfric's Longer *Life of St Martin* and its Latin Sources: A Study in Narrative Technique', *Leeds Studies in English*, 13 (1982), 23–41 (pp. 25–26).

[43] Biggs, 'Ælfric as Historian', pp. 292–93 and 297–98.

source text at this point) or because, were he drawing on a detailed account in the *Dialogues*, 'perhaps for personal or theological reasons he was offended by the suggestion of intimacy between the saint and a woman' who might have served as 'the intermediary between the saint and the cured person', as Biggs argues.[44] Should the latter be Ælfric's source text here,[45] the replacement may indicate an attempt on Ælfric's part to make Martin more impeccable as a man and more saint-like than in Sulpicius's account by suppressing in his narrative anything that may hint at behaviour less than appropriate of a saint. The attempt would explain a third 'strikingly different' account Ælfric gives in lines 178–89, where the saint appears as a man of virtue who cannot destroy a heathen temple, not because he is powerless but because the building is too strong for any human power, as Godden notes: 'in the *Vita*, Martin cannot destroy the temple because the heathens resist, and the angels simply keep them at bay while he demolishes it, whereas Ælfric says Martin cannot destroy the temple because of its strong construction, and the angels do the work for him'.[46]

Two additional passages may amplify Ælfric's representation of Martin as a saint without human imperfections. One of them, lines 154–60, derived from the *Vita*, cap. 12, tells how Martin spellbound a band of heathen men and released them when realizing his mistake (121.24–122.12). Godden points out that Ælfric gives a different account, 'failing to explain that Martin spellbound the heathens not in a gratuitous display of power but in the mistaken belief that they were engaged in devil-worship rather than a funeral'.[47] The 'failure' might have been deliberate, as suggested by two phrases (quoted below) that Ælfric uniquely introduces in his account. As Ælfric reshapes the story, Martin saw from afar the heathens carrying a corpse for burial *mid anpræcum gehlyde* 'with a horrible clamour' (line 155–56,[48] instead of with linen clothes spread over the corpse which misled the saint in the original account), and for that heathen practice he spellbound them momentarily but released them *for his godnysse* 'because of his kindliness'[49] (lines 159–60). Ælfric has apparently transformed a story of the saint's misplaced use of miraculous power into a veneration of his goodness.

The other passage (lines 229–38), an account of the devil tempting Martin, shows an interesting case of similar revision combined with a distinctive vocabulary which reinforces it:

> ÆCHom II, 39.229 Hwilon com se deofol on anre digelnysse mid purpuran gescryd. and mid helme geglengd to ðam halgan were þær he hine gebæd. and cwæð þæt he wære witodlice se hælend; Þa beseah martinus wið þæs sceoccan leoht. gemyndig on mode. hu se metoda drihten cwæð on his godspelle be his godcundan tocyme. and cwæð to ðam leasan mid gelæredum muðe; Ne sæde ure hælend þæt he swa wolde beon mid purpuran gehiwod. oþþe mid helme scinende. þonne he eft come mid engla ðrymme; Ða fordwan se deofol dreorig him fram. and seo stow ða stanc mid ormætum stence. æfter andwerdnysse þæs egeslican gastes.[50]

---

[44] Biggs, 'Ælfric as Historian', pp. 292–93.

[45] Biggs discusses the two passages in comparison with the corresponding narratives in the *Lives of the Saints* to argue that Ælfric draws on Alcuin's condensed *Vita* rather than Sulpicius's *Dialogues* for some part of the *Catholic Homilies* life of the saint.

[46] Godden, *Commentary*, p. 629, note to lines 178–89.

[47] Godden, *Commentary*, p. 628, note to lines 154–60.

[48] Godden says that 'the reference to their noise [...] is perhaps due to Alcuin's brief summary' (*Commentary*, p. 629, note to lines 154–60).

[49] *The Dictionary of Old English*, ed. by Angus F. Cameron, Ashley Crandell Amos, Sharon Butler, and Antonette diPaolo Healey (Toronto: Centre for Medieval Studies, University of Toronto, 1986–) cites this passage as an example of the word *godnes* used of persons in the sense 'kindness, benevolence, generosity' (s.v. 2.a.ii).

[50] 'Once the devil came, in a secret place, clothed with purple, and with a crown adorned, to the holy man, where he

The saint, as Ælfric represents him here, shows not even a momentary sign of being in doubt about the identity of the figure before him, as he apparently is in the *Vita*, cap. 24, where he remains silent when first spoken to and is urged to acknowledge what he sees: 'Martine, quid dubitas credere, cum uideas?'[51] (134.12–13); all this is followed in the narrative of the *Lives of Saints*. Ælfric's Martin in the homily does not hesitate to respond, recalling Christ's words in the Gospel. This is one of the two biblical references Ælfric gives in the homily. But like the other reference (a quotation of Ps 117.6 in lines 77–78, drawn from the *Vita* 116.12–13), this reference is derived from the *Vita* (134.15–18). Ælfric neither dwells on it nor expands it with commentary, but abridges it and hastens to the closing remark about the devil vanishing. The devil in turn is given a representation which is similarly reduced but relies more on symbolism, with just two features — *mid purpuran gescryd. and mid helme geglengd* 'clothed with purple and adorned with a crown' — picked up to the exclusion of other realistic details of his appearance given in the *Vita*. The contrast between the two figures, one representing the heroic saint and the other the tempter and Antichrist, is intensified by a distinction mentioned earlier concerning the mode of speech assigned to them — that is, assertive direct speech assigned to the former ('cwæð [...]; Ne sæde ure hælend [...] ðrymme') and indirect speech to the latter ('cwæð þæt he wære [...] hælend'), 'downgraded' from two direct speeches in the *Vita*. In his direct speech itself, the saint announces his triumph using a contrasting vocabulary which reflects Ælfric the homilist's own voice — *gehiwod* 'feigned' in reference to the devil's false appearance (as against the narrative *gescryd* 'clothed' in an earlier sentence)[52] and *mid engla ðrymme* 'with a host of angels' in reference to the Advent. The two epithets are original with Ælfric, though the speech itself and its biblical reference are in the *Vita*. Nor are the epithets used in Ælfric's later telling (*ÆLS* 31.764–69), which repeats the narrative *gescryd* in the saint's speech and has no equivalent to *mid engla ðrymme*. In fact, this later version, following the *Vita* closely, lacks any of the features seen above to be characteristic of the passage of the homily. They are homiletic features which show Ælfric adapting the narrative he found in the *Vita* to his own purpose, focusing upon the saint's unswerving devotion and his *gelæredum muðe* 'learned mouth' and incorporating the moral into the narrative.

V

The final part of the homily, introduced with the rubric *De Eius Obitu*, is an account of the saint's last days (lines 270-313) followed by a post-mortem event (lines 314–32). For the former, Ælfric draws upon Sulpicius's *Epistula Tertia*, a letter to his mother-in-law Bassula, in which he supplements his *Vita*, apparently written while the saint was alive, with a description of his death and its circumstances. It is a full description linked into one large story, with five consecutive scenes: the saint's foreknowledge of his own death, his journey to one of his monasteries to settle a discordance among the monks, his announcement of his impending

---

was praying, and said that he verily was Jesus. Martin then looked on the fiend's splendour, mindful in mind how the Creator Lord said in his gospel of his divine advent, and he said to the false one with learned mouth, "Our Saviour said not that he would be so habited in purple, or with crown shining, when he should come again with a host of angels." Then the devil vanished from him sad, and the place stank with an exceedingly great stench, after the presence of the terrific spirit.'

[51] 'Martin, why do you hesitate to believe, when you see?'
[52] Ælfric uses the verb *hiwian* in reference to a woman who pretended to be ill (line 112).

death and the disciples' bewailing, the saint on his deathbed, and his passing away. Ælfric follows this seamless succession closely, and the homily is now not shortened from the source so drastically. Still, Ælfric sometimes abridges boldly. Thus, when the saint hears the lamentations of the disciples in the third scene, he is assigned only one speech to make to God, which is condensed from the two speeches, intervened by narrative sentences, in the *Epistula* (148.16–17; 148.21–149.2). The abridged speech is not only much briefer but is more resolute, with the God-trusting supplication 'beo ðin willa .a. weroda drihten'[53] placed at its end (line 295). Again, the disciples, having made lamentations and pleas, are no longer present in the third scene, though they continue to have a role there in the *Epistula* (149.8–18), worrying about the saint's illness and trying in more than one way to make him comfortable as he lay on the earth. By removing the disciples from the scene, Ælfric leaves Martin alone in prayer, facing death and devil heroically, and hastens to the last moment, which he introduces with the phrase *oð þæt* 'until', a formula he often uses to introduce a climax:[54] 'and ne geswac his gebeda. oð þæt he sawlode'[55] (lines 299–300).

As before, Ælfric intersperses this condensed narrative with affective epithets which are original with him and which help to make the *sententia* of the narrative explicit as a substitute for comments. The epithets occur with intense concentration in two passages that describe Martin confronting the devil (devil himself and devil in simile). Thus, in the second of the five scenes, the saint, en route to a monastery, sees some fowls pursuing fish in a river and calls them *ehtende* 'chasing; persecuting' (line 276), likening them to the devils who *grædelice gripað to grimre helle* 'greedily snatch to the grim hell' the unwary (lines 278–79, with a striking alliteration). In the later passage describing the saint on his deathbed, the confrontation is intensified by more distinctive epithets for the saint and the devil:

> *ÆCHom* II, 39.300 He geseah ðone deofol standan swiðe gehende. and hine orsorhlice axian ongann; Þu wælhreowe nyten to hwi stenst ðu þus gehende? Ne gemetst þu on me. aht witniendlices. Me soðlice underfehð se heahfæder Abraham. into his wununge on ecere wynne; Æfter ðisum worde gewat seo sawul of ðam geswenctan lichaman sona to gode.[56]

The contrast between *orsorhlice* for one and *wælhreowe* for the other closely parallels the contrast in the earlier passage on the saint and Emperor Julian (see III) — a parallelism which reinforces the representation of the saint and his adversary as types rather than individuals; and the homiletic formulas such as *on ecere wynne* and *gewat seo sawul of ðam geswenctan lichaman* in the following clauses reinforce that approach to the narrative. None of the four phrases (except perhaps *wælhreowe*) is prompted by the *Epistula* (where we read: 'haec locutus diabolum uidit prope adsistere. quid hic, inquit, adstas cruenta bestia? [...] Cum hac ergo uoce spiritum reddidit'[57] (149.16–19)), and *on ecere wynne* is an addition not found in the telling in the *Lives of Saints* (*ÆLS* 31.1368).

---

[53] 'be thy will for ever, Lord of hosts!'
[54] Ælfric employs this conjunctive phrase earlier in lines 62, 87, 112, and 159. For Ælfric's usage in comparison with the phrase in prose romance, see my study 'Stylistic Features of the Old English *Apollonius of Tyre*', in Hiroshi Ogawa, *Studies in the History of Old English Prose* (Tokyo: Nan'undo, 2000), pp. 181–204 (pp. 193–95).
[55] 'and ceased not his prayers until he expired.'
[56] 'He saw the devil standing very near at hand, and began fearlessly to ask him: "Thou bloodthirsty beast, why standest thou thus at hand? Thou wilt not find in me aught that is punishable; but me will the patriarch Abraham receive into his dwelling in eternal joy." After these words, the soul forthwith departed from its afflicted body to God.'
[57] 'Having spoken these words, he saw the devil standing close at hand, and exclaimed: "Why do you stand here, thou bloody monster? [...]" As he uttered these words, his spirit fled.'

Then follow in rapid succession words for 'light' and 'shining' and other colourful expressions, all bearing obvious symbolism and describing in a long and poetic sentence the glory in which the saint's body is raised to heaven:[58] 'His lic wearð gesewen sona on wuldre. beorhtre ðonne glæs. hwittre ðonne meoloc. and his andwlita scean swiðor þonne leoht. þa iu gewuldrod to ðam toweardan æriste'[59] (lines 307–10). Ælfric probably owed much of the idea and material for this 'colourful description' (and the surrounding descriptions of the angels singing and the lamentations) to some preceding version or versions, as Godden points out.[60] But the arrangement is his own. *His lic* comes first, before *his andwlita*, unlike the order in the *Epistula* (149.19–150.1); and the balanced clauses are bound closely by the alliteration of *wuldre* and its derivative *gewuldrod*, a key feature that may well be Ælfric's own addition, judging from a variant reading of the *Epistula* which is otherwise very close to Ælfric's wording here.[61]

Ælfric finally turns to a post-mortem event which enhances the sanctity of the saint — a contest between the people of Tours and Poitiers for a superior claim to his body. It is at this point that Ælfric for the first time gives us an indication that what we have been reading is a preaching text, for he uses the verb *gehyran* 'hear' in introducing the narrative (*Is eac to gehyrenne* 'It is also to be heard' (line 314)), implying the presence of an audience he addresses. This is matched by another mark of preaching — a reference to the saint's feast on which the homily is delivered — which occurs immediately following the telling of the contest: 'On ðisum dæge gewat se halga wer to gode. mærlice of worulde. mid micclum wundrum geglencged'[62] (lines 328–29, with a striking alternation of alliterations on 'w', 'g' and 'm').[63] This poetic address to the audience trails off into a prayer for the saint's intercession and the final doxology. These last lines would seem rather abrupt, as there was nothing to match them at the homily's opening, neither a reference to the saint's feast nor a naming of source texts which would have helped to authorize the following homily. Whether this omission of a standard opening was deliberate or not is difficult to say with certainty. But it may tell its own tale of Ælfric's 'change of heart about the genre', showing the homilist already breaking away from the conventional form of hagiographical homily, much as he departs from the conventional division of narrative and commentary, in the present homily.

VI

Ælfric's life of Martin is a hagiographical homily which, like his other later works of the genre in the *Catholic Homilies*, no longer shares his earlier features such as 'a saint as preacher' and commentary and discussion of doctrinal issues prompted by the narrative.[64] But it has new recurrent features which sustain him in adapting the hagiographical narrative for his preaching purpose. Ælfric achieves this homiletic mode in narrative by deploying two

---

[58] For a study of the 'light' symbolism in Old English, see Hugh Magennis, 'Hagiographical Imagery of Light and Ælfric's "Passion of St Dionysius" ', *Leeds Studies in English*, 37 (2006), 209–28.

[59] 'His corpse forthwith appeared in glory, brighter than glass, whiter than milk, and his face shone more than light, then already glorified for the future resurrection.'

[60] Godden, *Commentary*, pp. 632–33, note to lines 296–313.

[61] See Godden, *Commentary*, pp. 632–33, note to lines 296–313.

[62] 'On this day the holy man departed to God, gloriously from the world, with great miracles adorned.'

[63] Letson ('The Form', p. 425) has noted that the homily has 'an *uton* passage' (inviting the audience to pray for Martin's intercession) and 'the customary doxology', but does not mention the opening *Is eac to gehyrenne [...]*.

[64] See Godden, 'Experiments in Genre', p. 266.

powerful techniques. For one thing, he often abridges the account given in his source texts, paring the narrative to the saint and his immediate adversaries and those of their actions which reinforce his emphases in the homiletic framework into which he recasts a hagiography and thereby developing a prose which is 'striking in its starkness'. This feature of style has a thematic consequence. Focusing on the progress of action which he tells mostly with the assertive verb forms in the preterite tense, Ælfric presents the hagiographical events and their meanings as truths, projecting the omniscient author as a homilist, and represents the protagonist saint as a man of absolute sanctity, occasionally to the point of heroicization (see IV). Based on this manipulative use of narrative style, Ælfric has produced a hagiographical narrative which embodies within itself the *sententia* of the events it recalls; Ælfric gives the *sententia* in narrative form, rather than in commentary.

The *sententia* Ælfric gives in this way is reinforced by the other of his distinctive techniques in this homily — the use of affective epithets designed to sharpen the antithesis of 'a protagonist saint and his adversary' and 'good and evil', which is typically seen in the descriptions of the saint in conflict with Emperor Julian and the idol-worshippers (see III and IV, respectively). As a result, the epithets are often formulaic. One consequence of this formulaic vocabulary is its emphasis on the saint and his adversary as types rather than individualized examples of the type. Another consequence is what would seem as a 'misplaced' use of an epithet, seen at least once in this homily in the use of the phrase *þæt læne lif* 'the transitory life in this world'. Its implication is exactly what is called for in describing the saint's passing away as 'he ferde fram eallum frecednyssum ðises lænan lifes to his leofan drihtne'[65] (lines 270–72). But it seems slightly incongruous as an epithet for a man who has just been restored to life by virtue of the saint's prayer, to the joy and wonder of his mother and the people watching them: 'he sona aras to ðam lænan life þe he ær forlet; Þurh ðam tacne gelyfdon of ðære leode gehwilce on ðone lifigendan god. ðe hine to life arærde'[66] (lines 149–52).

Seen in a wider perspective, the formulaic vocabulary is obviously related to what Godden calls 'universalizing hagiographic diction',[67] common in the later hagiographical homilies in the *Catholic Homilies*. The epithets 'se halga', almost invariably the epithet for Martin from line 77 onwards, and 'se wælhreowa' referring to Emperor Julian and the devil, are the clearest examples of such diction, as he notes.[68] But usage is more flexible and varied in other vocabulary items. For example, the word *geswæs* 'gentle, pleasing' is used both in the sense of Christian charity (in 'He wæs swiðe geswæs eallum swincendum', lines 24–25 (see above, n. 21), and 'ða ungeðwæran preostas ðreade [...] and on sibbe gebrohte mid geswæsre lare', lines 283–84)[69] and in the sense of sweet words of flattery (in 'He nolde olæcan ænigum rican mid geswæsum wordum', lines 251–52).[70] More interesting are words meaning 'to shine'. While they usually refer in this homily to a saint (Martin or Hilary) with their obvious symbolism, as in 'the colourful description' of Martin passing away (lines 307–10; see V), and also in

---

[65] 'he went from all the perils of this miserable life to his dear Lord.'
[66] 'he forthwith arose to the poor life that he had before left. Through this miracle all of that people believed in the Living God, who had raised him to life.'
[67] Godden, 'Experiments in Genre', p. 280.
[68] Godden, 'Experiments in Genre', p. 280.
[69] 'rebuked the discordant priests [...] and brought them in peace with kind advice.'
[70] 'He would not flatter any powerful man with sweet words.' Elsewhere Ælfric uses the phrase *mid geswæsum wordum* in referring to John's teaching (*ÆCHom* I, 4.204). On this example, see Robert K. Upchurch, 'Homiletic Contexts for Ælfric's Hagiography: The Legend of Saints Cecelia and Valerian', in *The Old English Homily: Precedent, Practice, and Appropriation*, ed. by Aaron Kleist (Turnhout: Brepols, 2007), pp. 265–84 (pp. 281–82).

Sententia *in Narrative Form*

'hilarium [...] scinende swa swa tungel. on soðre lare' (lines 60–61) and 'men gesawon scinan færlice æt his [Martin's] hnolle swilce fyren clywen. swa þæt se scinenda lig his locc up ateah' (lines 241–43),[71] they are occasionally used with descriptive purpose, as in referring to the shining sword ('ðam scinendan brande', line 191)[72] of a man who threatens to kill the saint and the devil's splendour ('þæs sceoccan leoht', line 232). In these last two cases, the relevant words serve to represent the adversaries sensationally, emphasizing them as a foil to the saint who is steadfast in confronting the dangers. This mixture of the two uses, universalizing and descriptive, might be worth a fuller consideration in comparison with other late hagiographical homilies in the *Catholic Homilies*, such as those on Cuthbert and Benedict.[73]

As I noted in passing where appropriate in the preceding analysis, the hagiographical diction, primarily a reinforcement of the *sententia*, is often also an important element of the alliterative prose in which much of the homily is written. Examples not mentioned previously include the poetic *folde* 'earth' in 'he hit underfenge feallende to foldan. and hi hit forcurfon' (line 165; see IV), the single occurrence of the poetic *metod* in 'gemyndig on mode. hu se metoda drihten cwæð [...]' (lines 232–33), beside the four common words for 'God' (*god*, *drihten* (the usual form in the saint's speeches), *crist*, and *hælend*),[74] and the alliteration combined with wordplay on words of related meaning in 'he gehælde an mæden mid halwendum smyrelse gehalgodes ele' (lines 152–53). Frequent alliteration is another hallmark of the Martin homily shared by other later hagiographical homilies in the *Catholic Homilies*, notably the one on Cuthbert, and as such it needs to be examined in more detail than I have been able to consider in this study, both in its own right and in relation to the later form of Ælfric's rhythmical prose as he uses it in the *Lives of Saints* and other works.[75] How this and other rhythmical features can be seen at work in enhancing the effect of the narrative method Ælfric deploys in the Martin homily and how they represent, in a more regularized and mature way, an organizing principle of the narrative style in his later hagiographies are problems that remain to be explored in studying Ælfric's changing attitude to the genre and its consequences for his use of language and his prose style.

---

[71] Lines 60–61: 'Hilary [...] shining as a star with true learning'; lines 241–43: 'men saw suddenly shining on his crown as it were a fiery circlet, so that the shining flame drew up his locks'. Szarmach calls the first of these an 'imagistic line' and notes that Ælfric uses 'no similes' in the corresponding part of his later version ('Ælfric Revises', p. 50).

[72] Godden notes: 'Neither source has anything as colourful as *scinendan brande* (line 191)' (*Commentary*, p. 630, note to lines 189–96).

[73] On the diction in the life of Cuthbert, see Godden, 'Experiments in Genre', pp. 278–79; and Peter Clemoes, 'Ælfric', in *Continuations and Beginnings: Studies in Old English Literature*, ed. by E. G. Stanley (London: Nelson, 1966), pp. 176–209 (p. 206).

[74] For *foldan* in line 165, see Roberta Frank, 'Poetic Words in Late Old English Prose', in *From Anglo-Saxon to Early Middle English*, ed. by Malcolm Godden, Douglas Gray and Terry Hoad (Oxford: Clarendon Press, 1994), pp. 87–107 (p. 96). As for *metod*, M. R. Godden has pointed out that there are five uses of the word in Ælfric, all 'in passages where he was experimenting with a form of alliterating rhythmical prose': 'Literary Language', in *The Cambridge History of the English Language. Volume I: The Beginnings to 1066*, ed. by Richard M. Hogg (Cambridge: Cambridge University Press, 1992), pp. 490–535 (p. 498). See further Godden, 'Ælfric's Changing Vocabulary', *English Studies*, 61 (1980), 206–23 (pp. 217–19).

[75] On the development of Ælfric's rhythmical prose, see *Homilies of Ælfric: A Supplementary Collection*, ed. by J. C. Pope, *Early English Text Society*, o. s., 259 and 260, 2 vols (London: Oxford University Press, 1967–68), i, pp. 105–36; and James Hurt, *Ælfric* (New York: Twayne Publishers, 1972), pp. 125–37.

Infinitival Complements with the Verb *(ge)don* in Old English: Latin Influence Revisited

Olga Timofeeva

Introduction

The emergence of the accusative-and-infinitive constructions (ACI) with causative *(ge)dōn*[1] 'to do, make' — such as *þu dydest minne broðer his god forlætan* discussed below — and *to*-verb-phrase (VP) constructions with *(ge)dōn* — *He dide ðone king to understanden* — has been described in secondary literature as both 'ultimately due to Latin influence'[2] and as a native Old English development.[3] The former claim is based on the evidence from the Old English translations, in which *(ge)don* with infinitival complement is used to render Latin ACI constructions with causative *facere* 'to make';[4] while the latter relates the rise of this construction to variation and change in the argument structure of *(ge)don*, which can be employed as a three-place verb 'to give, grant' taking NP-*to*-VP complements, and as a two-place verb 'to make' taking ACI and *that*-clause complements.[5]

My aim in this article is by no means to produce a final judgement on this debate but to show that both claims about the origin of the *(ge)don* with infinitival complement describe

---

[1] I use the spelling *(ge)don* to refer collectively to both the prefixed verb *gedon* and the simplex *don*.

[2] Morgan Callaway, Jr., *The Infinitive in Anglo-Saxon* (Washington, D.C.: Carnegie Institution, 1913), p. 205; cf. Alvar Ellegård, *The Auxiliary 'Do' : The Establishment and Regulation of its Use in English*, Gothenburg Studies in English, 2 (Stockholm: Almqvist & Wiksell, 1953), p. 54; Manfred Scheler, 'Altenglische Lehnsyntax: Die syntaktischen Latinismen im Altenglischen', Ph.D. dissertation (Berlin: Freie Universität, 1961), p. 99.

[3] e.g. James Finch Royster, 'Old English Causative Verbs', *Studies in Philology*, 19 (1922), 328–56 (p. 345); Olga Fischer, 'The Origin and Spread of the Accusative and Infinitive Construction in English', *Folia Linguistica Historica*, 8.1–2 (1989), 143–217 (pp. 187–9); Bettelou Los, *The Rise of 'To' -Infinitive* (Oxford: Oxford University Press, 2005), pp. 134–36.

[4] Causative *facere* with ACI complements is attested already in Classical Latin, but becomes widespread only in Late and Medieval Latin, with variation being still possible between ACI, *ut*-, and *quod*-complements. See Alfred Ernout and François Thomas, *Syntax latine* (Paris: Librairie C. Klincksieck, 1953), pp. 296–303 (p. 329); R. A. Browne, *British Latin Selections, A.D. 500–1400* (Oxford: Blackwell, 1954), pp. xxvii–xxviii; Veikko Väänänen, *Introduction au latin vulgaire* (Paris: Éditions Klincksieck, 1981), pp. 139–40; Michele Fruyt, 'Grammaticalisation and Latin', in *Historical Linguistics 2003: Selected Papers from the 16th International Conference on Historical Linguistics, Copenhagen, 11–15 August 2003*, ed. by Michael Fortescue, Eva Skafte Jensen, Jens Erik Mogensen and Lene Schøsler (Amsterdam: Benjamins, 2005), pp. 131–39 (pp. 131–32). The Latin part of my research corpus represents the two later varieties of Latin.

[5] Los, *The Rise of 'To'-Infinitive*, p. 136.

the situation only partially. In the long diachrony, these claims can actually complement each other. In other words, while the Latin-based hypothesis better describes early and classical Old English, the native-based one applies more to late Old English and the transitional period. Moreover, I suggest that although the calques of the Latin *facere*-ACI are indicative of Latin influence in this domain of syntax, transformations of these structures in Old English translations are equally meaningful and can signal important incompatibilities between the two language systems. I also show that in many cases a close philological analysis of the wider context of a particular text reveals intricate syntactic dependencies between what are considered original Old English compositions and their Latin sources. It seems, therefore, necessary to distinguish an intermediate category of texts that are not translations proper, in that they do not go back to one particular source text, nor are they original Old English texts because they exhibit affinities to one or more Latin sources. Before I proceed to the contrastive analysis of my Latin and Old English data, I will briefly describe my research corpus.

The research corpus, its scope and timeframe

The corpus that I used for this study consists of two contrasted samples: a) Sample 1 — written Old English as independent from Latin as possible, based on a selection from the *York-Toronto-Helsinki Parsed Corpus of Old English Prose* (*YCOE*)[6] and representing five text types: laws, charters, correspondence, chronicle narrative, and homily/life narrative (274,757 words); and b) Sample 2 — written Old English closely dependent on the Latin originals, based on editions of two gloss texts, five translations, and Latin originals of these texts, representing four text types: hymns, religious regulations, homily/life narrative, and biblical narrative (180,622 words).[7]

Working with Sample 2, I made syntagmatic comparisons between the Latin originals and Old English translations of edited texts, and documented all the possible renderings of *facere*-ACI constructions into Old English. For Sample 1, I retrieved data (e.g., *(ge)don* with infinitival or *that*-clause complements) by using CorpusSearch programme, and checked them still against the searches in the *Dictionary of Old English Corpus* (*DOEC*), to make sure that I got all the relevant instances of *(ge)don* within my *YCOE* selection. I use normalised orthography in examples from the *YCOE* and occasionally extend them if some important context is needed. Analysing data from Sample 1, I also consulted the online database of the *Fontes Anglo-Saxonici*, which enabled me to trace some of the infinitive constructions in the original Old English texts back to their Latin prototypes.

---

[6] *The York-Toronto-Helsinki Parsed Corpus of Old English Prose* (*YCOE*), compiled by Ann Taylor, Anthony Warner, Susan Pintzuk and Frank Beths (University of York, 2003), <http://www-users.york.ac.uk/~lang22/YcoeHome1.htm> [accessed 18 February 2011].

[7] The size of the samples may look small to corpus linguists, but it should be kept in mind that surviving Old English accounts only for some 3,000,000 words, a major of part of this consisting of glosses, translations and manuscript variants of essentially the same texts (*The Dictionary of Old English Web Corpus* (*DOEC*), ed. by Antonette diPaolo Healey and others (Toronto: University of Toronto, 2009), <http://tapor.library.utoronto.ca/doecorpus> [accessed 18 February 2011]), so that a balanced and representative contrastive corpus is really difficult to compile. Historical linguists working with this material basically have to make the best of the available data, which, as I am going to show below, is very restricted both socially and linguistically. A detailed description of the corpus and criteria used for the selection of texts can be found in Olga Timofeeva, *Non-finite Constructions in Old English, with Special Reference to Syntactic Borrowing from Latin*, Mémoires de la Société Néophilologique de Helsinki, 80 (Helsinki: Société Néophilologique, 2010), pp. 3–8.

Since the early 1990s, the accepted periodisation of Old English has been the fourfold distinction represented in Table 1.[8] In this study, however, the amount of my data did not allow me to retain this division, especially in the two early sub-periods, so I had to lump OE1 and OE2, and OE3 and OE4 together; I refer to this twofold periodisation as early Old English (eOE) and late Old English (lOE), respectively.

OE1	–850
OE2	850–950
OE3	950–1050
OE4	1050–1150

Table 1. Periodisation of Old English in the *Helsinki Corpus*

Analysis

1. Old English causative verbs

In Old English basic syntactic causatives are formed of the negative causative *lætan* 'to let, allow' and positive causative *hātan* 'to order, command' plus infinitive. I will give a brief overview of these two verbs before I proceed to the analysis of *(ge)don*.

With causative *lætan* two syntactic patterns prevail: *lætan* + bare infinitive of transitive verbs with implicit causees (*lætan*-Inf, 55 per cent of infinitival constructions with *lætan* in my data) and *lætan* + bare infinitive of intransitive verbs with explicit accusative causees (*lætan*-ACI, 45 per cent), cf. (a) and (b) below:

(.1) (a) *[se cyng...] let   niman   of hire eall þæt heo ahte*
       the king   let-PAST take-INF of her   all   that she owned

   [the king...] made-take/took from her all that she owned (ChronE 1048.82; late Old English)

   (b) *7   a   hi   leton   heora feonda wærod   wexan*
       and ever they let-PAST their enemies' army-ACC grow-INF

   and they would let their enemy's army grow (ChronE 999.11; late Old English)

The constructions with implicit causees seem fairly co-lexicalised[9] and the majority of the tokens (c. 77 per cent of *lætan*-Inf constructions in my data) follows the word order in which the infinitive directly follows the main verb.[10] In these, *lætan* appears to be used primarily as

---

[8] *Early English in the Computer Age: Explorations through the* Helsinki Corpus, ed. by Matti Rissanen, Merja Kytö, and Minna Palander-Collin, Topics in English Linguistics, 11 (Berlin: Mouton de Gruyter, 1993); Merja Kytö, *Manual to the Diachronic Part of the 'Helsinki Corpus of English Texts' : Coding Conventions and Lists of Source Texts*, 3rd edn (Helsinki: University of Helsinki, 1996).

[9] Co-lexicalisation occurs when the main verb and complement verb form one unit and share one set of grammatical relations. See, e.g., Michael Noonan, 'Complementation', in *Language Typology and Syntactic Description, vol. 2: Complex Constructions*, ed. by Timothy Shopen (Cambridge: Cambridge University Press, 1985), pp. 42–140 (p. 75).

[10] Timofeeva, *Non-finite Constructions in Old English*, pp. 95–101; cf. Noonan, 'Complementation', pp. 73–6; Talmy

Infinitival Complements with the Verb '(ge)don' in Old English

the marker of implicative causation, as in (1a). Typically, causees in such sentences are either unimportant or, more rarely, retrievable from previous context.[11] Since many Old English texts are historical narratives (varying from chronicles to hagiographies), with more or less standard sets of events, their sequences and end points, *lætan*-Inf construction seems to an extent to be genre-specific. When Anglo-Saxon kings in these texts make their commands, the main thing is that they are fulfilled, regardless of who carries them out.[12]

With *lætan*-ACI constructions, the word order *lætan*-NP$_{Acc}$-Inf prevails (60 per cent of *lætan*-ACI constructions in my data); while yet another portion of material (28 per cent) consists of collocations, such as *lætan-faran/gangan* 'to let-go, release', which, again, could be seen as co-lexicalised items, with *lætan* marking both causation and transitivity.[13]

Lætan never takes *to*-infinitive complements,[14] but it can take finite clausal complements. Their frequency, however, is quite low, with all tokens coming from late Old English. Moreover, these typically demonstrate a shift in the semantics of *lætan* from causation to cognition, along the lines 'let > allow > admit > consider'.[15]

Although co-lexicalised structures with *lætan* are attested already in eOE, frequency-wise *hatan* appears to be the default verb of causation — in the YCOE, it is about nine times more frequent than *lætan*, let alone other verbs of causation.[16] *Hatan* takes bare-infinitive complements with implicit causees (*hatan*-Inf, 78 per cent of my data on *hatan*), bare-infinitive complements with explicit accusative causees (*hatan*-ACI, 14 per cent), and finite subjunctive and indicative complements (*hatan*-that, 9 per cent), cf. the examples in 2(a–c) below.

(.2) (a) *ond   he het   wyrcan   gyldeno godgeld ond seolfrene*
        and   he order-PAST   make-INF gold   idols   and silver

        and he made [people] make gold and silver idols (Mart 5 [Kotzor] Jy19, A.5; early Old English)

    (b) *7 Se cyng het   þone   arcebisceop Wulfstan þærto*
        and the king order-PAST   the-ACC archbishop Wulfstan thereto
        boc   settan
        charter set-INF

        and the king ordered-to/made archbishop Wulfstan prepare a charter to this end (Ch 1460 [Rob 83] 8.126; late Old English)

    (c) *forðanþe Crist het,   þæt mann æte   þæt*
        for   Christ command-PAST that man   eat-PAST-SUBJ the-ACC
        husl
        host

     Givón, *Syntax: An Introduction*, 2 vols (Amsterdam: Benjamins, 2001), ii, pp. 59–63.
[11] Cf. Bruce Mitchell, *Old English Syntax*, 2 vols (Oxford: Clarendon Press, 1985), §3763; Taro Kageyama, 'AGR in Old English to-infinitives', *Lingua*, 88 (1992), pp. 91–128 (p. 113); David Denison, *English Historical Syntax* (London: Longman, 1993), p. 189; Los, *The Rise of 'To'-Infinitive*, pp. 15–16.
[12] Cf. Los, *The Rise of 'To'-Infinitive*, pp. 103–4.
[13] Timofeeva, *Non-finite Constructions in Old English*, pp. 101–6.
[14] Cf. Fischer, 'The Origin and Spread of the Accusative and Infinitive', pp. 187–90; Los, *The Rise of 'To'-Infinitive*, p. 107.
[15] e.g., *Manige men leton þæt hit cometa wære* 'many people allowed/thought that it was a comet' (ChronE 1097.21); see Timofeeva, *Non-finite Constructions in Old English*, pp. 106–7.
[16] The absolute number of examples of *lætan* with infinitival complement is 131 and of *hatan* 1167 (Timofeeva,

for Christ commanded that man ate the host (ÆLet 1 [Wulfsige Xa] 84.101; late Old English)

With implicit causees, direct sequences of *hatan* and infinitive, as *het wyrcan* in (2a), are less frequent than *lætan*-Inf (only about 26 per cent of the *hatan*-Inf constructions). Moreover, many of them tend to occur in collocations of *hatan* with a verb of utterance, such as *hatan-secgan* 'to command to say, make known'.[17]

Causative *hatan* with explicit accusative causees is less frequent and allows a lot of variation in the order of the constituents belonging to this construction. Most typically, however, it follows the pattern *hatan*-NP$_{Acc}$-Inf, in which an object of the infinitive (2b) or an adverb may intervene between the accusative causee and the infinitive.[18] Just as *lætan*, *hatan* never takes *to*-VP complements in Old English. Most importantly perhaps, *hatan* allows variation between infinitival and finite complements (2c). Finite complements typically occur in contexts that imply that there is no co-temporality between the causing and caused events, no direct contact between the causer and causee, that the causer exercises only weak control over the causee, which may retain its own intentionality.[19] This suggests that finite complements after *hatan* code weaker causation, compared to infinitival complements.

To conclude, Old English typically employs two verbs to code strong causation: *lætan* and *hatan*. Both of them seem to develop more grammatical meanings towards the later Old English period: *lætan* follows the semantic path of 'allow > let > make', and *hatan* that of 'tell > order > make'. Further, they contrast with other causative verbs (both strong, such as *nīedan* 'to force, urge', and weak, such as *tǣcan* 'to show, instruct, direct') in that (i) they are much more frequent, and (ii) show a clear preference for infinitival complements. Yet, we know that the Middle English period saw the rise of another causative construction, that of *don* with infinitival complements.[20] We are now going to see whether this development can already be seen in the Old English data. I will first present my material from the independent Old English texts (Sample 1) and the data from the *Dictionary of Old English* (*DOE*), and then compare it against the Old English renderings of the Latin *facere*-ACI construction in translations (Sample 2).

2. *(ge)don* in original Old English texts[21]

In my selection from the *YCOE* (Sample 1), *(ge)don* with infinitival complements is to be found only in late Old English texts.[22] For example, in Ælfric's *Catholic Homilies I*, there are two occurrences within the same passage (3a). Although this collection of homilies is an original

Non-finite Constructions in Old English, pp. 95, 108). Cf. Royster, 'Old English Causative Verbs', p. 351; Ellegård, *The Auxiliary 'Do'*, pp. 48, 55.

[17] Timofeeva, *Non-finite Constructions in Old English*, pp. 109–13.
[18] Timofeeva, *Non-finite Constructions in Old English*, pp. 116–17.
[19] Timofeeva, *Non-finite Constructions in Old English*, pp. 117–18; cf. Givón, *Syntax*, pp. 43–49; Willem B. Hollmann, 'Synchrony and Diachrony of English Periphrastic Causatives: A Cognitive Perspective' (unpublished doctoral thesis, University of Manchester, 2003), pp. 146–49, <http://www.lancaster.ac.uk/staff/hollmann/WBH_PhD_causatives.pdf> [accessed on 18 February 2011].
[20] e.g., Royster, 'Old English Causative Verbs', pp. 342–45; Ellegård, *The Auxiliary 'Do'*, pp. 43–7, 118; Los, *The Rise of 'To'-Infinitive*, p. 135.
[21] This section is an extended version of the sub-section (GE)DON in my dissertation (Timofeeva, *Non-finite Constructions in Old English*, pp. 126–28).
[22] Cf. Callaway, *The Infinitive in Anglo-Saxon*, p. 205.

work, many of its episodes (as is often the case with medieval vernacular compilations) go back to Latin sources (3b).

(.3) (a) *swa swa þu dydest minne broðer his god forlætan [...]*
so as thou do-PAST my-ACC brother his god forsake-INF [...]
swa do ic eac þe forlætan þinne god
so do-PRES I also thou-ACC forsake-INF thy god

as you made my brother forsake his god ... so (will) I also make you forsake your god (ÆCHom I, 31: 446.214; late Old English)

(b) *sicut tu fecisti fratrem meum ut*
as thou make-PERF brother-ACC my-ACC that
relinqueret deum sum [...] ita te ego
forsake-IMPERF-SUBJ-3SG god his [...] so thou-ACC I
faciam derelinquere deum tuum
make-FUT-INDIC forsake-INF god thy

as you made my brother forsake his god ... so will I make you forsake your god

Although it cannot be assumed that the two *(ge)don*-ACIs above are used independently of Latin, it is remarkable that the subjunctive complement of the Latin source *ut relinqueret* is changed into a second (linearly the first) ACI. This transformation has to do with the fact that Old English *(ge)don* does not allow an accusative NP in the main clause if it is followed by a finite complement — it always appears in the construction *do that* ..., never in *do NP that* ...,[23] which perhaps makes a word-for-word rendering of *tu fecisti fratrem meum ut relinqueret* impossible. I suggest that in the analysis of the structural correspondences between source and target texts, such texts as Ælfric's *Catholic Homilies* should be classified as intermediate between original Old English compositions and translations.

Five more infinitival complements with *(ge)don* are found in the later extension of the *Peterborough Chronicle* (c. 1155). Three of these (ChronE 1123.55, ChronE 1127.25, ChronE 1128.10) are *to*-infinitives, occurring in a collocation *don to understanden(ne)*, e.g.

(.4) *He dide ðone king to understanden þet he wolde mid alle*
he do-PAST the-ACC king to understand-INF that he would withal
forlæten þone minstre
forsake the minster

he made/gave the king to understand that he would give up the monastery completely (ChronE 1128.10; late Old English)

Los suggests that *don to understandenne* is a set phrase and analyses *don* in such contexts as a three-place verb with the sense 'to give, grant', deriving 'from a reanalysis of the [_ NP NP] frame' of the kind *to do someone a favour*.[24] My own proximity searches in the *DOEC* produced 6 tokens of *don to understandenne*: LS 22 (InFestisSMarie) 11, Eluc 1 (Warn 45) 99, Ch 1101 (Harm 49) 2, ChronE 1123.55, ChronE 1127.25, ChronE 1128.10. There is also

---

[23] Fischer, 'The Origin and Spread of the Accusative and Infinitive', p. 188; Los, *The Rise of 'To'-Infinitive*, pp. 134, 136.
[24] Los, *The Rise of 'To'-Infinitive*, p. 135.

one example with a bare infinitive *deþ understandan* glossing Latin *facit intellegere* in LibSc 78.26. Together with Los's findings,[25] these statistics seem to suggest that the use of the *to*-VP complement was very limited (more on this below). My fifth example, however, contains a bare infinitive:

(.5) þat   te   king   sende efter   him   7   dide   him   gyuen   up   ðat
     that the   king   sent   after   him   and do-PAST   he-DAT   give-INF   up   the

     abbotrice   of   Burch   7   faren   ut   of   lande
     abbacy   of   Peterborough   and   go-INF   out   of   land

   that the king sent after him and made him give up the abbacy of Peterborough and leave the country (ChronE 1132.9; late Old English)

Once again, this example is very late and may reflect a new development within the causation paradigm. On the surface, it may seem that the structure contains a dative causee. However, this late in the Old English period the distinction between the accusative form *hine* and the dative *him* (which eventually contaminated both grammatical meanings) was not properly maintained (similarly in (ChronE 1140.21)). Moreover, my evidence on unequivocally native use of bare infinitives with *(ge)don* is limited to (ChronE 1132.9) and (ChronE 1140.21).

Overall, finite complements after *(ge)don* prevail[26] — 33 instances in Sample 1 (as opposed to seven infinitival complements discussed earlier in this section). Two examples of *that*-complements will suffice:

(.6) 7   dyde   þa   mid   drycræfte   þæt   ðær   comon   micele
      and   do-PAST   then   with   magic   that there come-PAST-INDIC   big

      hundas   7   ræsdon   wið   Petres   weard
      dogs   and   rush-PAST-INDIC   towards   Peter

   and he made then by magic that big dogs came there and rushed towards Peter (ÆCHom I, 26: 395.189; late Old English)

(.7) He   deð   þæt   fyr   cymð   ufene,   swylce   hit   of
      he   do-PRES   that   fire   come-PRES-INDIC   from above   as if   it   of

      heofonum   cume
      heaven   come-PRES-SUBJ

   he will make the fire come from above, as if it come from heaven (WHom 4: 62.143; late Old English)

As has already been observed, these constructions do not contain causees in the main clause. It is worth mentioning that *(ge)don* with finite complements is equally frequent in early and later Old English (0.99 per 10,000 words and 0.96 per 10,000 words, respectively, with data from the complete *YCOE* being taken into account). However, in both periods its use — just as with the use of ACI complements — is mostly limited to translated texts and compilations.

To sum up this subsection, *(ge)don* with NP-*to*-VP complements seems to occur mainly in set phrases, while the evidence on *(ge)don*-ACIs does not suggest that the construction was in wide circulation before the transition from the Old to Middle English period. I will now compare my corpus findings to the data in the *don* and *gedon* entries in the *Dictionary of Old English*.

---

[25] Los, *The Rise of 'To'-Infinitive*, pp. 135–6.
[26] Cf. Royster, 'Old English Causative Verbs', pp. 337–43.

3. *(ge)don* in the Dictionary of Old English

The *DOE* lists examples of causative *(ge)don* under *don* III.A (10 instances) and *gedon* 2.a. (9 instances). Of these, five examples are from glosses imitating Latin *facere* (4 occurrences) and *fingere* 'to make, pretend' (1 occurrence) with infinitival complements: PPs 67.6; PPs 103.30; LkGl (Li) 24.28; PsCaA 1 7.58; MkGl (Li) 6.39. Six more examples are either found in overt translations from Latin or in compilations based upon several Latin sources: ÆCHom I, 31 446.214 (discussed above in ex. 3a); Bede 4 24.334.16; LS 7 (Euphr) 315; ChrodR 1 80.68; HomU 7 163; LS 1.1 (AndrewBright) 165.[27] Both groups therefore have to be viewed as Latin-based.

Further, five examples appear to be set phrases similar to those described in the previous sub-section. These contain *(ge)don* with *to*-VP (4 occurrences) or bare infinitive (1 occurrence): CP 46.357.4; ÆCHom II, 18 170.35; Or 3 9.69.28; and two versions of Prov 1 1.9. The NPs in these examples are either nominal dative or pronominal indistinguishable between dative and accusative. The complement VPs in all five occurrences share the same verb *witan* 'to know', which seems to suggest a pattern — *(ge)don* with a verb of cognition, (attested outside Sample 1 and the *DOE* with *understandan*, *witan*, and *ongietan* 'to perceive, know', in CP 35.237.21 and Solil 1 40.9).[28]

Three examples of *(ge)don*-ACI remain. Of these, the only one unequivocally independent of Latin is ChronE 1132.9, which I have already discussed in (5). The other two examples — ÆLS (Basil) 123 and ÆLS (Swithun) 375 — are from Ælfric's *Lives of Saints*, again a collection of texts that does not have one concrete original behind it, but rather draws on several medieval Latin writers, similar Latin compilations of lives and homilies, and quotations from the Bible. The latter, for instance, is a quotation from Romans 12.20:

(.8) (a) *gif him þyrste ðu do him*
if he-DAT thirst-PRES-SUBJ thou do-IMPER he-DAT
drincan
drink-INF/-ACC-SG
if he is thirsty, you give him drink/water (ÆLS (Swithun) 375; late Old English)

(b) *si sitit, potum da illi*
if thirst-PRES-INDIC drink-ACC-SG give-IMPER he-DAT
if he is thirsty, give him drink (Rm 12.20)

The form *drincan* in (8a) can be interpreted both as an infinitive *drincan* 'to drink' and as a noun *drinca* 'drink' in the accusative singular. The second option seems to me more likely, since the Latin original also has a noun in the accusative singular *potum*. Moreover, *An Anglo-Saxon Dictionary* quotes this example in its entry on the noun *drinca*.[29] The rendering of the

---

[27] Susan Rosser suggests that the source of this Old English homily 'is most likely to have been a Latin translation of the Greek Acta [sanctorum] similar to that printed by Blatt (1930), although the Old English translator's source was clearly much closer to the Greek Acta than this Latin version is' (Susan Rosser, 'The Sources of Blickling Homily 19 (Cameron C.B.3.3.1)', in *'Fontes Anglo-Saxonici' : World Wide Web Register*, <http://fontes.english.ox.ac.uk/> [accessed on 18 February 2011]). Accordingly, I was able to trace the *gedon*-ACI construction in this text back to its Greek prototype in *Acta Andreae et Matthiae*, ch. 21: Franz Blatt, *Die lateinischen Bearbeitungen der Acta Andreae et Matthiae apud anthropophagos* (Giessen: Alfred Töpelmann, 1930), p. 72, l. 13.

[28] Cf. Ellegård, *The Auxiliary 'Do'*, pp. 39–40.

[29] Joseph Bosworth and T. Northcote Toller, *An Anglo-Saxon Dictionary* (Oxford: Oxford University Press, 1898),

imperative *da* with *do* in Old English may be a case of transfer from the source text, triggered by the phonological similarity of the two forms; more commonly, however, Latin *dare* is translated into Old English with *sellan* 'to give, supply' or *giefan* 'to give, grant'.[30]

Overall, the *DOE* data seems to support my earlier findings in the *YCOE*: causative *(ge)don*-ACI constructions in original Old English texts are extremely rare,[31] and it is, moreover, very difficult to rule out Latin influence in Old English collections of lives and homilies. The evidence on *to*-VP constructions with *(ge)don* is much more consistent, suggesting that the pattern typically occurred in set phrases, in which the *to*-VP constituent was a verb of cognition. We are now going to see how *facere*-ACIs were dealt with in overt translations from Latin.

4. *(ge)don* in translations from Latin

As has been observed in sub-section 1, the basic causative verbs in Old English are *hatan* and *lætan*, which typically take infinitival complements. If Latin originals contain such verbs as *iubeo* 'to order, command', *praecipio* 'to tell, command', or *permitto* 'to allow, permit', and an ACI complement, their translation into Old English is quite straightforward — *hatan* renders *iubeo* and *praecipio*, *lætan* renders *permitto*, and ACIs are rendered by ACIs. Overall in Sample 2, this translation strategy accounts for c. 38 per cent of all renditions of Latin ACIs with verbs of causation.

The statistics change, however, when Latin authors use ACIs after causative *facere*. These constructions are rendered by *(ge)don*-ACIs only in glosses, see example (9) below:

(.9) (a) *doeð   hie   cwaecian*
do-PRES-3SG   she-ACC   tremble-INF

(he) makes her (the earth) tremble (VespPs 103.32; early Old English)

(b) *facit   eam   tremere*
do-PRES-3SG   she-ACC   tremble-INF

(he) makes her (the earth) tremble (VespPs 103.32; early Old English)

In translations, two major strategies can be observed (see Table 2): the translators either retain the infinitival complement and change the main verb (c. 30.5 per cent) or they retain the main verb, rendering *facere* with *(ge)don* and the ACI with a finite complement clause (also c. 30.5 per cent). Let us consider the former option first, using Wærferth's translation of Gregory's

---

s.v.; cf. Los, *The Rise of 'To'-Infinitive*, p. 32.

[30] Cf. a quotation from the glosses to the *Lindisfarne Gospels*: 'Soðlice se ðe sylð drinc eow calic fulne wæteres' ('truly, whoever gives you a drink [from] a cup full of water'; MkGl (Li) 9.41) and its Latin source: *Quisquis enim potum dederit vobis calicem aquae* (Mk 9.41). The context is conspicuously similar, but *dederit* (future II of *dare*) is translated with *sylð* (present of *sellan*).

[31] A comprehensive survey of other attestations is available in Callaway, *The Infinitive in Anglo-Saxon*, pp. 33, 110–11, 118, 120, 130, 304; Royster, 'Old English Causative Verbs', pp. 337–8; and Ellegård, *The Auxiliary 'Do'*, pp. 48–54.

Dialogues (ex. 10)[32] and then the latter, using the Old English homily on St Chad, based on Bede's *Ecclesiastical History* (ex. 11).[33]

(.10) (a) *Quem   [...] calcare   ipsos paucissimos racimos*
         who-ACC   press-INF those very few   bunches
         fecit
         do-PERF-INDIC-3SG

   he made him press those very few bunches [of grapes] (GD i.9.78.30)

(b) *het   hine   wringan   þa   feawa geclystru þære*
    order-PAST-3SG he-ACC press-INF those few   bunches of the
    byrgena
    grapes

    he made him press those few bunches of grapes (C 58.16; early Old English)

The Latin *fecit* is rendered by *het*, the most common causative verb in Old English and one that prefers infinitival complementation, which allows the preservation of the ACI.

(.11) (a) *et   hos   septem fratres   huc   uenire   facito*
         and those-ACC seven brothers-ACC hither come-INF do-IMPER-2SG

   and make those seven brothers/monks come here (HE iv.3.340.16)

(b) *⁊ gedo   þu þet heo   hider cuman   þas   ure*
    and do-IMPER thou that they hither come-PRES-SUBJ those our
    seofen broðru
    seven brothers

    and make our seven brothers come hither (Chad 172.112; early Old English)

Above, the main verb *facito* is translated literally as *gedo þu* and the ACI has to be replaced with a finite complement clause. The transformation looks logical here since *facere*-ACI has future reference and the main verb cannot be construed as implicative (as has been observed in 2.1, the distinction between implicative and non-implicative causation is typically coded in Old English with infinitival and *that*-clauses, respectively).

Several other means to render *facere*-ACI are found in the late-OE translation of Genesis (early 11th century).[34]

(.12) (a) *Fecitque   eum   ascendere   super currum   suum secundum*
         do-PERF-and he-ACC ascend-INF into   chariot his   second

   and he made him [Joseph] ascend his second chariot (Gn 41.43)

(b) *⁊ sette   hyne   on hys oþer cræt*
    and set-PAST he-ACC on his other cart

---

[32] *Dialogues Grégoire le Grand*, ed. by Adalbert de Vogüé, Sources Chrétiennes (Paris: Éditions du Cerf, 1978); *Bischofs Wærferth von Worcester Übersetzung der Dialoge Gregors des Grossen*, ed. by Hans Hecht, Bibliothek der angelsächsischen Prosa, 5 (Leipzig: Wigand, 1900), MS C.

[33] *Bede's Ecclesiastical History of the English People*, ed. by Bertram Colgrave and R. A. B. Mynors (Oxford: Clarendon, 1969); *The Life of St. Chad: An Old English Homily*, ed. by R. Vleeskruyer (Amsterdam: North-Holland Publishing Company, 1953).

[34] Genesis, in *Biblia Sacra Iuxta Vulgatam Versionem*, ed. by Bonifatio Fischer, Iohanne Gribomont, H. F. D.

and he set him in his second chariot (Gn 41.43; late Old English)

The Latin *fecit eum ascendere* is translated by the morphological causative *sette hyne*, while below the infinitive is simply omitted.

(.13) (a) Absque liberis   me   esse   fecistis
         without children I-ACC be-INF do-PERF-2PL
         you have made me be without children (Gn 42.36)

   (b) Bearnleasne   ge   habbað   me   gedonne
       childless-ACC ye   have-PRES-2PL I-ACC do-PART
       you have made me childless (Gn 42.36; late Old English)

Thus, the Old English translation contains a small clause, with the adjective *Bearnleasne* replacing the PP *Absque liberis*.

Ellegård reports four occurrences in the *Old English Heptateuch* in which *facere*-ACIs are rendered into Old English as *lætan*-ACIs.[35] All of them contain intransitive verbs in the ACI: *requiescere – restan* 'to rest', *decurrere – yrnan* 'to run', *stare – standan* 'to stand', and *viuere – libban* 'to live'.

Summing up, the amount of replacement and restructuring in target texts seems to suggest a kind of incompatibility between the Latin *facere*-ACI and the Old English complementation patterns with *(ge)don*.[36] Although *(ge)don* is the closest equivalent of *facere* in its basic meaning, as a two-place verb it prefers *that*-clause complements (although these too are mostly restricted to Latinate contexts), while as a three-place verb it prefers *to*-VP complements, whose meaning is best described as 'to grant to do something', with a clear tendency to be used with verbs of cognition. I agree with Los that competition exists between ACI and *that*-clause, rather than between ACI and *to*-VP.[37]

	ABS NOS	REL NOS
facere rendered with *hatan*, Inf retained	7	30.44%
don + *þæt*-clause	7	30.44%
morphological causative	5	21.74%
facere rendered with *bebeodan*, Inf with *þæt*-clause	2	8.7%
Inf omitted	1	4.35%
main verb omitted	1	4.35%
TOTAL	**23**	**100%**

Table 2. Old English renderings of Latin *facere*-ACIs (excluding glosses)

Discussion

Although we have seen that causative *(ge)don* with ACI complements are generally Latin-based in both sub-periods of Old English, in this socio-historical setting, the term *syntactic*

Sparks and W. Thiele (Stuttgart: Deutsche Bibelgesellschaft, 1969); *The Old English Heptateuch*, ed. by Samuel Crawford, Early English Text Society, o. s., 160 (London: Oxford University Press, 1922).

[35] Ellegård, *The Auxiliary 'Do'*, p. 52.
[36] Cf. Ellegård, *The Auxiliary 'Do'*, p. 52.
[37] See Los, *The Rise of 'To'-Infinitive*, p. 136.

borrowing should be used with caution. The reason for caution lies first of all in the specificity of the Anglo-Latin language contact in the historical Old English period, with its paucity of oral communication between speakers of Latin and speakers of English.[38] The situation can be described as one in which a socially defined group of people acquires literary competence in L2 (Latin) via studying, reading, copying, and glossing it. The use of L2 is promoted through schooling and is restricted almost entirely to the domain of religion, while the speech community as a whole remains essentially monolingual.[39]

The association of bilinguality, i.e. literacy in Latin (taken broadly — from passive familiarity to high proficiency), with affiliation with the holy orders is widely accepted among Anglo-Saxonists.[40] The size of this bilingual group can be estimated to be between 0.27 and 0.55 per cent of the population.[41] The bilinguals are very few, and, more importantly, they are also the group responsible for most of the literary production in Old English. The contemporary records of the period in both Latin and Old English are, thus, representative only of one per cent of the population at most. With such figures, language contact may only result in a limited number of lexical borrowings, while the prospect of structural borrowing would not look very promising.[42] Latin influence in the domain of causative constructions, addressed here, should therefore operate within the outlined social group, affecting the overall language situation but to a negligible degree. With this in mind, to refer to these constructions as borrowings would not be quite accurate. But what are they then?

In their recent studies of contact-induced grammaticalisation, Bernd Heine and Tania Kuteva describe syntactic borrowing as a process of grammatical replication which supposedly takes several stages.[43] At first speakers of the replica language (R) notice that the model language (M) has a grammatical category (Mx).[44] They then create an equivalent category (Rx), using linguistic material available in their own language (R), and eventually the new category is grammaticalised.[45] Time-wise these stages relate 'to a gradual process [...] and may involve several generations of speakers'; the grammaticalisation stage in particular 'may extend over centuries'.[46]

---

[38] Olga Timofeeva, 'Anglo-Latin Bilingualism before 1066: Prospects and Limitations', in *Interfaces between Language and Culture in Medieval England: A Festschrift for Matti Kilpiö*, ed. by Alaric Hall, Olga Timofeeva, Ágnes Kiricsi and Bethany Fox, The Northern World, 48 (Leiden: Brill, 2010), pp. 1–36.

[39] Cf. Leo J. Loveday, *Language Contact in Japan: A Sociolinguistic History* (Oxford: Oxford University Press, 1996), pp. 19–20.

[40] See, e.g., Hugh Magennis, 'Audience(s), Reception, Literacy', in *A Companion to Anglo-Saxon Literature*, ed. by Phillip Pulsiano and Elaine Treharne (Oxford: Blackwell, 2001), pp. 84–101 (pp. 86–89).

[41] For the details of the calculation and references, see Timofeeva, 'Anglo-Latin Bilingualism before 1066', pp. 12–16.

[42] See the 'borrowing scale' proposed in Sarah G. Thomason and Terrence Kaufman, *Language Contact, Creolization, and Genetic Linguistics* (Berkeley: University of California Press, 1988); and Sarah G. Thomason, *Language Contact* (Edinburgh: Edinburgh University Press, 2001); cf. Donald Winford, *An Introduction to Contact Linguistics* (Oxford: Blackwell, 2003).

[43] e.g. Bernd Heine and Tania Kuteva, 'On Contact-induced Grammaticalization', *Studies in Language*, 27 (2003), 529–72; *Language Contact and Grammatical Change* (Cambridge: Cambridge University Press, 2005).

[44] The terms *model language* and *replica language* were initially introduced by Uriel Weinreich in 1953. Model languages provide the model for transfer, and replica languages make use of the model. See Uriel Weinreich, *Languages in Contact: Findings and Problems*, Publications of the Linguistic Circle of New York, 1 (The Hague: Mouton, 1968), pp. 7–8, 30–31 (first publ. New York: Linguistic Circle of New York, 1953).

[45] Heine and Kuteva, 'On Contact-induced Grammaticalization', pp. 533, 539; *Language Contact and Grammatical Change*, pp. 80–81, 92.

[46] Heine and Kuteva, 'On Contact-induced Grammaticalization', p. 533.

The early stages of contact-induced grammaticalisation are related to discourse characteristics of a replicated grammatical structure. It is essential to distinguish between pragmatic and categorial aspects of grammatical replication, as grammaticalisation, including contact-induced grammaticalisation, starts out 'with pragmatically motivated patterns of discourse that may crystallise in new, conventionalised forms of grammatical structure'.[47] Thus the earlier stages of contact-induced grammaticalisation can be described as discourse-pragmatic, referring to such parameters as context and frequency. As long as the replica unit remains pragmatically marked, it is termed 'use pattern' rather than category. In contact situations, new (replicated) use patterns or, more commonly, infrequent (native) 'minor use patterns' may become more frequent and less marked, that is, develop into 'major use patterns',[48] which is represented graphically in Table 3.

stage	0	Ia	Ib	II	III
	minor use pattern		> major use pattern		
		incipient category		> full-fledged category	

Table 3. Discourse-based vs. categorial structures in grammatical replication (Heine and Kuteva, *Language Contact and Grammatical Change*, p. 75)

The distinction between the discourse-based and categorial structures seems to be particularly useful for the study of Old English data, as in situations of written language contact, we may be dealing with translation-induced grammaticalisation that is initiated by the mechanism of grammatical replication, leading to the establishment of translation conventions/patterns that may or may not give rise to full-fledged categories.

The distinction between category and use pattern is emphasised in Werner Koller's 1998 study of the role of translation in the history of German. He suggests that the influence of translation patterns on target language can be seen on the level of *system innovations* (*Systeminnovationen*, i.e. innovations in the language system) and *norm and style innovations* (*Norm- und stilistische Innovationen*, i.e. innovations in particular text types).[49] Similarly, Nicole Baumgarten and Demet Özçetin claim that the 'frequent translation of source text structures by grammatical, but less used linguistic structures of the target language can, over time [...] marginalise other linguistic means used for the particular communicative function in the target language'.[50] Thus, a translation pattern may spread to original texts in the target language and produce a minor use pattern, typically within the text type that corresponds closest to the source text type. This minor use pattern (norm and style innovation) may eventually develop into a category (system innovation).

---

[47] Heine and Kuteva, *Language Contact and Grammatical Change*, pp. 40–122, esp. p. 70.

[48] Heine and Kuteva, *Language Contact and Grammatical Change*, pp. 44–62; cf. Lars Johanson, *Structural Factors in Turkic Language Contacts*, trans. by Vanessa Karam (Richmond: Curzon Press, 2002), pp. 10–11; 'Remodeling Grammar: Copying, Conventionalization, Grammaticalization', in *Language Contact and Contact Languages*, ed. by Peter Siemund and Noemi Kintana, Hamburg Studies on Multilingualism, 7 (Amsterdam: Benjamins, 2008), pp. 61–79 (pp. 69–70).

[49] Werner Koller, 'Übersetzungen ins Deutsche und ihre Bedeutung für die deutsche Sprachgeschichte', in *Sprachgeschichte: Ein Handbuch zur Geschichte der deutschen Sprache und ihrer Forschung*, ed. by Werner Besch, Anne Betten, Oskar Reichmann and Stefan Sonderegger (Berlin: Mouton de Gruyter, 1998), pp. 210–29 (p. 212).

[50] Nicole Baumgarten and Demet Özçetin, 'Linguistic Variation through Language Contact in Translation', in *Language Contact and Contact Languages*, ed. by Peter Siemund and Noemi Kintana, Hamburg Studies on Multilingualism, 7 (Amsterdam: Benjamins, 2008), pp. 293–316 (pp. 294–95).

It has to be pointed out that to become a category both contact-induced and translation-induced grammatical innovations have to be supported by intense and prolonged contact and continuous translation tradition. These two approaches can, therefore, describe Old English data on *(ge)don*-ACI only in a limited way. I suggest that they can be legitimately applied to account for glosses, translations and written Old English more generally in terms of translation patterns developing into minor use patterns. But there is little evidence to substantiate further evolution to the categorial (system) level.

Furthermore, formal grammatical replication is not the only outcome of contact-induced language influence. Heine and Kuteva point out:[51]

> [I]f we find that speakers regularly translate category Mx of language M by using category Rx in language R, then we will say that this is an instance of translational equivalence between Mx and Rx — irrespective of the grammatical structure of the categories concerned.

Indeed, it should be emphasised that translational equivalence does not (necessarily) imply structural equivalence between Mx and Rx. The latter is better described in terms of structural isomorphism, while the former reflects a search for a closest equivalent of Mx,[52] which relies on previous translation experience and continues an established translational convention.[53]

If we apply these assumptions to the written Old English data, we shall see that in fact there are several translation equivalents for the Latin *facere*-ACI:

1) *(ge)don*-ACI (infrequent, mostly limited to lOE),

2) *(ge)don-þæt*-clause (rather frequent, used in both sub-periods),

3) *hatan/lætan*-ACI (rather frequent, used in both sub-periods),

4) morphological causatives (limited to one text in my corpus, but attested elsewhere by other scholars,[54] perhaps unproductive because many of the old morphological causatives had become polysemous in Old English, while new causatives stopped to be formed along the old derivational patterns[55]).

As (3) and (4) are well represented in the original Old English writings, I restrict the following discussion to (1) and (2).

Ellegård observes that '*facere ut* is normally rendered *do that* in [Old] English, whereas *facere ac*[*cusative with infinitive*] is generally changed, mostly into *do that*'.[56] Thus, *(ge)don-þæt*-clause has two models in Latin, while *(ge)don*-ACI only one, although ex. (3a) may suggest that an equivalence relation exists also between *facere-ut*-clause and *(ge)don*-ACI, which can perhaps be seen graphically as represented in Figure 1.

Equivalence rests on previous translation experience, which in the Old English setting can be envisaged as both individual translation experience and the experience of reading and copying existing glosses and translations. It seems therefore, that indeed repeated translation (experience) of the same Mx creates a convention, or *translation use pattern*.

Once we have a pattern, we may expect it to spread from translated to original texts within the same text type. This should be a particularly well motivated expectation in Old English, since most of the prose text types were actually created through the imitation of

---

[51] Heine and Kuteva, *Language Contact and Grammatical Change*, pp. 222–25.
[52] Johanson, 'Remodeling Grammar', p. 77.
[53] Cf. Heine and Kuteva, *Language Contact and Grammatical Change*, pp. 223, 225.
[54] See Ellegård, *The Auxiliary 'Do'*, pp. 49–51.
[55] Royster, 'Old English Causative Verbs', pp. 328–32.
[56] Ellegård, *The Auxiliary 'Do'*, p. 52.

corresponding Latin text types. My analysis of Old English data shows a clear development in this direction: outside glosses, eOE prefers the *(ge)don-þæt*-clause (whose use is mostly restricted to translations), while lOE employs both the *(ge)don-þæt*-clause and *(ge)don*-ACI, and both structures are seen to creep into texts that occupy an intermediate position between translations and independent Old English texts (see sub-section 2; absolute figures are given in Table 4).

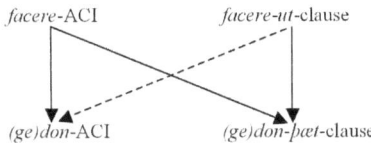

Figure 1. Translation equivalence between the complements of *facere* and *(ge)don*

		eOE	lOE
(ge)don-ACI	translations	0	2
	intermediate	0	7
	independent	0	2
(ge)don-þæt-clause	translations	46	30
	intermediate	0	54
	independent	3	7

Table 4. Distribution of ACI and finite complements with *(ge)don* (based on counts from the complete *YCOE*)

As discourse innovations or minor use patterns these two constructions may or may not find their way into the language system. The two occurrences of *(ge)don*-ACI in the *Peterborough Chronicle* seem to support the former scenario (see ex. 5). Language-internal development, however, cannot be ruled out for two major reasons: common Old English is completely undocumented, while cognates of causative *(ge)don* are attested at various stages in the development of Frisian, Dutch and German.[57] I will, however, have to stop at the lOE stage as the arrival of the Romance-speaking elite in 1066 and the partial discontinuity of the old written tradition make it impossible to trace the initial scenario further, but definitely call for more research into the development of causative constructions in ME.

Conclusions

Corpus analysis has shown that both hypotheses of the origin of infinitival complements with *(ge)don* highlight important linguistic points but omit many no less important details. Accordingly I divide my conclusions into two parts.

As far as the 'native' hypothesis is concerned, the distinction between *(ge)don* with NP-*to*-VP complements and *(ge)don*-ACIs is crucial not only in terms of argument structure and

---

[57] Nils Langer, *Linguistic Purism in Action: How Auxiliary 'tun' was Stigmatized in Early New High German*, Studia

the semantics of *(ge)don* but also in the examination of the diachronic development of the two structures. NP-*to*-VP complements occur mainly in set phrases with verbs of cognition, and their use shows no dependence on Latin sources from eOE onwards. The evidence on *(ge)don*-ACIs, on the other hand, does not suggest that the construction was in wide circulation before the transition from Old to Middle English period. Not only are they rare in original Old English texts, but the scribes seem generally reluctant to render *facere*-ACIs with their structural equivalents. Moreover, many of the texts that are classified as original Old English, and therefore can supposedly be used to support the claim about the native development of *(ge)don*-ACIs, on closer examination reveal affinities with one or more Latin sources.

The 'Latin' hypothesis holds only for *(ge)don*-ACIs, particularly before the OE4 period, into which the two examples from the *Peterborough Chronicle* belong (see sub-section 2). The claims about syntactic borrowing, however, should not be made too hastily in view of the small size of the corpus of surviving Old English texts, their general dependence on Latin sources, and the social background of their authors. I suggest that translation-induced-interference analysis should be applied instead. In the course of studying, reading and translating from Latin, speakers of Old English become aware of the category *facere*-ACI in Latin. They create two translational equivalents for this category: *(ge)don*-ACI and *(ge)don*-*þæt*-clause. These equivalents in due course become translation patterns and thus have a potential to spread outside translations. The statistics presented in Table 4 show that frequency-wise this potential was higher for *(ge)don*-*þæt*-clause.

Furthermore, typological analysis of the Old English causatives (outlined briefly in 1) shows that native constructions were available and that the basic positive causative verb was *hatan*. It seems reasonable to hypothesise that as long as the central position of *hatan* remained unshaken, there was little room for new developments within the causative paradigm. Therefore the decline of *hatan* in ME and the rise of *do* and *make* should perhaps be investigated as complementary processes.[58]

Linguistica Germanica, 60 (Berlin: Walter de Gruyter, 2001), pp. 12–98.

[58] The diachronic development of ME causatives is investigated by Brian Lowrey in 'Les verbes causatifs en anglais: une étude diachronique du moyen-anglais à l'anglais moderne', unpublished Ph.D. dissertation (University of Lille, 2002).

The present study was supported by the Academy of Finland Centre of Excellence funding for the Research Unit for Variation, Contacts and Change in English at the Department of English, University of Helsinki.

Errata to Domenico Pezzini, 'An Edition of Three Late Middle English Versions of a Fourteenth-Century *Regula Heremitarum*'

Issue 40 of *Leeds Studies in English* (2009), 65–103, published Domenico Pezzini's 'An Edition of Three Late Middle English Versions of a Fourteenth-Century *Regula Heremitarum*'. Regrettably, the author was not able to communicate all his corrections to the proofs prior to publication. Here follows a list of substantial errata, including all those affecting the edition itself. A corrected version of the article, implementing the corrections listed and a few other minor alterations is available online via <http://leeds.ac.uk/lse>.

p. 77, l. 12: þey *for* ney
p. 78, l. 23: per *for* oper
p. 79, l. 20: desiderare *for* deisderare
p. 79, l. 28: residuum *for* residdum
p. 82, l. 16: iaceat *for* iacet
p. 84, l. 23: chapito*ur* is *for* chapito*ur*. is
p. 85, l. 12: chapito*ur*. *for* chapito*ur*
p. 86, l. 4: of[66] *for* <or>[66] of
p. 86, fn. 66: Lat. 'alicuius hominis sive status'. A,S,B may have read 'sive/seu' as 'sui'. *for* or] Lat. 'sive'.
p. 87, l. 6: ou*er for* ou*er* ou*er*
p. 88, l. 15: turtamyzacion *for* turtamyȝacion
p. 88, fn. 106: turtamyzacion *for* turtamyȝacion
p. 89, l. 2: Complyne *for* complyne
p. 89, fn. 118: health *for* heath
p. 90, l. 19: Holy *for* holy
p. 90, l. 23: Mateyns *for* mateyns
p. 91, l. 4: noster *for* Noster
p. 91, l. 12: Maria *for* maria
p. 91, l. 19: Maria *for* maria
p. 91, l. 20: salutis *for* salutes
p. 92, l. 10: IX *for* XI
p. 93, l. 20: Patri *for* patri

Errata to 'Three Middle English Versions of a Regula Heremitarum*'*

p. 93, l. 28: gode *for* Gode
p. 93, l. 33: IX *for* ix
p. 97, l. 14: noþer [þ]ey²¹⁸ by hyme, ther-off nor slandar thame. *for* noþer ney by hyme, ther-off nor slandar thame.²¹⁸
p. 97, fn. 218: þey] *ney*. This sentence is difficult to interpret. It should render the Latin 'ne detur religiosis occasio malignandi in eum', a caveat justifying the rule that the hermit should wear a habit not like one of any religious order. It seems that a phrase has been omitted. The version in A is of no help since this Latin sentence is not translated. *for* This sentence is difficult to interpret. It should render the Latin 'ne detur religiosis occasio malignandi in eum', a caveat justifying the rule that the hermit should wear a habit not like one of any religious order. It seems that a phrase has been omitted. The version in A cannot be of any help since this Latin sentence is not translated.
p. 98, l. 3: ȝole *for* ȝole
p. 98, l. 7: ȝole *for* ȝole
p. 101, l. 4: for *for* ffor
p. 101, l. 32: God *for* god
p. 102, l. 6: Lord *for* lord
p. 102, l. 9: cumunyth of *for* cumunyth (?) of
p. 102, l. 14: Lorde *for* lorde

REVIEWS

Rachel Koopmans, *Wonderful to Relate: Miracle Stories and Miracle Collecting in High Medieval England*. Philadelphia: University of Pennsylvania Press, 2011. viii + 337 pp. ISBN 978-0-8122-4279-9. £42.50.

> When I was on the isle of Thanet, I went walking along the seashore with a knight who had asked me there for his edification. We considered those things that were marvels of God there and drew from them material for good conversation. From there the conversation turned to father Dunstan, as every time I find occasion for speaking about him I always obtain the greatest benefit. Recalling that name, the knight paled, and breathing deeply as if in pain he said, 'Oh, how ungrateful I am, I who am forgetful of his great kindness' (p. 19)

The story above, recounted by Koopmans in the first chapter of *Wonderful to Relate: Miracle Stories and Miracle Collecting in High Medieval England*, is emblematic of both the subject matter and the methodology of this fascinating and important book. Koopmans uses this anecdote, recounted by Osbern of Canterbury in his collection of the miracles of St Dunstan, to highlight what she understands to be the key aspect of miracle stories in high medieval England: the greater importance of their oral to their written form. Here, the memory of a miracle is shared between Osbern and the anonymous Knight of Thanet. The miracle is remembered between members of the same community, retold, and, finally written down: 'then, seeing those who were present, I presented to them in words what I now produce in letters', Osbern concludes (p. 20). It is the spectre of forgetting, Koopmans argues, more than the demands of propaganda or avarice, that was the main impetus for the fashion for miracle collection that emerged, peaked, and then subsided in high medieval England.

Wonderful to Relate analyses the seventy-five or so surviving miracle collections from high medieval England for what they can tell us not just about high medieval religious culture or the cult of saints, but more generally about the relationships between orality and literacy, monastic culture and lay culture, history and written record. The introduction insists we rewrite our understanding of at least this corner of medieval English literary history. It is worth quoting in full a passage that amounts to a manifesto:

> English miracle collections were written in the same monastic contexts and frequently by the same authors who produced other Latin prose texts of the period. In terms of numbers of authors, miracle collecting was actually a more important and mainstream literary activity in England than the writing of chronicles. The creation of miracle collections is usually thought to have been driven by the pressures of cults and the immediate political needs of monastic communities. Except in studies of pilgrims, disease, illness and the

like, it has been rare for miracle collections to be considered as a body. But the stark rise and fall of miracle collecting in high medieval England demonstrates that we need to think in terms of broader patterns of production, to read individual collections within these broader patterns, to weigh the influence of specific authors, to formulate explanations for peaks and troughs in the popularity of miracle collecting, and to recognize the miracle collection for what it was: a defining genre and major literary phenomenon of the long twelfth century. (p. 2)

Wonderful to Relate rises to the challenge it presents here. Its ten chapters fall loosely into three sections. The first two chapters set the scene and articulate the book's methodology. The centrepiece of this methodology is a focus on the 'oral creation and circulation' (p. 11) of miracles, especially as 'personal stories'. Here Koopmans argues that 'many of the repetitive similarities between stories in different collections were not the results of writers working to set models. Rather, these similarities were already a feature of the oral stories the collectors heard' (p. 6). Chapters Three through Seven write the literary history of English miracle collections by focusing chronologically on the important miracle collections and their key developments. Thus Chapter Three begins with the observation that no miracle collections were produced in England in the troubled years between 800 and 950, and it moves on to consider the sole pre-Conquest miracle collection, Lantfred of Fleury's *Translation and Miracles of Swithun*. Koopmans reorients our understanding of this collection from the context of English monastic reform, back to Fleury, with its history of miracle collecting, and suggests that the first 'English' miracle collection was in fact intended for a non-English audience. This may, in part, explain why English miracle collecting had to wait for yet another foreign monk, this time Goscelin of St Bertin, before the 'fad' really got underway. Chapter Four considers Goscelin of St Bertin's career as a professional hagiographer in post-Conquest England. Koopmans attributes much of the structure, form and meaning of the standard format of the miracle collection to Goscelin's pioneering lives of Wulfsige, Edith and Kenelm. Chapters Five and Six turn to the native English miracle collectors, Osbern and Eadmer of Canterbury. Reading Osbern and Eadmer's lives of St Dunstan against one another, Koopmans traces a developing tension in the treatment of the oral sources of miracles. Chapter Seven describes the shifts in miracle collecting from the 1140s–1170s to the 1170s–1200. It also serves as something of an introduction to the final three chapters, which focus on the collections of miracles of St Thomas Becket: those of Benedict of Peterborough and William of Canterbury. Three appendices on the manuscripts and relationship between these collections support the analysis here.

At the same time as it focuses on these case studies, *Wonderful to Relate* constructs an overarching narrative that describes English miracle collecting as falling into two main phases. The first, c. 1080–1140, arranged miracles into medium-sized collections that intend to preserve current oral stories, and which present themselves as self-consciously attempting to preserve the past from oblivion. In this, they share the impulse of post-Conquest historiography. The second phase, from c. 1140–1200 sees collections grow longer, while the individual narration of miracles becomes shorter: the collecting impulse shifts from recording in-house gossip to a desire to add as many witnesses as possible. And for the first time, these witnesses prominently include lay persons. Here, the influence on the development of the canonization dossier is seen. In the thirteenth century, as Koopmans describes in the conclusion to the book, miracle collections are still produced, but the *exemplum* overtakes the miracle as the narrative of choice.

The critical interventions of *Wonderful to Relate* are many and important. In particular, Koopmans' untangling of the relationships between the Becket miracle collections will be invaluable. In many cases, she reorients traditional interpretations and offers new perspectives. For example, Koopmans disputes Southern's argument that the impulse behind miracle collecting reflected the need for and importance of a written record, as well as those arguments that see in miracle collections a propaganda for the monastic reform movement directed at the laity. Here, however, I was sometimes left wondering if her central argument that the chief motivating factor behind the collection of miracles was a desire to preserve the past takes her texts a bit too much at face value. After all, this study does such a good job of presenting these miracle collections as key and central cultural documents that it is difficult not to see them performing variously in multiple contexts. Nevertheless, throughout this study, Koopmans' insistence on unearthing and attending to the 'personal stories' that, she argues, were the lifeblood of the tradition of miracle collecting – and, indeed, of the cult of saints more generally – offers up a series of engaging anecdotes, such as the story of the Knight of Thanet, which make this book a pleasure to read and which make these miracles come alive once more.

HEATHER BLURTON UNIVERSITY OF CALIFORNIA, SANTA BARBARA

Massimo Verdicchio, *The Poetics of Dante's 'Paradiso'*. Toronto: University of Toronto Press, 2010. xi + 177 pp. ISBN 978-1-4426-4119-8. $45.00.

According to the author, *The Poetics of Dante's 'Paradiso'* came from a desire to continue the critical reading of the *Inferno* and *Purgatorio* established in his earlier work *Reading Dante Reading*, which identified the *Commedia* as a text with a predominantly ironic tone. The criticism of the characters in Paradise, which Verdicchio believes the poet intended, 'required on Dante's part the use of a very subtle irony, which, while upholding their status as blessed souls, exposed their earthly flaws … in *Paradiso* there is no punishment, only … an ironic smile that serves as a *contrapasso* for these souls' (p. x). The analysis of *Paradiso* is sequential, dedicating a chapter to each heaven, each beginning with a quote from the *Convivio* referencing the connection made in that work between the heaven and its respective science. While this mode of reading relies on accepting a continuity between the thought of the *Convivio* and *Commedia* which is not uncontroversial, it nevertheless acts as a productive lens for interpretation which would merit more consistent and detailed analysis.

Prologues I and II establish Verdicchio's rationale for reading the *Commedia* as primarily a work of social and linguistic critique. He puts forward a case for seeing in the figures of the *veltro* of *Inferno* I and the DXV of *Purgatorio* XXXIII respectively the *Commedia* itself and Dante the poet, whose joint role is to critique the Church and Empire. The subsequent argument is largely dependent on one's acceptance of this interpretation, though perhaps sufficient grounds for reading the *Commedia* as biting comment could be found without recourse to such an elaborate and therefore vulnerable interpretation. Furthermore, in the book as a whole the author has chosen to minimise engagement with other critical works which, while allowing for a certain purity of argument, also at times impoverishes it. Prologue II establishes 'the poetics of *Paradiso* as an allegory of irony' as only this mode of reading recognises Dante's intention to reveal the deception and 'empty rhetoric' (22) of language.

The chapters dedicated to the heavens of the Moon, Mercury and Venus argue that by connecting the heaven with its respective science Dante is encouraging us to see the souls met there as two-sided, their words concealing another truth. The partial illumination-partial truth manifested in the image of the moon spots and suggested by the heaven's relation to grammar leads to the suggestions that the moon's principal characters are engaged in acts of deception. In Mercury, Justinian, the representative of Empire, is suggested to be an unreliable, anti-example of justice when the narrative of his actions is read in the light of their historical context. The souls in Venus, principally Charles Martel representing the House of Anjou, are revealed as lacking maturity, development, and self-knowledge, still equating love with pleasure and being misled by its language.

In opposition to those who read these cantos as a manifestation of the intellectual and spiritual harmony of Dante's religious thought acting against the corruption of the Church, Verdicchio reads the heaven of the Sun as characterised by religious conflict and by Dante's desire to highlight the blessed souls' earthly flaws, thereby carrying out a critique of the Church. However, because other ways in which Dante engages with Dominicanism and Franciscanism in the *Commedia* as a whole are not addressed, it is difficult to substantiate the argument beyond these cantos. That these cantos — and those in the heaven of Saturn — criticise the corruption of the religious orders, is somewhat self-evident.

The following six chapters continue to emphasise the ironical tone of the *Paradiso* to prove that its message is to be found by seeking beyond the literal words and reading the characters and events in the light of certain historical facts. In Verdicchio's analysis of the heaven of Mars, Cacciaguida is presented as characterised by 'greed and evil', as the 'caesar responsible for Florence's civil wars' (p. 81), whose real historical actions undermine his positive heavenly projection. This furthermore make implausible the historical Dante's familial relationship to him. On the heaven of Jupiter, the disharmony, which marks this canto, is demonstrated and stress placed on the reference to the corrupt princes of the earth so that 'the story of the Monarchy as told by the Eagle is a story of corruption, debauchery ... Justice is nowhere to be found' (p. 112). In analysing the heaven of Fixed Stars, Verdicchio suggests that Dante undermines the three apostolic figures by reference to 'historical' details which appear to counteract their virtues. The arguments here are weakened by the selectiveness of those details listed, lack of further references, and assumptions about the poet Dante's thinking, which do not always ring true. For example, contrary to casting Peter as the example of anti-faith, one could argue that it is precisely his doubt and later convictions which make him an accessible and humane example of human weakness and potential. Both here and elsewhere, some of the points (and terms, for example *piacer, disio*) which are raised could be made more convincing if placed in dialogue with these issues as they are present in the text as a whole. The analysis of the Primum Mobile reiterates the important theme of the misuse and deceptiveness of language. The role of the *Commedia* comes to be to teach proper, ironic reading. Verdicchio's analysis of the Empyrean relies heavily on his readers' knowledge of *Reading Dante Reading*, and undertakes only a cursory analysis of the figure of Beatrice and Dante's vision of the heavenly city.

Verdicchio's book is strongest in its call for a reading of the Paradiso which allows for a tone of critical irony, highlighting the essential deceptiveness and insufficiency of language. In its desire to give an 'oppositional' interpretation to the general positive view of the blessed souls, however, he goes too far (in his eagerness to support his interpretative stance) in asserting Dante's negative, critical tone. A more productive analysis may be produced by a recognition of the 'grey' areas of Dante's thought which instead of passing black and white judgements on humanity, engage with the problematics of being human in a vivified and eschatological context which is not simply driven by a desire to make a social point but is instead engaged in an exploration of human and divine nature.

RUTH CHESTER   UNIVERSITY OF LEEDS

Katharine Breen, *Imagining an English Reading Public, 1150–1400*. Cambridge Studies in Medieval Literature, 79. Cambridge: Cambridge University Press, 2010. x + 287 pp. ISBN 978-0-5211-9922-3. £58.00.

In her introduction to *Imagining an English Reading Public*, Katharine Breen explains that her book will chart the 'translation' of the Latin concept of *habitus* into a Middle English 'habit' that 'lies at the heart of — and conditions — late-fourteenth-century contests over vernacular authorship'. (As later chapters explain, medieval grammarians claimed that *habitus* — which in this context can be loosely defined as the conscious cultivation of virtue — could be acquired only through the study of grammar, and therefore of Latin.) These 'contests' are initiated by the 1381 revolt, in which William Langland's *Piers Plowman* was subjected to a radicalized interpretation. 'After 1381', Breen explains, 'English authors had to confront the fact that their texts were potentially available to anyone who could read or even speak the mother tongue'. She labels the result for Middle English authors a 'shift in imagined audience' (p. 10).

In the development of her thesis, Breen shows that she can be an intelligent, industrious researcher. However, there are some serious problems with her presentation and interpretation of this research. The most serious is that she has buried, in the next-to-last section of her last chapter, an acknowledgement that her thesis is untenable — at least for her main example, *Piers Plowman*. I can only assume that this acknowledgement was exacted by a reviewer, but what I find disturbing is that having made it, Breen did not then revise her claims about post-1381 literature.

Obviously, I must now substantiate my own claim about Breen. To do that, I provide a close reading of parts of Chapter 5, which is titled '*Piers Plowman* and the Formation of an English Literary *Habitus*'. In this chapter, Breen examines Langland's revisions of the C-text as an attempt to 'habituate' potential non-latinate readers and thus avoid the kind of misinterpretations exhibited by the 1381 rebels. In doing so, she encounters two examples that seem to point in the opposite direction, suggesting that Langland was seeking to limit rather than broaden his audience. In an effort to minimize the impact of these examples, she employs increasingly questionable strategies.

The first example is Conscience's complicated grammatical metaphor in the third passus of the C-text. Breen describes the metaphor as 'a gatekeeper or shibboleth' (p. 187), one that 'sorts authorized from unauthorized readers based on their grammatical knowledge and mastery of difficult syntax'. She seeks, however, to soften this conclusion, noting that the rendering of the grammatical terms into English suggests 'that English can be an appropriate vehicle for activating or developing a virtuous *habitus*' (p. 189). Breen then turns the focus back to the less educated, 'lower-common-denominator' audience, pointing out that Conscience, and his ally Reason, only confuse the king with their grammatical terms, while Will later comments that education is expensive. Accordingly, she concludes, Reason and Conscience 'give Will conditional permission to continue writing in hopes that the specifically literary reading his dream visions demand can stand in for the linguistic and moral work of habit-formation usually carried out "in Cloystre or in scole" ' (p. 198).

Breen's paraphrase of Reason's and Conscience's words to Will is not supported by citation from or reference to the text, other than the 'cloister or school' quote (which is not attributed but derives from Reason's sermon to the realm; B.10.300, C.5.154). The only likely source I could find are these lines, which come just after Will has concluded his apologia in Passus 5 by hoping he may yet attain God's grace:

> 'Y rede the', quod Resoun tho, 'rape the to bigynne
> The lyif þat is louable and leele to thy soule'.
> '3e, and contynue!' quod Conscience; and to þe kyrke Y wente. (C.5.102–04)

Apart from occurring two *passūs* away from the dilemma they supposedly resolve, nothing in these lines matches Breen's paraphrase of them. They do not concern writing, dream visions, or an attempt to habituate the wider population; they conclude with Will going not to his desk but to church. Thus, the gatekeeping function of the grammatical terms in Passus 3 remains intact.

The second challenge to Breen's thesis comes in the section titled 'Haukyn's Habit' (pp. 209–16). Here she acknowledges that Langland's fullest exploration of the difficulties facing those who lack grammatical habituation occurs in the B-text. Haukyn the Active Man, 'yhabited as an heremyte' (B.13.284), offers a compelling example of the frustrations of human sin, yet he is replaced in the C-text by a weakened and de-personalized figure, Activa Vita. Breen concludes this section with the observation that 'over the course of Langland's revisions, good *habitūs* become more closely associated with a highly literate elite … and more of a long-term administrative goal than an immediate personal imperative' (p. 216). I can see this statement only as an acceptance that Langland responded to the 1381 revolt by directing his text to a more, not less educated readership.

Yet Chapter 5's next, and last, section immediately tries to smooth over the closing admission of the previous one. 'Despite this [i.e., Langland's] retrenchment — or perhaps because of it', Breen begins, 'Langland's C-text revisions present the search for a workable vernacular habitus as a major problem in *Piers Plowman*' (p. 216). The chapter's closing summary confusingly mixes acknowledgement of C's greater reliance on elite literacy with insistence that it was reaching out to the unlettered more than earlier versions, while periodically folding both B and C into assertions such as that Langland's 'unhabituated readers are invited to use the poem as a makeshift means of acquiring a vernacular *habitus*' (p. 221). (At no point does Breen discuss how uneducated readers were meant to engage with the large amount of allusive Latin in C as in all versions of *Piers Plowman*.)

In her introduction, Breen claims that her study

> examines these [post-1381] writers' attempts to adapt or 'translate' the established conventions of Latin reading into usable vernacular forms as well as their efforts to compensate for the fact that their readers, unschooled in Latin grammar, could not be counted on to have satisfied any prerequisites before picking up their texts. (p. 10)

Breen let this statement stand on page 10, despite having acknowledged, on page 216, that 'over the course of Langland's revisions, good *habitūs* become more closely associated with a highly literate elite'. And if Breen's contention doesn't hold for *Piers Plowman* it basically doesn't hold for the whole book. This is because the canon Breen cites as exemplary of the 'shift in imagined audience' consists of only three works: *Piers*, John Mirk's *Instructions for*

Parish Priests, and Chaucer's *Treatise on the Astrolabe*. Yet Mirk's *Instructions* is a standard pastoral manual intended, obviously, for priests (although, admittedly, for ignorant ones), while Chaucer's *Astrolabe* presupposes a reader with the money and time to invest in acquiring and learning to use a complex astronomical instrument. On this showing, the late fourteenth-century 'crisis' Breen attributes to English literature in general really applies only to *Piers Plowman*, and Chapter 5 reveals that it doesn't apply to *Piers Plowman* either.

Breen's book has other problems as well. Her exposition is often jumbled, and thus hard to follow. The appropriateness or relevance of texts she chooses to analyze can be hard to see, and the ground of her commentary and arguments keeps shifting. She never establishes a stable definition of *habitus* (at times, it seems that any move to denounce vice or praise virtue can be labeled 'habituation'), while her model of *habitus*-acquisition is unsatisfactory. Her claims for what primary texts allegedly reveal often exceed anything I can see happening in the sources as quoted. As we have seen, in order to make her argument she sometimes misrepresents primary texts via paraphrase or cherry-picking of examples. There are also important gaps in her coverage: hardly any consideration of the programme of educating the laity in religious observance that followed the Fourth Lateran Council of 1215 — surely a major early effort at lay 'habituation' — and no attention paid to England's other vernacular, French, or to the pragmatic realities of manuscript access and reading modes.

In reviewing problematic books, one traditionally looks for and highlights the areas in which useful contributions are being made. In this case, so much of Breen's analysis seems like ventriloquism — the author making the texts say what she wants them to say — that one can never feel confident about her readings. I can only hope that in her future work, the author will combine her considerable abilities with a more rigorous approach to the material.

JOYCE COLEMAN   UNIVERSITY OF OKLAHOMA

Peter Brown, *Authors in Context: Geoffrey Chaucer*. Oxford: Oxford University Press, 2011. xvi + 254pp. ISBN 978-0-1928-0429-7. £8.99.

This affordable paperback aims to be both 'compact and comprehensive', to offer 'a wide-ranging account of the medieval society from which works such as *The Canterbury Tales* and *Troilus and Criseyde* sprang'. I opened it hoping to find a book that would be a good starting-point for undergraduates struggling to make sense of Chaucer's world, and was partly satisfied.

There are seven chapters, all of which combine history with literary analysis: 'The Life of Geoffrey Chaucer', 'The Social Body', 'The Literary Scene', 'Society and Politics', 'Intellectual Ideas', 'Science and Technology' and 'New Contexts'. The book's greatest strength is that it provides summaries of relevant contextual information that can be hard to find so helpfully and succinctly presented elsewhere: there are excellent accounts, for example, of the Peasants' Revolt, guilds, named individuals in Chaucer's circle, the four humours, and the Hundred Years' War. The best of these involve a sensitive examination of their relation with Chaucer's poetry. Anyone wanting to know about Chaucer's response to the Black Death or Lollardy should find this book a great place to start. More on religious practice beyond Lollardy would not have gone amiss, but it is hard to criticise omissions from such a short book. Some of the more literary material also reads as fresh and interesting: the analysis of how the Wife of Bath uses social networks and navigates textual culture is invaluable, and the section on 'Personal Identity' under 'Society and Politics' will be a good resource for helping students to think about the pilgrim portraits in the *General Prologue*, as well as the performance of identity in the *Merchant's Tale*.

However, in general the material on literary cultures and contexts was less well done than the more strictly historical. 'London as a Literary Scene' moves eccentrically from the *Parson's Tale* to *Sir Gawain and the Green Knight* to *Piers Plowman* — and back again to the *Parson's Tale* — with only a short and incoherent discussion of *Sir Thopas* making a real connection between Chaucer and his native literary inheritance. First we are told that Chaucer mercilessly lampoons popular romance, then that his narrator 'does not properly understand the genre' (p. 99) – claims that, if not mutually exclusive, would at least bear clearer exposition. The section on 'Manuscript Culture', which asserts that a single accurate copy of a literary work was used to produce subsequent copies (p. 90), simplifies things to a degree that seems likely only to generate confusion among those trying to understand what the fragments in the *Canterbury Tales* are, or why some lines appear in some manuscripts but not others. The section on patronage, too, cries out for a clear articulation of what the reason for Chaucer's annuities might have been if they were not given for literary productions.

In fact, that struck me as a recurrent problem with this book. As all teachers know, it can be hard to explain phenomena that you have read about and explained a hundred times without skipping a few crucial points along the way: they are so familiar to you that they seem almost self-evident. But readers using this book as an introduction to Chaucer's world will not find it self-evident, for example, what a 'valettus' is – Chaucer's role when serving Lionel, earl of Ulster — and are unlikely to find the gloss 'yeoman' much help (p. 46). The oblique statement that 'land ownership counts for more than ownership of property and possessions' (p. 30) does not say much to someone who does not already know that knights typically owned more land than merchants. On astrology, while Brown's opening claim that the stars were a description of what would come to pass rather than actually directing events on earth (p. 171) is clear enough, he later asserts that the planets 'directly influenced … human experience, identity, and behaviour' (p. 173), which left me scratching my head wondering how the author's perspective had changed.

The literary readings also tend to be a little flat, eliding critical controversies rather than exposing areas of ambiguity and disagreement in ways that might stimulate further reading and thought. To give just one example, Brown argues that the *Knight's Tale*'s Palamon and Arcite have entirely opposing perceptions of the world, and that Arcite 'sees Emelye as a woman to be won by force and enjoyed physically' (p. 160). This in itself is probably an over-reading, but crucially, Brown makes no reference to the opposing critical view – that Palamon and Arcite are virtually indistinguishable except in terms of their fortunes. The final chapter extends analysis to modern reception of Chaucer in film, on TV and on stage, and comes down rather stuffily against the comic postmodernism of Helgeland's *A Knight's Tale* (2001) and in favour of Chaucer as 'icon of national identity' evoking 'ancient spiritual values' in Powell and Pressburger's 1944 *A Canterbury Tale* (p. 198).

This book will be useful resource for those teaching Chaucer to refresh their memories about historical contexts: it is quick to read and reliable. As an introduction for students, it will work best when there is ample class time to tease out its full implications.

CATHY HUME   NORTHWESTERN UNIVERSITY

Dinah Hazell, *Poverty in Late Middle English Literature: The 'Meene' and the 'Riche'*. Dublin Studies in Medieval and Renaissance Literature, 2. Dublin: Four Courts Press, 2009. 234 pp. ISBN 978-1-84682-1155-4. £50.00.

Dinah Hazell's book provides a wide-ranging survey of representations of poverty in late fourteenth-century literature. It is structured by four topics or categories: 'Aristocratic', 'Urban', 'Rural', and 'Apostolic' poverty. Each section provides the reader with a brief 'socioeconomic overview' and a selection of descriptions of the place of poverty in a variety of texts. The breadth of texts discussed is unusual and interesting, and includes work on diverse genres.

The section on 'Aristocratic' Poverty includes discussions of five Middle English romances: *Ywain and Gawain*; *Sir Amadace*; *Sir Cleges*; *Sir Launfal*; and *Sir Orfeo*. The chapter on 'Urban' poverty contains some brief discussion of *Havelok*; 'London Lickpenny'; Hoccleve's *Regiment of Princes*; Chaucer's *Prioress's Tale*; and *The Simonie*. The section on 'Rural' poverty is dedicated to more substantial discussions of Chaucer (again), in the form of the *Clerk's* and *Nun's Priest's Tales*, and of the various Shepherds' Plays in the York, Chester, Coventry and Towneley cycles (with a natural emphasis on the Towneley *Prima* and *Secunda Pastorum*). The chapter on 'Apostolic' poverty is largely focused on anticlerical and antifraternal themes, such as those in Gower's *Vox Clamantis*, *The Land of Cockaygne*, and *Pierce the Ploughman's Crede*. An interesting inclusion here, though, is Richard FitzRalph's Latin antifraternal text *Defensio Curatorum*. The 'positive' representation of clerical poverty is then detailed in texts such as the *South English Legendary*, Capgrave's *Life of Gilbert* and (interestingly) the romance *Sir Gowther*. A final chapter, 'solutions and attitudes', describes some of the different forms of relief that were afforded to the poor in the Middle Ages, from individual alms-giving to institutional charitable programs originating in monastic houses or hospitals.

From the list of works cited in the last paragraph alone, it should be clear that this is a very wide survey of the subject across a very broad (even eccentrically broad) sample of texts. Despite this breadth, there are particular strong points. The material on *The Simonie* in chapter two is substantial, and that on the *Clerk's Tale* in chapter three — concerning the psychological effects of poverty on Griselda — is interesting. The regular appearance of sections dedicated to socio-economic history provides a census of useful starting points, though sometimes at the risk of appearing to breeze through an awful lot of different topics rather briefly.

In the main, though, this is a book which may be most useful for scholars new to the material. As a compilation or anthology of texts on the representation of poverty, it may find use as a teaching aid for, particularly, the development of dissertations or theses on the subject of poverty and its literary representation in the later medieval period. As a book, though, it has some serious problems.

Hazell tends to try to cover a huge amount of material and the cost is a scattershot approach which often tends towards superficiality. While a quotation from Michel Mollat's classic *The Poor in the Middle Ages* (1986) begins the book, the equally important work of Bronislaw Geremek in *Poverty: A History* (1994) is strangely lacking from the intellectual framework of the book. Also, for example, while the 'socioeconomic overview' for the chapter on Apostolic Poverty does mention the importance of mendicantism (pp. 134–37), it does not mention some of the best scholarship on it, such as the historical work found in K. B. Wolf's *The Poverty of Riches: St Francis of Assisi Reconsidered* (2003), or the work (albeit not on later fourteenth century English writing) in Nick Havely's *Dante and the Franciscans: Poverty and the Papacy in the 'Commedia'* (2004).

Moreover, while the extensive selection of texts is a good thing, the selection of the overarching, organizational categories seems rather misjudged. The entire first chapter on Aristocratic poverty is strikingly out of place. As Hazell herself writes, poverty frequently appears in these texts as 'transitory and transitional and serves as a basis for the examination of moral and social concerns' (p. 16). Poverty here is a kind of narrative topos, a way of plunging the protagonist into a situation of trial. That such representations of poverty might be interesting in themselves is fair — one might think of the suggestions of penitential activity in, for example, Malory's *Morte Darthur* — but to place them in such a formative position in a survey (and thereby suggest that they are central to the subject as a whole) seems ill-conceived.

The discussion of poverty in the texts also sometimes seems to lose focus. Phenomena such as particular literary themes or historical contexts appear for a paragraph and then disappear again, leaving the reader with an odd sense of having read a sequence of hazily-related abstracts rather than a sustained argument or exploration of a topic. For example, in the first chapter, we move from land economy to definitions of romance as a genre, to a survey of arguments about audience, within six pages, without any sense of how these different things are relevant to a wider intellectual argument about the material. Similarly, the textual discussions themselves sometimes seem to disintegrate into shorter discussions of distinct things. It is not clearly articulated, for example, how the issue of poverty in *Ywain and Gawain* relates to the discussion of 'trouthe' in Arthurian romance (pp. 26–30).

One also wonders if the book is meant to be read in tandem with Anne M. Scott's *Piers Plowman and the Poor* (2004, also from Four Courts Press), as the appearances made by Langland's poem here are rather brief and sporadic. While Hazell does suggest in the introduction (p. 11) that *Piers Plowman* has often been the focus of work on representations of poverty in medieval literature, its absence from sustained discussion in the book is something of a drawback. Few other texts in this period — perhaps none — are so deeply concerned with the issue of poverty, in terms which are at once both economic and spiritual. It might be that Langland's explorations of poverty do not really fit into the rather static categories that Hazell imposes on the material here. Langland is deeply interested in the idealization of poverty, for example in the shape of Christ who, Langland writes, in 'pouere mannes apparaille pursueþ vs euere' (B 11.185). As some scholars — Lawrence M. Clopper particularly — have argued, it may be that Langland has a particular interest in the charismatic form of voluntary poverty offered by Franciscanism. At the same time, Langland shows a detailed and sharply contemporary concern for the failings of clerical poverty, and in the problems of social categorization and spiritual worth that accompany such figures as 'able-bodied' beggars and itinerant ecclesiastics. These multifarious intersections between Langland and Hazell's subject should have made *Piers Plowman* central, rather than peripheral, to the book.

MIKE RODMAN JONES   UNIVERSITY OF NOTTINGHAM

Dana M. Oswald, *Monsters, Gender and Sexuality*. Gender in the Middle Ages, 5. Cambridge: Brewer, 2010. viii + 227 pp. ISBN 978-1-8438-4232-3. £50.00.

This book represents an ambitious project: to interrogate medieval notions of the body and the boundaries of identity as they played out within a range of medieval literary contexts and two discrete periods, that is to say Anglo-Saxon times and the later Middle Ages. Building on other recent treatments of sexed and gendered identity formation (such as Jeffrey Jerome Cohen's *Of Giants* and Caroline Walker Bynum's *Metamorphosis and Identity*), Oswald argues for a radical shift in attitudes towards the body as a stable entity between the early and later periods, tracing that shift via close attention to the bodies of the monstrous 'other' as revealed in a range of texts from both periods. Defining that 'other' in her introduction, Oswald argues for the monster within medieval texts as falling into one of three categories: the more than human; the less than human; and the hybrid human. In turn, these monstrous categories each serve to 'present a different type of commentary' on the human body (p. 6), and all tend to be culturally specific and therefore contextually contingent. For Oswald, such definitions of monstrosity also rely heavily on culturally specific notions of a human 'essence' which has its visible boundaries constantly challenged by the incursion, or threatened incursion, of the monstrous. For Oswald, too, it is clear from the interplay between the human and the monstrous in the texts under scrutiny that the monstrous also serves as a means of (re)writing cultural beliefs. This is the case not only in an historiographical writing context but also in the context of narratives of sex, gender and sexual identity.

Oswald concentrates on a number of texts whose monsters have already been subject to some considerable scrutiny in recent years, as well as to gender analysis, offering readings of varying closeness in each case. Chapter One, for example, focuses primarily on the extraordinary illustrations of those monstrous and 'indecent bodies' which populate three manuscript copies of the Anglo-Saxon *Wonders of the East*. Here Oswald argues for the primacy of this text, and its dialogic interaction between word and image, as a means of determining the often troubled relationship between sexuality and identity, building considerably on Cohen's earlier treatment of the monsters in this text. Chapter Two, meanwhile, focuses closely on *Beowulf*, offering an intense reading of the failed heroic masculinity of its eponymous protagonist as exposed by the fearsome Grendel and his monstrous mother. Here, Oswald's attention to linguistic, imagistic and contextual detail again allows her both to illuminate and extend some of the work already undertaken in this vein and is probably the most successful of the four chapters making up this book. Chapter Three fast-forwards to the fourteenth century and the Middle English *Mandeville's Travels*, in which a range of female monsters enter the spotlight. To my mind this chapter is a little less convincing than the others, avoiding the kinds of close readings and intensive analyses so prevalent in the previous chapter, for example. Another small point is that its treatment of the hybrid 'dragon woman' (pp. 131–38), enchanted daughter of Hippocrates, who can only be redeemed by the kiss of a man, inadvertently opens up the surprising omission of any discussion of the dragon-monster of *Beowulf* in the previous chapter (an oversight which ends up haunting this book by its absence, perhaps). The final chapter, which usefully combines the *Alliterative Morte Arthure* and the strangely troubling romance *Sir Gowther*. Here Oswald argues concertedly for the prevalence during the later period of what she terms the 'transformative monster', who is seemingly capable of becoming (re)assimilated into society, and therefore of being 'redeemed' in a way that Anglo-Saxon monsters were not. Oswald's selections and readings in this book are generally both interesting and engaging and offer important and sometimes intricate insights into the role played by the monstrous within the confusing matrix of sex, gender and identity in the Middle Ages. Moreover, Oswald extends the scope of the earlier treatments on which she builds by drawing on an eclectic range of poststructural theories of sex, gender and identity as propounded by, for example, Julia Kristeva, Eve Kosowski

Sedgewick, Judith Halberstam, Judith Butler, and Gayle Rubin, to name but a few. Whilst at times this range threatens to manipulate some readings and disrupt overall cohesion, it is never intrusive or gratuitous. Indeed, Oswald's use of this methodological tool succeeds in uncovering the excessive multivalence of the monster and its ability to mean different things in different contexts and to threaten different types of boundaries within changed epistemologies. Here, therefore, lies the most significant contribution of this book to our understanding of how the monstrous comprises an ever-present 'identity machine' within medieval texts: Oswald seizes the Derridean notion of 'the trace' as her central tool for unpicking the problems inherent to any form of representation, writing or otherwise. If for Derrida absence and presence are always in play within language, then as Oswald demonstrates in this book, 'the trace of the monster in the text declares its presence through its absence' (14).

Monsters, Gender and Sexuality offers a strong and convincing case for the spectral presence — or trace — of the monster as always already haunting a sexed and gendered human imaginary and its texts. As such, it proves itself a valuable addition to our understanding of how, in its infinite manifestations, the monstrous operates as a 'machine' for both the construction and the policing of human identities.

LIZ HERBERT McAVOY   SWANSEA UNIVERSITY

Kiriko Sato, *The Development from Case-Forms to Prepositional Constructions in Old English Prose*. Studies in Language and Communication, 88. Bern: Lang, 2009. 231 pp. ISBN 978-3-03911-763-5. £45.00.

Kiriko Sato's 2009 book is based on her Ph.D. dissertation, defended at the University of Tokyo in 2006. Focusing on Old English syntax, it has the ambitious aim of showing why, when and how variation between old case-forms and new prepositional constructions arose, leading to the eventual prevalence of the prepositonal constructions. It examines six semantic relations that can be expressed by both case-forms and prepositional constructions: 1) *instrumentality/manner*, 2) a closely related *accompaniment*, 3) *point in time*, 4) *duration of time*, 5) national *origin*, and 6) place *specification* (with parts of the body). In addition, Sato looks at one syntactic construction — augmented vs. non-augmented *dative absolute*. The investigation is divided into seven chapters, six of them being case studies of six respective texts or sets of texts: the *Parker Chronicle*, Old English *Boethius*, Old English *Bede*, Ælfric's *Catholic Homilies* and *Lives of Saints*, and Wulfstan's *Homilies*, with chapter 7 providing a summary and conclusions. Six appendices list full inventories (a total of 1,937 examples) of Sato's chosen constructions in the selected research corpus.

Each case study begins with a survey of previous research on the text concerned, goes on to an overview of absolute and relative numbers of case-forms vs. prepositional constructions, and then discusses the six semantic relations and the dative absolute in more detail. The not unexpected conclusion of chapter 7 is that prepositional constructions increase towards the late Old English period with considerable variation remaining still among the selected functions and texts (e.g., Wulfstan is about as conservative as the Old English *Boethius* in his use of instrumental case forms).

The way Sato analyses her data gives the impression of a solid dissertation. She has good points to make about the stylistic side of the two constructions; for example, she observes that

Ælfric's use of dative absolutes in his later work can be explained by the fact that many of them rhythmically fit into a verse half-line and are thus preferred by Ælfric on stylistic grounds.

As a whole, however, the book does not go much beyond a positivist description of syntax. At no point does Sato discuss, adopt or criticise any of the more recent approaches to typology or historical corpus studies, such as grammaticalisation or variationist approaches. Nor does she clearly define her own approach, which unfortunately has a more immediate bearing on the selection of research data and methodology. For example, it remains unclear how and why the research texts were selected. It is evident that they have been grouped into early and late texts and that this division was intended to make the "chronological development" (p. 18) observable, but apart from all the six texts being prose, they hardly make a uniform set of comparanda. While the early Old English sample — the *Parker Chronicle* (studied in Plummer's edition rather than Bately's more recent one), *Bede*, and *Boethius* — does provide 'a wide variety of styles' (p. 20), *Bede*, moreover, having Mercian elements, this is not quite the case with the late Old English sample — Ælfric's *Catholic Homilies* I and II, his *Lives of Saints*, and Wulfstan's *Homilies*, with texts by Ælfric amounting to 91 per cent of this sample and 64 per cent of the whole research corpus. Statistics in particular highlight the weak points of Sato's selection. It has been observed above that even relative figures show that the development from case-forms to prepositional constructions is far from straightforward. Normalised frequencies could have been even more revealing. Table 1 gives my own calculation based on Sato's absolute numbers (p. 171) and the word counts for the six texts in the *York-Toronto-Helsinki Parsed Corpus of Old English Prose*.[1] In fact, we can see that case-forms are more frequent in the late *ÆLS*, and *WHom* than in the early *Bo*, while prepositional constructions are more frequent in the early *Bede* than in the late *ÆCHom* and *WHom*, which makes Sato's main claim about prepositional constructions having 'increased substantially from the early to the later OE periods' (p. 184) look slightly suspect.

date	texts	case-forms	prepositional constructions
early	ChronA	86	16
early	Bede	33	30
early	Bo	8	13
late	ÆCHom	3	23
late	ÆLS	14	39
late	WHom	16	26

Table 1. Normalised frequencies per 10,000

What further complicates the matter is the selection of data within the studied texts. It remains unexplained why only thirty-four nouns are considered suitable for the investigation of the instrumentality/manner relation and how this list of nouns was arrived at, why the study of the accompaniment relation includes the noun *werod* only, and the study of point in time the nouns *dæg*, *niht*, *tid*, and *gear*, but not, say, *winter*. Similar decisions were made in connection with the remaining three semantic relations (pp. 22–23) but again the reasons

---

[1] Compiled by Ann Taylor, Anthony Warner, Susan Pintzuk and Frank Beths (University of York, 2003), <http://www-users.york.ac.uk/~lang22/YcoeHome1.htm> [accessed 6 May 2011].

behind them are not explicit. With dative absolutes, Sato only considers constructions that have parts of the body as their nominal elements, e.g., *upahafenum handum* 'uplifted hands' (dative plural), which, as before, limits the validity of her conclusions. First of all, she records a single example of this type of dative absolute in early OE (corresponding to a remarkable 100 per cent in statistics on p. 178), while all her late examples are from Ælfric. Second, according to my estimate, absolute constructions with parts of the body are a type that can only amount to some 10 per cent of dative absolutes in OE.[2] Further, many among them are fossilised and should properly be interpreted through a collocational analysis; and so forth.

Sato says (pp. 17, 184) that her study was inspired by the desire to prove that Bruce Mitchell whose opinion I would like to reproduce here was in the wrong:

> for what it is worth, my own impression is that — perhaps contrary to what we might expect — little significant change in the comparative percentages of case-forms alone and of prepositions + case-forms in those contexts where both are possible can be detected in the extant OE monuments.[3]

Well, she did try to challenge his opinion, but the old Bruce remains unshaken.

OLGA TIMOFEEVA   UNIVERSITY OF ZURICH

---

[2] Olga Timofeeva, *Non-Finite Constructions in Old English, with Special Reference to Syntactic Borrowing from Latin*, Mémoires de la Société Néophilologique de Helsinki, 80 (Helsinki: Société Néophilologique, 2010), pp. 34–45.

[3] Bruce Mitchell, *Old English Syntax*, 2 vols (Oxford: Clarendon Press, 1985), I, §1225.

Also published by *Leeds Studies in English* is the occasional series:

LEEDS TEXTS AND MONOGRAPHS

(ISSN 0075-8574)

Recent volumes include:

Approaches to the Metres of Alliterative Verse, edited by Judith Jefferson and Ad Putter (2009), iii + 311 pp.

The Heege Manuscript: a facsimile of NLS MS Advocates 19.3.1, introduced by Phillipa Hardman (2000), 60 + 432pp.

The Old English Life of St Nicholas with the Old English Life of St Giles, edited by E. M. Treharne (1997) viii + 218pp.

Concepts of National Identity in the Middle Ages, edited by Simon Forde, Lesley Johnson and Alan V. Murray (1995) viii + 213pp.

A Study and Edition of Selected Middle English Sermons, by V. M. O'Mara (1994) xi + 245pp.

Notes on 'Beowulf', by P. J. Cosijn, introduced, translated and annotated by Rolf H. Bremmer Jr, Jan van den Berg and David F. Johnson (1991) xxxvi + 120pp.

Úr Dölum til Dala: Guðbrandur Vigfússon Centenary Essays, edited by Rory McTurk and Andrew Wawn (1989) x + 327pp.

Staging the Chester Cycle, edited by David Mills (1985) vii + 123pp.

The Gawain Country: Essays on the Topography of Middle English Poetry, by R. W. V. Elliot (1984) 165pp.

For full details of this series, and to purchase volumes, or past numbers of *Leeds Studies in English*, pleased go to <www.leeds.ac.uk/lse>.

www.ingramcontent.com/pod-product-compliance
Lightning Source LLC
Chambersburg PA
CBHW081355230426
43667CB00017B/2839